THE
LOW-CARB
BIBLE

Publications International, Ltd.

Contributing Writer: Elizabeth M. Ward, M.S., R.D., is a registered dietitian, freelance writer, and nutrition consultant who has worked as a nutrition counselor at Harvard Vanguard Medical Associates. She is the author of *Pregnancy Nutrition: Good Health for You and Your Baby* and coauthor of *Live Longer & Better: A Lifestyle Guide with Recipes.* Her articles have appeared in the *Los Angeles Times, The Boston Globe, Environmental Nutrition, Fitness, American Baby,* and *Shape Fit Pregnancy,* and she frequently appears on local and national television.

Nutritional Analysis: Linda R. Yoakam, M.S., R.D., L.D.

The nutritional information that appears with each recipe was submitted in part by the participating companies and associations. Every effort has been made to check the accuracy of these numbers. However, because numerous variables account for a wide range of values for certain foods, nutritive analyses in this book should be considered approximate.

Photo credits:
©**Lou Chardonnay/Corbis:** 6 (top), 13; **SuperStock:** 6 (center), 72; **Deborah Van Kirk:** 71 (bottom center & bottom right).

All food photographs *except* those on pages 193 and 219 copyright © Publications International, Ltd.

Pictured on the front cover: *(clockwise from top):* Chocolate Peanut Butter Ice Cream Sandwiches *(page 290),* Asian Chicken Kabobs *(page 220),* and Pork Chop Paprikash *(page 170).*

Pictured on the back cover: *(bottom right)* Grilled Red Snapper with Avocado Papaya Sauce *(page 156)* and *(bottom left)* Main Dish Chicken Soup *(page 168).*

This book is for informational purposes and is not intended to provide medical advice. Neither the Editors of Consumer Guide © and Publications International, Ltd., nor the author or publisher take responsibility for any possible consequences from any treatment, procedure, exercise, dietary modification, action, or application of medication or preparation by any person reading or following the information in this book. The publication of this book does not constitute the practice of medicine, and this book does not attempt to replace your physician or other health care provider. Before undertaking any course of treatment, the author, editors, and publisher advise the reader to check with a physician or other health care provider.

The brand-name products mentioned in this publication are trademarks or service marks of their respective companies. The mention of any product in this publication does not constitute an endorsement by the respective proprietors of Publications International, Ltd., nor does it constitute an endorsement by any of these companies that their products should be used in the manner recommended by this publication.

contents

get the lowdown on low carb

You want to go low carb, but you want to do it right. You want to lose weight without harming your health, you want a diet that will fit your personality, your tastes, and your life, and you want your weight loss to last.

That's not too much to ask, is it? Not when you have *The Low-Carb Bible* at hand. It's designed to help you create a low-carb lifestyle that will fulfill all of these needs.

The Low-Carb Bible guides you from the very start of your low-carb weight-loss quest. And it's there as you progress, to help you make smart, safe choices and get the most from your weight-loss efforts.

The first section of the book, Know Your Low-Carb Options, explains the fundamentals of low-carb dieting, discusses the science that supports its usefulness, and provides warnings about conditions that make low-carb dieting less than desirable. It also includes reviews of popular low-carb plans. The review for each diet describes the reasoning behind its approach to weight loss, the kinds and amounts of foods allowed, how flexible it is, how it might impact your health, and more.

Then, in the second section, Personalize Your Low-Carb Plan, you'll find tools to help you create or tailor a low-carb plan to ensure you get the nutrients your body needs without all the processed foods and empty carbs that do little for your body but pack on pounds. You'll find expert advice on building a low-carb lifestyle that includes plenty of enjoyable physical activity, provides a huge variety of tasty food choices, and works in the real world.

Finally, in the last section, Enjoy Low-Carb Recipes, you'll be amazed to discover the many scrumptious dishes, including desserts, that can be a part of your low-carb plan. The accompanying nutritional information makes it easy for you to plan meals that meet your needs for weight loss, health, and eating pleasure.

You can make low-carb dieting work for you. You just need to know how to take the greatest advantage of its weight-loss potential while preserving your health and preventing the boredom that has sunk many a diet in the past. In other words, you just need to keep *The Low-Carb Bible* nearby. So enjoy weight loss for a change!

know your low-carb options

With all the low-carb diets out there, how do you know which one's right for you? After all, just because a diet worked for a friend or celebrity doesn't mean it will work for you. To help you decide, this section provides you with an understanding of the basics of low-carb dieting, what the research says about it, and what warnings you need to be aware of. You'll also find reviews of popular low-carb diet plans, with information and ratings to help you figure out which one suits you and your lifestyle best.

low-carb fundamentals

A diet is a diet, right? Not according to low-carbohydrate diet proponents, who say they have a better way to shed weight and to keep it off for good. To grasp the logic driving the low-carb revolution, you need to understand the role that carbohydrate, fat, and protein play in the body and how they are used for energy.

the basic idea

Dr. Atkins' New Diet Revolution, The Zone, and *The South Beach Diet* are

just a few examples of low-carb diet programs. Although they may differ in their approach and style, all low-carb diets have a single uniting principle: Too much dietary carbohydrate causes weight gain and prevents weight loss. Low-carb diets cut down the amount of carbohydrates you eat rather than focusing on cutting calories or fat, the usual targets of weight-loss programs.

Some of the low-carb diet plans eliminate more

carbohydrates than others. Dr. Atkins, for instance, allows only 5 percent of daily calories to come from carbohydrate, while *The Zone* allows 40 percent. Traditional diet recommendations call for 50 to 55 percent of calories from carbohydrate.

carbohydrates: the culprit?

Why do low-carb proponents finger carbohydrate instead of fat (or protein) as the culprit in weight gain or the inability to lose weight? It has to do with the way the body stores blood glucose as fat.

Carbohydrate is found in breads, cereals, rice, pasta, and other grains; fruits and vegetables; dairy products; and processed foods as added sugar. It is broken down into glucose (the kind of carbohydrate that cells use for energy) during digestion and released into the bloodstream. Glucose is the preferred energy source for most tissues, including the brain, which requires a constant source of fuel for peak function. Your body maintains tight control over blood glucose levels. After you eat carbohydrate, blood glucose is higher than normal. To clear the excess, the pancreas releases insulin, a hormone, into the blood-

are also easily depleted if you go without food for 12 to18 hours, which dieters sometimes do when they fast. The body's muscle tissue packs more than three times the amount of glycogen—about 300 grams—but the muscles' glycogen stores can only be used to provide the muscles with energy; they can't be used to fuel the rest of the body.

stream. Insulin facilitates the transfer of glucose from the blood into your cells. Of the three macronutrients (carbohydrate, protein, and fat), carbohydrate causes the greatest and speediest spike in blood glucose levels and, as a result, the largest release of insulin. This, as you'll see, is an important factor for low-carb diet advocates.

Some of the carbohydrate that is not used to meet immediate energy needs becomes glycogen, which is stored in the liver and the muscles for future use. Insulin also facilitates the processes that allow glycogen to be stored in the liver and muscles. The liver can stockpile between 70 and 90 grams of glycogen. When blood glucose levels fall between meals, the stockpile is raided to keep blood glucose levels within normal range. Liver stores are easily depleted when you're on a low-carb diet since liver glycogen stores are below par when your diet is consistently low in carbohydrates. Liver stores

Carbohydrate confusion

Not all carbs are bad, even to low-carb diet proponents. There are two basic types of carbohydrate: simple and complex. It's very important to distinguish between the two.

Simple carbs include table sugar, honey, molasses, and the high-fructose corn syrup found in a variety of processed foods, including salad dressings, crackers, cereal, and soda. Simple carbohydrates are also found naturally in fruit, as fructose, and in dairy products, as lactose.

Complex carbohydrates include starch and fiber, and they are found in foods such as grains, corn, and potatoes. Complex carbs provide important nutrients, including vitamins, minerals, fiber, and phytonutrients, which are disease-fighting plant compounds. If you  drastically reduce complex carbohydrates in your diet, you will lose out on these crucial nutrients and may jeopardize your health, both short- and long-term.

However good they taste, most foods that contain simple carbohydrates aren't worth much from a nutritional standpoint. Your body receives virtually no nutritional benefit from cakes, cookies, and candy, and little nutrition from white or brown-colored bread, white rice, white pasta, and other processed foods. Foods packing simple carbohydrates can add inches to your waistline and set off food cravings, leading you to consume even more of them.

So, when low-carb proponents advise you to go easy on carbs, they're primarily talking about simple carbohydrates. You can still eat fiber-filled carbohydrates, such as beans, whole-wheat products, and fruits and vegetables.

What happens when the liver and muscles are filled to the brim with glycogen? Extra carbohydrate is converted to fat and stored in your cells. Again, this process is facilitated by insulin. That's why low-carbohydrate proponents maintain that eating a low-carb diet will help you lose weight. If you don't provide your body with a lot of carbohydrate, your body won't produce a lot of insulin, so it won't be storing as much fat. The less fat stored in your cells, the thinner you will be. That's the premise.

the ketosis controversy. When you eat a very low-carbohydrate diet every day, glycogen stores in the liver become low. Less glucose is available to fuel your cells, prompting the body to turn to fat stores for energy. The liver converts fat to acidic substances called ketones that can be used for energy. This induces an abnormal metabolic condition called ketosis, which is defined as the presence of high levels of ketones in the blood.

Some low-carb proponents encourage ketosis, seeing it as a sign of successful fat-burning. Others do not. It's easy to see why some diet plan authors shy away from ketosis. The rapid fat burning that produces ketosis disturbs the body's chemical balance. What's worse, it may lead to dehydration. In an effort to restore balance, the body eliminates ketones through the urine, causing increased urination.

Another unpleasant side effect of ketosis is bad breath.

protein power

Low-carb diets are nearly always high-protein diets, and they may also be high in fat. The reason? Only carbohydrate, fat, and protein provide your body with the calories (energy) it needs to function. When you drastically curb consumption of one of the three energy-producing nutrients (in this case, carbohydrates), you need to increase your intake of one, or both, of the others (in this case, protein and/or fat), even when weight loss is the goal.

Life would be impossible without protein, found in foods such as meat, eggs, poultry, seafood, dairy products, and legumes. Protein is necessary for relaying messages in the nervous system and brain; balancing fluid; absorbing nutrients; and producing enzymes, hormones, connective tissue, muscles, antibodies, and other substances that affect growth, development, and overall health. Unlike carbohydrate and fat, protein is not stored in the body, so you need to eat enough protein every day. Digestion breaks protein down into its individual amino acids, which can be used to construct body proteins such as insulin, red blood cells, and digestive enzymes or to make glucose for energy.

Protein does not cause the sharp increase in blood glucose levels that carbohydrate does. Instead, protein produces a slower and steadier increase. As a result, the pancreas releases less insulin. Since insulin helps the body store glucose as fat, you will store less fat when you eat more protein and less carbohydrate. That is why low-carbohydrate proponents encourage dieters to eat more calories from protein. Still, if you eat more calories than you need in the form of protein, your body will store them as fat.

fat: friend or foe?

Dieters despise fat, but they are misguided. Fat provides the raw materials (fatty acids) for your body's production of many substances that drive life and sustain good health, including brain cells. For instance, fat transports vitamins A, D, E, and K and is required for their absorption.

Fatty acids are classified as either saturated or unsaturated (monounsaturated or polyunsaturated). Saturated

fats, found in foods including meat, cheese, and cream, contribute to clogged arteries and increase your risk for heart attack and stroke. Unsaturated fats, found in vegetable oils, nuts, avocados, and seafood, are considered good for your heart because they lower the levels of harmful fats and cholesterol in the blood.

Fat's bad reputation, from a weight-loss perspective, comes from the fact that it provides nine calories per gram. Compare that with carbohydrate and protein, both of which provide only four calories per gram. Fat, then, supplies more than double the calories of the other two macronutrients. The risk of overindulging in fat-laden foods when you're trying to lose weight is that you'll also be consuming a high-calorie diet, one that will add pounds rather than take them off.

But low-carb proponents have a different angle on fat. The number of calories it provides is only a part of fat's story, they say. Eating a higher-fat

When insulin goes awry

Chronically high insulin levels may result in insulin resistance (IR), which affects an estimated 60 to 75 million Americans. IR means you produce and release insulin into the bloodstream, but it's not enough to move glucose into the cells and out of the blood because the cells have become resistant to the action of insulin. As a result, blood glucose levels rise along with insulin concentrations. High-carb diets, particularly those packed with simple carbs, contribute to IR in some people. But being overweight and underactive are major contributors to the development of IR. In the majority of cases, IR can be reversed with weight loss, increased physical activity, or a combination of both.

In search of satisfaction

Eating more protein may be key to weight control because it promotes feelings of satisfaction in the brain. In fact, a high-protein diet may head off feelings of dietary deprivation that so often prompt dieters to throw in the towel. How much protein is safe to eat on a daily basis? For healthy people, 100 grams or less probably poses no health problems. About 15 ounces of meat, chicken, or fish provides 100 grams of protein, nearly double what most adults require.

A combination of fiber-filled foods and fluid fills you up and helps you feel satisfied for longer, too.

diet can help, rather than hinder, weight loss. That's because fat differs from carbohydrate and protein in another significant way: It causes little or no rise in blood glucose levels, so it doesn't provoke insulin release into the blood after digestion. Since insulin is the designated facilitator of fat storage, low-carb proponents say a high-fat diet that's also low in carbohydrates actually prevents the body from storing glucose as fat.

keeping control

It's important to control your blood glucose concentrations. A low blood glucose level makes you feel tired because it deprives your cells of the energy needed to function. On the other hand, a chronically high glucose concentration, often seen in people with uncontrolled diabetes, damages blood vessels, particularly the very small vessels that supply the eyes and kidneys with oxygen-rich blood.

The body favors balance, and most people have a built-in mechanism that works well to keep blood glucose levels in check. It dispatches the hormone insulin from the pancreas to reduce blood glucose levels after a meal or snack containing carbohydrate or protein. Between meals, when your blood glucose levels tend to drop, the pancreas releases the hormone glucagon, which directs the liver to liberate stored glucose (glycogen). This raises your blood glucose level. Glucagon facilitates the body's production of glucose from amino acids, thereby creating an additional energy source. Insulin is also used to store the calories you don't burn as body fat.

Low-carb diet proponents believe a diet high in carbohydrates causes weight gain and keeps you overweight because carbohydrates provoke the release of insulin into the bloodstream. Since insulin is responsible for fat storage, they say that too much insulin causes weight gain. Too much insulin coursing through your blood vessels is also unhealthy because it produces harmful changes in the vessels that supply the heart with blood, promoting heart disease.

what the research says

Low-carb eating plans produce weight loss, and that makes them popular. Despite their success, however, they are not widely accepted by the medical community. Is there a price to be paid for eating a low-carbohydrate diet? The verdict isn't in yet, but here's what we know so far.

the pros of low-carb eating

Doctors and nutritionists spent decades deriding Dr. Atkins' low-carbohydrate/high-protein/high-fat diet. Atkins, a cardiologist, maintained that his diet produced rapid weight loss and did not raise cholesterol levels, as health professionals were sure it would. Until recently, it was just the medical community's opinion against his. No independent controlled clinical trials had been done to assess the effectiveness of low-carbohydrate diets at producing weight loss or to measure their effect on cholesterol levels.

That changed when the results of two controlled clinical trials were published in the *New England Journal of Medicine* in May 2003. They showed that reducing the intake of carbohydrates and increasing protein intake

could be the ticket to weight loss and weight control, at least for some people. And, much to the medical community's surprise, they also showed that low-carb diets did not cause the expected increases in blood cholesterol that can lead to heart disease. In fact, the low-carb dieters had lower levels of triglycerides (harmful blood fats that can cause a buildup of plaque in the arteries) than those who followed a low-fat diet. In addition, the low-carb dieters had higher levels of HDL (good) cholesterol than their low-fat diet counterparts.

Both studies compared people following a low-carbohydrate diet with those following a more conventional low-fat, low-calorie diet. One study lasted six months, while the other lasted a year. These studies were

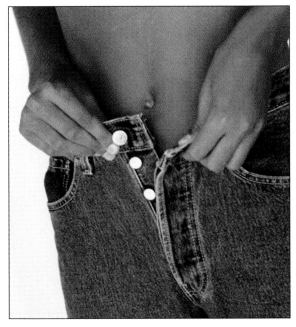

some of the first to follow low-carb dieters longer than 90 days.

The six-month study followed a group of 132 severely obese men and women; half were assigned to a low-carbohydrate diet similar to the Atkins diet and half were assigned to a low-calorie, low-fat diet. Although there was a high dropout rate (about 40 percent), of those who completed the study, the low-carb dieters lost more weight than those on the calorie- and fat-restricted diet (over six months, an average of 13 to 15 pounds compared to 4 to 7 pounds). The low-carb dieters also improved their insulin sensitivity and their triglyceride levels.

The 12-month study followed a smaller group of 63 obese men and women who were also randomly assigned to either a low-carb or a low-fat, calorie-restricted diet. The dropout rate, at 40 percent, was the same for this yearlong study. While the low-carb diet produced greater weight loss during the first six months of the study, the differences were not significant after one year. However, the low-carb diet was associated with a greater improvement in some risk factors for heart disease.

Two earlier studies received some attention prior to those published in the *New England Journal of Medicine,* and they also provide some indication that low-carb dieting may be beneficial. The Dr. Robert C. Atkins Foundation financed a study of 51 obese or over-weight people, which was conducted at Duke University. The results were published in the *American Journal of Medicine* in July 2002. Participants were placed on a diet of less than 25 grams of carbohydrate per day but were not restricted in their calorie intake. Only 20 percent of the participants dropped out of the study, and those that remained each lost between 8 and 31 pounds. In addition to the weight loss, participants' total cholesterol and low-density lipoprotein (LDL, the bad cholesterol) levels fell while their high-density lipoprotein (HDL, the good cholesterol) levels rose. However, this study had no control group for comparison.

A ten-week study of 24 overweight women, published in *The Journal of Nutrition* in February 2003, also found benefits to a low-carbohydrate diet. The group of 24 participants was divided into two equal groups. One group was put on a diet plan consisting of three-and-a-half times as much protein as carb (this was the high-protein group), while the other group was on a diet that supplied one-and-a-half times the amount of protein as

A look at the losers

There are thousands of diets to help you lose fat. What works best? The National Weight Control Registry (NWCR) is a research project that has identified nearly 4,000 people who have lost at least 30 pounds and kept them off for at least a year. How do they do it? About half of them lost weight on their own, while the other half used a formal weight loss program or consulted a health professional for guidance. No matter what their method for initial weight-loss, participants continue to follow a low-calorie, low-fat diet to keep the pounds off.

carb (this was the moderate-protein group). Each diet plan supplied the same number of calories—1,700 a day. The fat content (about 50 grams/day) was the same for both groups, so the diets differed only in the ratio of carbohydrate to protein. Both groups lost weight, which is no surprise given the reduced calorie intake. And both groups had improvements in their blood lipid levels. However, the high-protein group lost more body fat and spared more lean tissue (primarily muscle). In addition, the high-protein group expressed greater satisfaction with their diet and reported feeling more energetic than the moderate-protein group.

skepticism remains

Do the results of these studies mean that skeptics and critics of Atkins and other low-carb diet plans are ready to throw in the towel and join the low-carb bandwagon? Not really.

There is some evidence that a low-carb diet can leave the lean while burning the fat. The idea behind any diet is loss of body fat. But restricting calories often leads to a loss of desirable lean tissue (predominantly muscle), too. Preserving lean tissue prevents a drop in metabolism (your calorie-burning rate) because lean tissue burns more calories than fat. Curbing carbohydrate consumption

may be preferable to lowering protein intake because it seems to better preserve lean tissue. Research suggests that the ratio (relationship) of carbohydrate to protein is what preserves lean tissue.

Still, health care professionals doubt the worthiness of low-carb regimens. Here's why.

overall lack of proof. Conventional wisdom says it's the total number of calories consumed that determines whether you will lose weight and that no specific distribution of carbohydrate, protein, and fat can make you lose weight faster than any other. Since carbohydrates supply the same number of calories (four) per gram as protein and less than half the calories of a gram of fat (nine), it's counterintuitive to blame carbs alone for causing excess body fat.

When researchers examined 107 studies of low-carb diets that involved a total of 3,286 participants age 53 or younger, they found that decreased calorie consumption and the time spent on the diets were responsible for how much weight the participants lost, not the reduction in carbs alone. To be fair, the same article found no evidence for making recommendations for or against the use of low-carb diets for weight loss.

Many health professionals are intrigued by the recently published studies on low-carb diets, but they want longer studies to be done. It's only after following people for many years that the true effects of eating a low-carb diet will be revealed, they say. They have lots of questions: Will the expected harmful effects of a high-protein, high-fat diet show up later or will the decreased levels of triglycerides and increased levels of HDL (good) cholesterol found in the recently published studies continue long term? Will following a high-protein diet for years eventually enlarge the kidneys, promote the formation of kidney stones, and lead to gout, as many believe it will? Will a low-carb diet cause osteoporosis? And what about the brain, which relies on glucose to work efficiently? Will there be harm to brain function over the long haul? The medical community is waiting for the answers to these questions before it gives its verdict on low-carb dieting.

safety concerns. Any diet is dangerous when it severely restricts calorie and nutrient intakes, intentionally or not. Nausea, dizziness, constipation, fatigue, dehydration, bad breath, and appetite loss are among the reported effects of very low-calorie diets. Even the less extreme of the low-carb plans may be unsafe because they restrict

certain foods that help fight disease. For example, going without the recommended three servings of low-fat dairy foods for months or years means losing out on bone-building calcium and vitamin D. Consuming fewer than the five to nine suggested servings of fruits and vegetables (combined) leads to reduced intakes of beneficial antioxidant vitamins and phytonutrients, compounds found only in plant foods and considered valuable weapons in the battle against heart disease and cancer. And forgoing whole grains may increase your chances of developing diabetes and heart disease.

stick-to-it-ability. Both of the studies published in the *New England Journal of Medicine* had a high dropout rate—about 40 percent. These studies were only 6 or 12 months long, which does not bode well for the ability of dieters to stick with a low-carb regimen for the long term. The challenge of any diet is not just to help people lose weight but to help them make the lifelong changes in eating that will keep the weight off for good. Longer studies are needed to determine whether a low-carbohydrate diet can be a satisfactory way of eating for life, one that leads to permanent weight loss.

looking to the future

Low-carb diets, once the stepchild of the diet and health community, are finally getting the attention and scrutiny they deserve. That's great, since dieters have been experimenting with low-carb eating for several decades. But

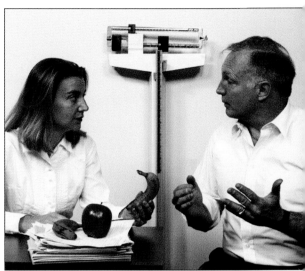

we still need the results of carefully constructed, long-running studies to make a final determination about low-carb dieting's effectiveness and its impact on health. In the meantime, it's unlikely that low-carb diets are harmful for most healthy people for a short period of time. But if you do go low carb, make sure you check with a health care provider who will monitor your blood cholesterol levels and your bone mass and who will check to make sure you are not developing kidney stones. Depending on how strict your low-carb regimen is, your health provider should also advise you about your need for vitamin, mineral, and fiber supplementation.

are low-carb diets for everyone?

Everyone can cut refined carbs

Even if you have a health condition that makes a strict low-carb diet unwise, much of the advice in this book is still valuable. Everyone can benefit from cutting back on "empty" carbs—the ones that come in foods such as cookies, white bread, bagels, and donuts—and empty calories. You'll need to check with your doctor first, but chances are you'll get the green light to trim refined carbs and add whole grains, fruits, and vegetables to your diet.

It's unlikely that any single type of diet is ideal for everyone. But low-carb diets can be particularly risky for certain groups of people. Here's how to decide whether you are in a high-risk group.

Low-carb diets are, by definition, high in protein, high in fat, or both. The protein content of the eating plan proposed by Dr. Atkins, as well as those in *Protein Power, Sugar Busters!,* and *The Zone* diets, is almost twice the Recommended Dietary Allowance of 50 grams for adult women and 63 grams for adult men. Why can that be problematic? Some health conditions make it more difficult to process the additional protein consumed in a low-carb diet, and others require a higher volume of carbohydrates to maintain good health.

processing protein

Eating extra protein places a burden on the liver and kidneys. Your body doesn't store protein, so these organs work harder to process it. The liver and kidneys are responsible for ridding the body of uric acid and ammonia, the substances that are left after the body digests protein. If you have a health condition that compromises the kidneys or liver, then you should not try a low-carb, high-protein diet. Since the liver and kidneys also process medications, be sure to check with your physician before starting a high-protein diet if you take any medication regularly. The additional protein could jeopardize your liver and kidney function.

diabetes and high blood pressure. People with diabetes and high blood pressure are at greater risk for kidney disease and are especially vulnerable to the detrimental effects of consuming large amounts of protein. And those with high blood pressure may also be compromised by the diuretic effects of ketosis.

gout. If you're prone to gout, bypass protein-packed diets. Uric acid can cause or aggravate gout, a condition characterized by painful uric acid deposits in the joints.

osteoporosis. Excess protein may also be harmful to bones, increasing your risk for osteoporosis, a bone disease that mostly strikes women after menopause but has its beginnings much earlier in life. In response to the acid environment produced by excessive protein intake, your kidneys direct bones to release calcium to buffer the acid. This can leach calcium from the bones if you don't eat a potassium-rich diet or supplement with calcium and potassium. Eating plenty of potassium-packed fruits and vegetables can counteract calcium loss because potassium also buffers acid. Getting at least 1,000 milligrams of calcium daily will help offset the calcium-wasting effects of protein, too. However, some low-carb diets tend to fall short in potassium and calcium because they restrict carbohydrate and dairy intake. The NeanderThin diet, for instance, prohibits all dairy products, and some of the diet plans forbid or drastically restrict dairy products during certain phases, which you could be in for long stretches of time and need to return to intermittently.

pregnancy and childhood. Pregnant and lactating women and grow-ing children should also steer clear of low-carb diets because they limit foods that foster a child's growth and development and may not satisfy energy and nutrient needs. In addition, too much protein in the diet puts unnecessary strain on a child's developing kidneys.

heart disease and cancer. Some low-carb diets don't restrict protein, fat, or calories. So while you're whittling your waistline, you could be clogging your arteries and increasing your cancer risk. This is especially true if you favor foods higher in total and saturated fat, such as meat, cheese, and cream, over lower-fat, high-protein choices including poultry, seafood, and yogurt. Unrestricted consumption of animal foods that are rich in total fat, saturated fat, and cholesterol, including meat and cheese, can raise low-density lipoprotein (LDL, bad cholesterol), an effect compounded by the relative absence of high-carbohydrate, high-fiber plant foods such as whole grains, fruits, and vegetables, which help keep blood lipids in check. Diets high in red meat and low in fiber may also increase cancer risk. Additionally, a low-carb diet may be missing many of the fruits, vegetables, and whole grains that contain cancer-fighting phytochemicals.

Turn down the heat

Low-carb diets pack a lot of protein-rich animal foods, which can increase your risk for cancer, depending on how you cook them. According to the National Cancer Institute, cooking beef, pork, poultry, and fish at high temperatures creates chemicals called heterocyclic amines (HCAs) that may increase cancer risk. Frying, broiling, and grilling produce the largest amounts of HCAs. Baking, steaming, slow cooking, and roasting produce the least. Meats that are partially cooked in the microwave oven before cooking by other methods also have lower levels of HCAs.

dr. atkins' new diet revolution

About the author

Robert Atkins, M.D., received his medical degree from Cornell University Medical School and went on to specialize in cardiology. In 1972, he published *Dr. Atkins' Diet Revolution*, one of the first weight-loss books to espouse low-carbohydrate eating. *Dr. Atkins' New Diet Revolution* first hit the bookstores in 1992 and has spent more than three years on *The New York Times* best-seller list. Dr. Atkins was the founder of the Atkins Center for Complementary Medicine in New York City. He passed away in April 2003.

the basic idea

Obesity is due to a malfunctioning metabolism, according to Atkins. He believes that people who are overweight do not metabolize carbohydrate properly because they are insulin resistant (see page 11 for an explanation of insulin resistance). You can't cure your faulty metabolism, Atkins says, but you can manage it by eating a very low-carbohydrate diet.

In Atkins' estimation, the high-carbohydrate (at least 50 percent of calories), low-fat diet preached by health professionals is the reason that Americans are rapidly becoming so unhealthy. That's because it promotes chronically elevated insulin levels, which he blames for what he calls the twin epidemics of obesity and diabetes. Atkins maintains that insulin overload in the blood promotes fat storage and encourages the development of type 2 diabetes. This "typical" American diet not only promotes obesity but also encourages irritability, fatigue, and sleeplessness. Atkins directs dieters, and anyone interested in protecting their health, to switch from a diet dominated by carbohydrate to a regimen that's comprised largely of fat and protein. In fact, Atkins cautions against turning his plan into a low-fat diet. He says that you must eat fat as the predominant calorie source, at least initially, because protein and carbohydrate provoke insulin release, while fat has no effect on insulin levels.

Avoiding the likes of bread, potatoes, rice, and fruit causes your body to become a fat-burning machine, using fat rather than carbohydrates for energy. This gives you what Atkins calls the "metabolic advantage." For Atkins, lipolysis—or fat breakdown—is the goal. When there are insufficient amounts of glucose to be burned for energy, the liver turns to fat stores instead. It converts fat to acidic substances called ketones. Lipolysis, then, results in ketosis, an abnormal metabolic condition caused by burning mostly fat to meet your energy needs. Stimulating lipolysis on a very low-carbohydrate diet suppresses your appetite and breaks the cycle of excess insulin in the bloodstream that in turn promotes fat storage, according to Atkins. And he believes the medical profession's concerns about the dangers of ketosis in healthy people are overblown. To make sure you're burning fat, Atkins recommends testing urine for ketones, the by-products of fat breakdown.

the plan

The Atkins Nutritional Approach requires no calorie counting or portion control. The theory is that as long as you choose from the acceptable foods, steering clear of most carbohydrates, you will lose weight no matter how much you eat.

The plan consists of four phases:

Induction lasts from two weeks to six months, depending on how much weight you want to shed. You're limited to 20 grams of carbohydrate a day (the amount in 1 cup fresh blueberries).

The Ongoing Weight Loss (OWL) phase lasts from two weeks to two months and allows you to add five grams of carbohydrate to your daily intake each week as long as you continue to lose weight. Weight loss during OWL is more gradual, but if your weight loss plateaus, you must stop adding carbs and may even need to cut back. The goal of OWL is to find your Critical Carbohydrate Level for Losing (CCLL), the maximum amount of carbs you can eat and still lose weight. You stay in OWL until you have just five to ten pounds left to drop.

During the Pre-Maintenance phase, which lasts a few weeks or a couple months, you add 10 grams of carbohydrate to your daily intake each week

until your weight loss slows to one pound per week or less. During Pre-Maintenance, your job is to discover your CCLM, Critical Carbohydrate Level for Maintenance, which is the amount of carbohydrate you can eat and maintain your present weight.

You enter the Lifetime Maintenance phase when you have arrived at your weight goal.

unique features

The Atkins Nutritional Approach is very low in carbohydrates (estimated range: 20 to 90 grams, or less than 10 percent of your daily diet), possibly the lowest of any of the low-carb eating regimens. (The average American diet includes about 50 to 60 percent of calories from carbohydrate, which amounts to at least 250 grams of carbohydrate a day.) After initially dropping carbohydrate intake to 20 grams a day, you gradually increase carbohydrate intake until you reach your weight-loss goal and discover the amount of carbohydrate you can eat every day without gaining weight. Ketosis is encouraged and seen as a sign of fat-burning success.

Atkins says exercise is essential to weight loss and optimum health. He encourages regular exercise.

Atkins recommends taking many nutritional supplements, especially from his own line.

Carbohydrate, protein, and fat allowances

- Carbohydrate: 20 grams a day in the Induction phase, gradually increasing to a maximum of 90 grams as long as weight loss is maintained.
- Protein: No set protein allowances.
- Fat: No set fat allowances.

Meal plan/ recipes

- More than 100 low-carb recipes and one sample meal plan for each phase of the diet.

the carbohydrate addict's diet

About the authors

Richard F. Heller, Ph.D., is a research biologist. His wife and professional partner, Rachael F. Heller, Ph.D., is a research psychologist and professor. Both were overweight as children and young adults, failing countless times at taking the weight off through "conventional" means. They are the founders of the Carbohydrate Addicts Center in New York City, where they conduct research about disordered eating and educate consumers about carbohydrate addiction.

the basic idea

The Hellers believe that most overweight people suffer from a genetically determined disorder, a food addiction caused by an imbalance in their body chemistry. That means being overweight is no more their fault than epilepsy or alcoholism. Carbohydrate addiction, then, is not something that can be solved by willpower. It can only be handled by regulating and restricting your intake of carbohydrates.

Those who have this disorder, say the Hellers, overproduce insulin in response to eating carbohydrates. Here's what happens: When you consume carbohydrates, your body releases far more insulin than it needs to rid the blood of the glucose that results from carbohydrate digestion. When too much insulin is in the blood, your brain fails to get the message that you are no longer hungry. You don't feel satisfied and likely will want to eat again soon. Carbohydrate addicts may recognize that the compulsion to eat again right after they finish a meal or snack is illogical, but they can't ignore the drive. They are never truly satisfied, so they repeatedly overeat and gain weight that they are unable to lose.

The Hellers hold that conventional diet plans (low-fat, high-carb) can't produce weight loss or weight control in carbohydrate addicts because these diets encourage eating carbohydrate several times a day. Even small amounts of carbohydrate can send a carbohydrate addict into the downward spiral of overeating.

how the plan works

The Carbohydrate Addict's Diet does not require calorie counting, and you don't need to keep track of grams of carbohydrate, fat, or protein. There are a few rules that dieters must adhere to, however. Carbohydrate consumption is restricted to a single "reward" meal each day. That meal must include equal portions of nonstarchy carbohydrates such as salad greens, protein, and starchy carbohydrates such as bread and pasta, and it must be consumed within one hour. You can have as many servings as you want during that one hour, but you must maintain the same proportions. Your other two meals must be free of starchy carbohydrates: They can include only protein and nonstarchy vegetables, such as leafy greens and cauliflower.

During the Entry Plan, which lasts two weeks and is designed for weight loss, you're allowed two low-carb meals and one Reward Meal a day. After the two-week period, you can choose from four different plans (A, B, C, or D), depending on your weight-loss goal. Each plan is based on the Entry Plan and includes one Reward Meal. In fact, the Entry Plan and Plan B are identical. Plan A is the same as the Entry Plan plus a low-carb snack. Plan C adds a salad to the Reward Meal, and Plan D encourages you to skip one low-carb meal a day and add a salad at your Reward Meal.

The Reward Meal may come as a surprise to professed carbohydrate addicts because it may include any food you want in any amount, including alcohol and dessert, as long as it is balanced proportionally to the other foods you eat at that meal. But the Hellers say that restricting the meal to 60 minutes limits insulin release into the bloodstream, no matter what you're eating. While they do encourage a wide variety of healthy foods for your Reward Meal, the Hellers believe there is no reason to forego favorite foods. It's up to you whether your Reward Meal is for breakfast, lunch, or dinner.

unique features

The premise behind The Carbohydrate Addict's Diet is that carbohydrates are addictive substances that encourage dependence and produce a habitual or excessive need to eat them. The Hellers detail the characteristics of carbohydrate addicts and offer a test for you to take to find out whether you suffer from carbohydrate addiction. Each day, you're allowed one carbohydrate-rich meal, such as the one shown here for example.

Carbohydrate, protein, and fat allowances

- There are no set guidelines for the amount of carbohydrate, protein, or fat in your diet. But high-carbohydrate foods must be confined to a single meal of no more than 60 minutes in duration.

Meal plan/ recipes

- Twelve days of low-carbohydrate menus are included, as is a chapter of low-carb recipes.

neanderthin:
eat like a caveman to achieve a lean, strong, healthy body

the basic idea

According to Audette, the trouble with our diet began when ancient man turned from hunting and gathering to agriculture and the domestication of animals for food. That's when humans became shorter than their predecessors and began dying earlier, he says.

Audette believes that foods made edible by modern civilization, including grains and milk, are the cause of many diseases, including obesity, that did not exist when humans ate a Paleolithic diet. Hunter–gatherers ate a wide variety of plants and animals, and Audette attributes their relative good health to that diet.

Audette believes technology has deeply compromised our health. Mass production of refined foods that are widely available and affordable, including white flour, canned foods, and sugars of all types, may have helped feed the growing population, but this has come at a huge human cost in terms of disease. He gives no scientific evidence, however, to support his claims. And, in fact, early humans may have suffered from arthritis.

Audette maintains that the modern obsession with a low-fat diet promotes weight gain. Low-fat diets, he says, have failed to control or conquer obesity. Americans should aspire to the meat-based caveman diet because it is so high in fat. Like other low-carb proponents, Audette believes that a high-fat diet will prevent the surges of insulin into the bloodstream that cause us to pack on calories as body fat.

Eating foods that are "free from technology" is the way back to good health, he claims. Audette wants to turn readers into urban (or suburban) hunter–gatherers, advising you to banish the "addictive" carbohydrates (such as any grain) that your diet is based on, as well as other foods that promote bad health and obesity. And he wants you to get moving, citing a sedentary lifestyle as one of the major pitfalls of modern life. Audette encourages regular physical activity for weight loss and better health.

how the plan works

Audette claims that diets based on calorie restriction fail. For that reason,

About the author

Ray Audette lectures, consults, and writes about Paleolithic nutrition. He is a falconer and avid hunter and gatherer in Dallas, Texas. Audette became intrigued by the Paleolithic-type diet as a way of managing his arthritis and diabetes, conditions that could not be controlled to his satisfaction by a conventional diet and medications. He claims his version of the caveman diet saved his life.

there are no calorie restrictions on this Stone-Age diet, and snacking is permissible. As long as you choose "technology free" foods, you can eat as much as you like. How do you decide whether a food is free from technology? Audette's acid test is whether a food would be edible when found in its natural state without using technology. Of note: Meat, poultry, seafood, and eggs *are* allowed on NeanderThin, but they should always be cooked first, as eating animal foods in their "natural" (raw) state raises the risk of food poisoning.

There is no cheating allowed on NeanderThin, because it encourages cravings for high-carb foods. Artificial sweeteners, coffee, and alcohol are not allowed; after all, they were unknown to ancient man. You are, however, allowed to indulge in a variety of foods, including meat, poultry, fish, rabbit, and squirrels. Since meat is the main attraction on NeanderThin, fat will be your primary calorie source. Starchy vegetables, including corn and potatoes, are not on the list of accepted foods. However, you will be allowed to enjoy other vegetables, such as leafy greens and broccoli. Audette advises eating them raw to minimize carbohydrate absorption.

There are two phases of the diet.

Phase I: For the first one to three weeks eliminate grains, beans, potatoes, milk, and refined sugars. Every day, drink 2 to 4 liters (about 68 to 140 ounces) chlorine-free water (municipal water supplies use chlorine to kill bacteria, but most bottled water companies do not).

Phase II: Once you've reached your desired weight, begin adding back carbohydrate-rich foods in small amounts (this is very vague in the book), including fruit and "sugary" vegetables, such as potatoes, beets, and yams. The bulk of your calories should continue to come from meats, nuts, seeds, and oils. Dairy products are prohibited.

unique features

The book reads more like an anthropology lesson than a diet program, and there is extensive information about the lifestyles of ancient humans and the evolution of food production.

The diet is largely based on animal foods and animal fat but eliminates all dairy products, even full-fat varieties.

NeanderThin encourages regular physical activity and provides a five-week exercise program that changes every day to mimic the varying activities of ancient hunter–gatherers.

Carbohydrate, protein, and fat allowances

- There are no set carbohydrate, protein, or fat allowances.

Meal plan/ recipes

- More than a quarter of this book is devoted to recipes and menu suggestions.

the protein power lifeplan

the basic idea

Our modern lifestyle has deviated from our ancestral one to the point where we are squandering our health, according to the Eades. They believe that while our diet has changed radically, our physiology has evolved imperceptibly. In essence, we are nothing more than cavemen in designer suits with cell phones.

The shift away from meat to a grain-based diet has been our undoing, say the Eades. Our meat-eating heritage cannot, and should not, be denied because it's actually linked to good health. Fossil records show that after agriculture arrived on the scene (about 10,000 years ago), human health, height, and longevity declined.

Why are grains so troubling? Their carbohydrate content, of course. The Eades argue that about 75 percent of adults overproduce insulin in response to carbohydrate consumption. A diet rich in sugar and starches (the typical American diet) results in insulin overload in the bloodstream. Abnormal metabolism of insulin is the primary reason for what the Eades characterize as the diseases of civilization: heart disease, diabetes, high blood pressure,

and elevated cholesterol and triglycerides in the blood, along with an array of other harmful conditions, including iron-storage disorder.

A high-carbohydrate, low-fat diet is not the panacea that health professionals had hoped for, the authors say. Promoting low-fat eating has not diminished the cluster of disorders caused by excess insulin. Eating more fat may be part of the answer to cutting back on carbohydrate intake, but the authors caution that all fat is not created equal. We may have evolved on a fat-packed diet, but our ancestors ate healthier fats, including the omega-3 kind found in seafood and in the fat of game animals. In addition, modern man consumes processed foods that contain trans fat, the type that "pollutes" cells and interferes with their function.

Reducing carbohydrate may be the primary route to better health, but the Eades take a more holistic approach. They concede that decreased caloric intake also works to reduce insulin levels in the blood but note that it's not nearly as effective as curbing carbohydrate consumption. The Eades prescribe exercise, arguing that our ancient ancestors were lean, fit, and

About the authors

Husband-and-wife team Michael R. Eades, M.D., and Mary Dan Eades, M.D., are also the authors of *Protein Power* and *The Protein Power Life-Plan Gram Counter.* They specialize in bariatric (weight control) medicine in Boulder, Colorado.

strong-boned. Stone Age exercise consisted of bursts of high-intensity activities that used the large muscle groups, followed by long sedentary periods. To that end, the Eades have designed a cavemanlike activity regimen that includes stretching, sprinting, leaping, and jumping.

We may be overloaded with iron as a result of our modern diet, say the Eades. If you are insulin resistant, they recommend getting an evaluation for iron-storage disorder, which they claim is a manifestation of excess insulin.

Nutrient supplements and prescription medication, as needed, are also part of their multifaceted program.

how the plan works

You begin by determining your protein and carbohydrate requirements. Detailed charts, based on height and weight, are provided to help you set the amount of protein you need. The Eades recommend everyone start at the Intervention level for carbohydrates, which allows less than 40 grams of Effective Carbohydrate Content (ECC)—the total carbohydrate content of a food minus the fiber content—per day. The amount of fiber is subtracted from the total carb content because fiber is not digested and is not converted to glucose. The authors provide a chart of the ECC for common foods and teach you how to evaluate the ECC of packaged foods. The Interven-

tion level lasts from a few weeks to several months, depending on your health and weight. Then it's on to the Transition level for carbohydrate intake for one to two months, then to the Maintenance level forever. Each successive level allows more carbs.

Once you know your protein and carbohydrate requirements, you choose one of three commitment levels. The least restrictive allows limited quantities of added sugars while the most restrictive approximates a caveman diet.

At every stage of the eating plan, you are encouraged to drink 64 ounces of filtered water daily.

unique features

The Eades use a sophisticated and sometimes complicated approach to low-carb eating. The eating plan can be difficult to figure out on your own. The authors provide in-depth explanations for their theories, using complex biochemical, physiological, and anthropological information. There are chapters devoted to cholesterol and health, antioxidants, diet and the immune response, peak brain function, and iron-overload disease. Each chapter provides a Bottom Line summary that highlights the main points. The plan promotes supplemental magnesium, chromium picolinate, alpha lipoic acid, and coenzyme Q_{10} to improve insulin receptor function.

Carbohydrate, protein, and fat allowances

- Carbohydrate: Intake is based on your current state of health, level of physical activity, and amount of weight you need to lose. Everyone should start with the Intervention level that restricts you to a maximum of 40 grams carbohydrate per day.
- Protein: Minimum requirements per meal vary with weight and height.
- Fat: Varies based on weight loss or maintenance goals. Cut back on fatty foods if you're not losing weight or start gaining. The plan encourages unsaturated fats and discourages most vegetable cooking oils and trans fats.

Meal plan/recipes

- Provides meal plans that account for your chosen carbohydrate intake and commitment level.

the schwarzbein principle:
the truth about losing weight, being healthy, and feeling younger

the basic idea

Schwarzbein's defining principle is: Your diet and other lifestyle habits determine your "metabolic age." The older your metabolism, the greater the chances for disease. When you avoid the lifestyle habits that accelerate aging, including a high-carb diet, stress, smoking, and excessive alcohol consumption, you naturally reduce the risk of the degenerative diseases that come with time, such as cancer, arthri- tis, and heart disease, while achieving ideal body composition.

One condition you *can't* avoid is insulin resistance (IR), according to Schwarzbein. She says everyone eventually develops it with time. IR occurs when cells resist insulin's com- mand to allow glucose to enter. When cells fail to respond to insulin, the pancreas pumps out more of the hor- mone until finally the level of insulin in the blood overwhelms the cells' resist- ance, forcing in glucose. IR translates into higher insulin levels in the blood- stream that, in turn, promote weight gain. IR earlier in life hastens metabolic aging, says Schwarzbein, and that

spells trouble for your health. The primary goal of avoiding accelerated metabolic aging is putting off IR for as long as possible.

Eating fat is central to delaying IR, says Schwarzbein, since low-fat diets backfire by promoting high insulin levels. Schwarzbein asserts that a calorie is not a calorie, as the current weight control dogma would have consumers believe. The body processes carbohydrate differently, she says. Since carbohydrate is not used as raw material to build body parts (cells), enzymes, or hormones, it must be used for energy only. You cannot lose weight simply by restricting calories, she says. You must eat a varied diet that includes protein, fat, nonstarchy vegetables, and carbohydrates in accordance with your metabolism, says Schwarzbein. Also, you must manage your stress, decrease stimulant use, get regular exercise, and take hormone replace- ment therapy, if needed, for optimum health.

Schwarzbein believes that your metabolism is resilient and you can constantly redirect its course. Her low-carb approach to weight loss and disease prevention is designed to heal your body by encouraging it to use stored fat, the result of excess blood glucose, for energy.

the plan

The ultimate goal of Schwarzbein's eating plan is to drop blood insulin levels from high to normal. There are no calorie limits, and you don't need to weigh and measure foods. Schwarzbein says focusing on numbers such as grams of fat and protein causes an unhealthy obsession with food. Carbs are the exception, however, at least during the initial phase of the regimen, when the goal seems to be to increase awareness. Schwarzbein reasons that once you become aware of the carbohydrate content of foods (she provides detailed charts), you will naturally curb your intake.

The plan is divided into two stages: the healing program and the maintenance program. During the healing phase, you drop carbohydrate intake below your current metabolic needs (details are given in the book about how to do this). The healing process continues until proper body composition is achieved. Although there is no test for this, Schwarzbein encourages dieters to go for a sleek, toned, slightly muscular look and "solid bones." In the maintenance part of the pro-

gram, you're encouraged to eat enough carb to meet your metabolic needs.

Each phase has a lifestyle component. For Schwarzbein, it's not enough to change your diet. She advocates exercise; the elimination of stimulants, including medications, caffeine, and alcohol; stress management; and hormone replacement therapy as components of her program to heal your metabolism and keep it on track.

unique features

This diet focuses on correcting metabolic disturbances to reduce body fat and to avoid premature aging and the diseases associated with it, including heart diseases and cancer. A healthy lifestyle is emphasized almost as much as a low-carb diet. Schwarzbein provides a lengthy chapter on serotonin, a feel-good neurotransmitter (brain messenger) that she says drops with poor eating and lifestyle habits, resulting in depression. The book provides instructions for vegetarians who want to follow Schwarzbein's plan.

Carbohydrate, protein, and fat allowances

- Carbohydrate: Intake depends on body composition, body weight, and activity level. Detailed guidelines are provided for carbohydrate intake.
- Protein: 60 to 70 grams of protein daily for women; 70 to 80 grams a day for men.
- Fat: No limit on fat consumption, but avoid unhealthy fats.

Meal plans/ recipes

- Provides four weeks of menus for vegetarians and mainstream eaters, as well as two dozen recipes.

the south beach diet

the basic idea

Carbohydrates, particularly the highly processed kind, are responsible for the bulk of our excess girth, reasons Agatston. Eating may put an end to your immediate hunger, but depending on what you eat, food can create cravings. The type of carbohydrate you eat matters because it influences food cravings that make and keep you overweight, and it affects insulin levels in the bloodstream. When the bloodstream receives an infusion of glucose after eating foods that cause rapid spikes in blood glucose, including white bread, potatoes, and cookies, the pancreas responds by releasing lots of insulin. But when you eat carbohydrates that are more slowly metabolized, such as high-fiber vegetables and unprocessed whole grains, insulin release is gradual. As a result, he says, food cravings and blood concentrations of glucose and insulin are better controlled, making it easier to lose weight and keep it off.

With the South Beach Diet, it's possible to correct the way you respond to the foods that caused you to pack on the pounds in the first place (i.e. "bad" carbohydrates). Not only will you lose weight, but Agatston claims you will alter your body chemistry to decrease the risk of diabetes, heart disease, and polycystic ovary syndrome, a condition that affects fertility.

With the exception of the first one to two weeks, the South Beach Diet is not a typical low-carb eating program. Instead of banning carbohydrates in general, it encourages eating good carbs, such as fruits, vegetables, and high-fiber grains—all foods that score low on the glycemic index. (See pages 68–69 for more details on the glycemic index.) And it doesn't give you license to eat saturated fat as do many low-carb diets. Agatston emphasizes eating healthy fats by encouraging a diet with lots of seafood, olive oil, nuts, and avocados. He says the problem with some low-carbohydrate diets is that they are packed with fat that harms your arteries and sets them up for clogging and for constriction, or clamping down, that blocks blood flow to major organs. In addition, Agatston asserts, high-fat meals can trigger a heart attack in certain people.

Agatston advocates exercise but says it's not necessary for losing weight. He says his diet will be effective regardless. However, he believes that regular physical activity is key for losing weight faster and for reducing insulin and glucose levels in the blood while promoting overall health.

the plan

Agatston theorizes that hunger undermines weight-loss plans, so you don't need to worry about counting calories, carbohydrate, fat, or protein on the South Beach Diet. The plan has three phases.

Phase One: For the first one to two weeks, you eat no bread, rice, potatoes, pasta, baked goods, fruit, or refined sugars in order to banish unhealthy cravings. There are no limits on the allowed foods, but meals should be of "normal size," enough to relieve your hunger and no more. The plan encourages snacking and dessert after dinner.

Phase Two: You begin to liberalize your carbohydrate consumption, but you must do so deliberately. Agatston recommends going slow when adding back carbs and paying close attention to your weight and how you feel. Your goal during this second phase is to eat more carbohydrate, preferably those with a low glycemic index (GI) score, while continuing to shed the pounds until you hit your weight target. The GI measures the degree to which eating a certain food increases blood glucose levels. A low GI score indicates the

food produces a slow rise in blood glucose concentrations. You shouldn't go overboard on low glycemic-index foods (typically foods such as whole grains and some legumes, including lentils, and unsweetened yogurt) either, says Agatston, because large portions will produce higher-than-desired blood glucose levels.

Phase Three: Now that you've achieved your goal weight, you know how many low glycemic index foods to eat without gaining weight. During this phase, which could also be called maintenance, you're allowed any food, including desserts on occasion.

unique features

The glycemic index is the cornerstone of Agatston's recommendations for carbohydrate intake after the first phase of the diet. The ultimate goal is arriving at a carbohydrate intake that allows you to maintain your weight.

The author devotes a lengthy chapter to diabetes, explaining how type 2 diabetes (the most common kind) develops and how to head it off. Another chapter details how to prevent heart disease.

Carbohydrate, protein, and fat allowances

- There are no set carbohydrate, protein, or fat allowances.

Meal plan/ recipes

- Includes two weeks' worth of menu plans for each of the three phases of the diet and dozens of recipes for each phase, many of which were created by Miami Beach restaurant chefs.

the new sugar busters!
cut sugar to trim fat

About the authors

Morrison C. Bethea, M.D., is a cardiothoracic surgeon and clinical professor of surgery at Tulane Medical Center in New Orleans. Sam S. Andrews, M.D., is an endocrinologist who specializes in obesity treatment. He is an associate professor of medicine at the Louisiana State University Medical School in New Orleans. Luis A. Balart, M.D., is the chief of gastroenterology at the Louisiana State University School of Medicine and is medical director of liver transplantation at Memorial Medical Center in New Orleans. H. Leighton Steward has been the CEO of a Fortune 500 energy company. His success with the Sugar Busters! diet and his family history of heart disease motivated him to help write the original *Sugar Busters! Cut Sugar to Trim Fat* book and to update it.

the basic idea

The "experts" are wrong, according to Sugar Busters! All calories are not created equal. The type of calories we eat matter more than how many, they say. Carbohydrates are responsible for raising insulin levels, which in turn promotes fat storage and inhibits the release of fat from cells for use as energy. Carbohydrates that are quickly absorbed, such as those found in white rice and potatoes, stimulate more of a rise in blood glucose than the carbs in foods such as whole grains. As a result, the authors believe the bulk of your diet should be derived from the "right" kind of carbohydrates.

Sugar Busters! is not a low-carb diet, say the authors. It's a correct-carbohydrate lifestyle that allows moderate amounts of healthy carbohydrates, protein, and fat. Fat is not the issue, the authors argue. In fact, the low-fat zealots have been misleading the public for decades. According to Sugar Busters! dogma, it's not necessarily the amount of fat you eat, but the fat you create from eating too many of the wrong kind of carbs that matters to your weight and to your health.

Insulin control is the key to permanent weight loss and the prevention of heart disease and diabetes. If you learn how to regulate insulin release into the bloodstream, you will be the master of your weight and your health, the authors contend. The Sugar Busters! diet is the key to insulin control.

the plan

There are no phases or different stages to the Sugar Busters! diet, but there are rules. These are the main ones: Eliminate white potatoes, rice, bread made from highly refined flour, corn products, beets, refined sugars, and beer from your diet. Concentrate on lean meats, poultry, and seafood while limiting foods rich in saturated and trans fats. Eat three to six meals a day plus snacks, but don't eat after 8:00 P.M. As for portion size, there are two simple rules: Don't overfill your plate, and don't go back for seconds. The authors approve of snacks, particu-

with food, not on an empty stomach. Beer is forbidden on this diet.

unique features

Sugar Busters! details in easily understood terms how digestion and metabolism work, and it helps readers relate these processes to the issues of insulin levels and health.

The diet's major goal is disease prevention, but it also stresses weight control and weight loss if you are overweight. The book contains chapters on women and weight loss; preventing childhood obesity; and how the Sugar Busters! diet helps head off and manage diabetes and heart disease.

The Sugar Busters! plan contains some food-combining rules, such as eating fruit by itself. It also recommends limiting fluids at meals and snacks to promote proper chewing and to prevent the dilution of digestive enzymes.

larly if they are a fruit. You're asked to drink between six and eight glasses of water every day and to limit alcohol to moderate levels. If you drink wine (preferably red), you should have it

Carbohydrate, protein, and fat allowances

- Carbohydrate: No set allowances, but averages at least 40 percent of calories.
- Protein: No set allowances, but averages 30 percent of calories.
- Fat: No set allowances, but averages 30 percent of calories.

Meal plan/ recipes

- No meal plans. Includes dozens of recipes.

suzanne somers'
get skinny on fabulous foods

About the author

Suzanne Somers is an actress and author of several diet books, including *Eat Great, Lose Weight*.

the basic idea

Somers continues to dispel what she believes is a myth, that fat is the enemy when it comes to weight control and good health, in this second book in the Somersizing series. Here she bashes the low-fat eating craze, with gusto. She contends there is plenty of proof that it's possible to eat fat and lose weight. Carbohydrates, rather than fat, are the enemy, says Somers.

Somers' ideas about the role of carbohydrates in weight gain are based primarily on the theories of Dr. Diana Schwarzbein, an endocrinologist and the author of *The Schwarzbein Principle* (see pages 28–29 for a review of Schwarzbein's diet plan). Schwarzbein maintains that scientific evidence proves high insulin levels are responsible for many health problems, including heart disease, high blood pressure, and obesity. And she claims the best way to control insulin levels—and reduce weight—is to decrease the amount of carbohydrates you eat.

Somers frequently refers to Schwarzbein's research and her conclusions about the roles of carbohy-drate, fat, and protein in weight loss and weight control. And Schwarzbein wrote a foreword for this book praising Somers' approach to low-carb eating.

Somers and Schwarzbein believe that conventional diets are filled with empty promises because they perpetuate a cycle of deprivation and overeating, resulting in weight gain. Somers' personal experiences with yo-yo dieting prompted her to conclude that high-carbohydrate, low-fat eating could not control her weight or keep her healthy.

According to Somers, you can reprogram your metabolism by eating fewer carbs and liberal amounts of fat. She says this type of diet retools the body to burn fat while providing a constant source of energy for cells. Somers' diet promises to restore hormonal balance, which she considers key to achieving ideal body weight and optimum health.

Avoiding sugar and starch is central to reaching the fat-burning state, says Somers, who recommends choosing foods with low glycemic index scores. The likes of bread, cereal, pasta, potatoes, and simple sugars promote hormonal imbalance by provoking insulin production and releasing an overload of it into the bloodstream.

But where Somers diverges from the typical low-carb diet plans is in her emphasis on careful food combining. Foods are divided into five basic categories: Pro/Fat, Veggies, Carbos, Fruit, and Funky Foods (primarily high glycemic index foods such as sugar and white flour). Foods in these different categories can only be eaten according to strict and somewhat complicated rules. For example, fruit must be eaten alone and on an empty stomach because it causes gas and bloating and may upset the digestion of other foods. And you must wait three hours between a pro/fat meal and a carbo meal.

how the plan works

On Level One, your job is to learn to eliminate from your diet all sorts of sugars; starchy foods including white flour, potatoes, and bananas; and "bad combo foods," such as nuts, olives, and low-fat milk and yogurt, and to separate foods into their Somersizing groups. Bad combo foods earn their label because they contain both carbs and fats. You are allowed to eat until you are full without counting calories or any other nutrient as long as you eat only those foods allowed on the diet in the correct combination. The goal of Level One is weight loss.

Once you have achieved your goal weight, you move on to Level Two for maintenance. By the time you reach Level Two, Somers says you will have trained your pancreas not to over-secrete insulin because you have been avoiding high-carbohydrate foods and eating more fat for so long. In addition, you will have directed your body to use fat reserves for energy by this point in the diet.

Level Two is less restrictive than Level One. It's okay to indulge your carbohydrate cravings, eating foods such as bread, potatoes, and even desserts. However, you must eat them only in moderation and infrequently. If you gain weight on Level Two, Somers recommends returning to Level One to lose it.

unique features

Somers' emphasis on food combining makes her plan somewhat different from the standard low-carb diet. There are two levels to the diet, and Somers encourages you to alternate between the two to maintain your weight for life.

Carbohydrate, protein, and fat allowances

- There are no set allowances for carbohydrate, protein, or fat.

Meal plan/ recipes

- More than 130 low-carb recipes for both levels of the diet.

the zone

About the author

Barry Sears, Ph.D., has worked as a researcher at Boston University and the Massachusetts Institute of Technology. His background includes developing drug delivery systems for cancer and heart patients. The males on his father's side of the family all died of heart disease in their early fifties, prompting Sears to seek a diet to prevent heart disease. In 1995, he published *The Zone,* which became number one on *The New York Times* best-seller list. He is the president of The Sears Technology Group.

the basic idea

Sears says the "Zone" is a metabolic state in which your body and mind function at their best. This state is achievable with the Zone diet he developed. When you're in the Zone, you are relaxed, yet alert and focused. Your body is strong and energetic, and it's working at peak efficiency at all times. According to Sears, being in the Zone slows the aging process; keeps colds and flu at bay; and helps ward off chronic conditions, including heart disease and cancer. Once you're in the Zone, you are able to tap into a virtually unlimited source of energy—your own body fat.

The reason we're not all in the Zone already is that we eat the wrong foods, says Sears, who maintains that much of the current dietary "wisdom" is dead wrong. The Zone diet is Sears' antidote to conventional dogma that carbohydrates are the cornerstone of healthy diets. Sears says humans are not genetically geared to eat the amount of carbohydrate they typically take in. He contends our digestive system was designed to process lean protein and natural carbohydrates such as those found in fruits and fiber-rich vegeta-

bles. As a result, most of us cannot handle high-carbohydrate diets. Eating carbohydrate causes insulin levels to rise and encourages fat storage, according to Sears. Too much insulin catapults you out of the Zone, where you gain weight; suffer from diabetes, heart disease, and a host of other ills; and feel sluggish.

Sears believes that food is much more than a fuel supply. He calls food the most powerful drug you'll ever encounter, contending that it directs the hormones that affect weight and health. For Sears, conventional weight-reduction diets are hormonally incorrect, which is why they fail.

how the plan works

Sears promotes a "beneficial" relationship (ratio) between protein and carbohydrate as part of a diet that is, by current recommendations, high in protein and modestly restricted in carbohydrate and fat content. He believes that the ratio he recommends, 40 percent carbohydrates, 30 percent protein, and 30 percent fat (40/30/30), is key to controlling insulin production, making it possible for you to burn excess body fat. The modest amount of carbohydrate in the Zone diet helps you to avoid ketosis. Plus, Sears says his eating plan allows the liver to maintain adequate glycogen stores.

Each meal and snack that you eat should contain the beneficial ratios of carbohydrate, protein, and fat. While it's not a low-fat diet per se, the Zone plan encourages lean protein choices, and it avoids most grain products, starchy vegetables, and certain fruit. Carbohydrate choices should be high-fiber and low on the glycemic index.

Before you jump right in to the diet, you must do a bit of math. The first step is determining your personal protein allowance by considering your current weight, percent body fat, and level of physical activity. (Sears provides detailed instructions for this.) Once you know how much you need, you can figure your carbohydrate and fat allowances. There is no need to count calories or grams of fat, protein, or carbohydrate. Sears has bundled foods into macronutrient blocks with predetermined portion sizes. Portions matter, so you do need to weigh and measure foods.

unique features

Sears has determined what he believes is the optimum ratio of carbohydrate, protein, and fat in the diet. Using his macronutrient blocks as a guide, you can always eat the proper ratio. Timing is also important to Sears. You shouldn't let more than five hours elapse without eating a Zone-balanced meal or snack.

Carbohydrate, protein, and fat allowances

- Carbohydrate accounts for 40 percent of calories on the Zone diet.
- Protein needs are unique and must be calculated by the individual but tend to amount to 30 percent of calories consumed for all dieters.
- About 30 percent of calories come from fat; unsaturated varieties are encouraged.

Meal plan/ recipes

- Contains some suggestions for meal planning and a chapter of low-carb recipes.

diets at a glance

Diet	Main features	Carb allowance	Protein and fat allowances	Ketogenic?	Flexibility rating
Dr. Atkins' New Diet Revolution	The lowest of the low-carb diets; high in fat	20 grams/day initially; up to 90 grams for maintenance unless you gain weight	No set allowances	Yes	3
Carbohydrate Addict's	Believes addiction to carbohydrates is a genetic disorder. Allows 1 unrestricted meal and 2 low-carb meals/day	None specified	None specified	No	3
NeanderThin	Advocates a return to meat-based, Stone-Age diet; discourages foods such as grains that utilize technology	None specified; dairy products prohibited	None specified	Yes	2
Protein Power LifePlan	Complex plan that can be difficult to use; delves into relationship between diet and disease	Less than 40 grams at the Intervention level; successive levels allow more	Protein varies with weight and height; fat based on weight-loss or maintenance goals	No	2

Diet	Main features	Carb allowance	Protein and fat allowances	Ketogenic?	Flexibility rating
Schwarzbein Principle	Goal is to heal metabolism by reducing carbs, exercising, and making other lifestyle changes	Varies, depending on body composition, weight, and activity level	At least 60 grams protein for women and 70 for men daily; no fat allowance	No	3.5
South Beach	Retrains how you metabolize carbs; emphasizes eating the right carbs (low glycemic index) and foods low in fat	None specified; emphasizes choosing low glycemic index foods	None specified	No	4
Sugar Busters!	Eliminates starchy and sugary foods while promoting lean animal foods and healthy fats. Has some food combining rules.	No set amount, but averages 40% of daily calories	No set amount, but averages 30% of daily calories for each	No	4
Suzanne Somers	Emphasizes food combining with somewhat complicated rules	None specified	None specified	No	4
The Zone	Moderate approach to low-carb eating that promotes a beneficial ratio of carb to protein for each meal and snack	40% of daily calories	30% of calories for each	No	4

personalize your low-carb plan

Make low-carb work for you. You've learned the fundamentals of low-carb dieting. And you've read the reviews of popular low-carb plans. Now it's time to get personal. Whether you're going to follow one of the reviewed diet plans or you want to create your own, you have to find ways to put the principles of low-carb living to work in your life, to make food and exercise choices that are in keeping with those principles but that also take your goals, your tastes, your lifestyle, and your health into account. You'll find what you need to do just that in this section. Consider it your personal low-carb tool kit, one that you can reach into time and again to ensure that your low-carb dieting efforts are moving you toward your weight-loss goals.

how to build your own low-carb diet

While the medical community has been slow to come around to low-carb eating, it's hard to argue with the benefits of the more moderate low-carb programs, such as The Zone and Sugar Busters!, that don't jeopardize your health for the sake of dropping a dress size. If the rationale and the evidence for low-carb dieting have convinced you to cut carbs, the challenge confronting you now is how to go about it. Do you want to follow one of the low-carb diet plans reviewed earlier or do you prefer a do-it-yourself approach?

tools for low-carb living

When you looked over the diet plans reviewed earlier, did any of them appeal to you? Or did some seem too restrictive while others require too much time and effort to figure out? Perhaps one plan seemed too good to be true while another doesn't eliminate enough carbs for you to lose weight.

If you didn't find just the right plan or a formalized approach feels too constricting, you still can adopt a low-carb lifestyle. All you need are the right tools. In this section, we give you those tools so you can fashion a personalized weight-control plan that works by combining conventional wisdom (you must cut calories to lose weight) with low-carbohydrate eating.

getting started: write it down!

To make real changes to your diet, you must be conscious of what you eat. Only then can you alter your diet in a way that will produce weight loss.

The best way to raise your consciousness is to keep track of the foods you eat with a food diary. Why log every morsel? Because it's easy to believe that you avoid simple sugars (carbs), such as table sugar, corn syrup, and fructose, when in reality your diet may be full of these expendable carbohydrates. Food diaries force you to spot sugar sources on food labels and to record the carbohydrate content of processed foods.

Keeping track of what you eat also helps you monitor portion sizes, which influence carbohydrate intake. Portion sizes have grown so large in America today that most of us don't have a clue about what a single serving is supposed to be. According to the Food Guide Pyramid, a single serving of pasta, for instance, is a half-cup. A single serving according to the Nutrition Facts panel is one cup. But what you're likely to eat, or what you're likely to be served in a restaurant, is a two-cup portion—four times the single serving allotment on the Pyramid and double the single serving size on the Nutrition Facts panel. The more you keep track of portion sizes, the less likely you'll be to overeat and thwart your weight-loss attempts. Try to weigh and measure foods for at least a few days to get accustomed to amounts and sizes. After that, you should be able to accurately eyeball foods and estimate the serving size. For more on portion sizes, see page 70.

Since emotions often play a role in when, where, and how much food you eat, use your journal to keep track of your mood when you eat as well as where you happen to be (in front of the television, standing at the kitchen counter). Also rate how hungry you are on a scale of one to five, with one being the lowest score. All of these bits of information will help you understand how your emotional state affects your eating habits.

Purchase a sturdy notebook that fits in your pocketbook or briefcase. You'll need to bring your food log with you everywhere to ensure accurate accounting. Trying to recall what you ate hours later may lead to faulty reporting, especially when you conveniently forget snatching a few of your child's french fries or popping a few pieces of candy in your mouth while driving. After a few days of diligent observance, look for patterns in your eating behaviors. Use food labels and the counter on pages 74–113 to tally your daily intake of carbohydrate grams. Aim for 100 to 150 a day for a lower-carb diet.

Still not losing?

You've curbed carbs, but you've yet to shed a pound. What gives? Here are some reasons why you may not be losing weight.

- Medications: Some medications work against weight loss, including insulin and steroids, such as prednisone. Check with your physician and pharmacist to establish a link between medicines you take on a regular basis and your weight.
- Nibbling: Dieters often underestimate their nibbling, which can amount to hundreds of calories every day. To prevent noshing during meal preparation—or any other time of the day—sip water, chew gum, or nibble on low-carb vegetables such as celery. You can also brush your teeth when tempted to nibble; the minty-fresh flavor of the toothpaste makes food taste bad.
- Large portion sizes: Whenever you're baffled by what the scale says, record what you eat for a few days to discover problem areas. Weigh and measure foods to track portion sizes.
- Exercise: Relying on diet alone to shed pounds takes longer and reduces your chance of keeping the weight off for good. Consider walking more. Already exercising? Change your routine around. Weight training preserves and builds muscle tissue, which burns more calories than fat.

label reading: in search of sugar

You have to be a bit of a detective to discover hidden sources of carbohydrate. But you don't need an advanced degree or special skills to uncover them. Most of the time, the information is right under your nose on the Nutrition Facts panel or the ingredient list of any food product.

the nutrition facts panel

The Nutrition Facts panel takes the guesswork out of the carbohydrate content of any packaged food you buy. It lists the total carbohydrate content as well as the amount of dietary fiber and sugars in a single serving. If you're interested in calories, you'll find a listing for them, too.

The listing for grams of total carbohydrate and fiber are the most valuable figures for carbohydrate-counters because they help you fit foods into your daily carbohydrate allowance. Foods that are higher in fiber are also lower on the glycemic index scale, so

they make excellent choices. Aim for at least 25 grams of fiber every day.

A word of caution about the Nutrition Facts panel. It's possible to think that milk, plain yogurt, and cheese contain added sugar and that they are unhealthy because they lack fiber. But neither is the case. Lactose, the primary carbohydrate in milk, is considered a sugar and is listed as such on food labels. It's not an added sugar but one that occurs naturally. And dairy products are naturally fiber free. That's because only plant foods provide fiber. But that doesn't make dairy products unhealthy. They're very important sources of bone-building calcium and vitamin D.

a carbohydrate by any name

There are so many names for sugar, it's important to familiarize yourself with all of them or you could end up unwittingly eating a high-carb diet even as you're trying to cut back. You probably recognize the word sucrose as a stand-in for the word sugar. It's the white stuff you add to coffee, tea, and baked goods. But processed foods, including croutons, spaghetti sauce, and salad dressing, pack a variety of added sugars. Sugar goes by many names in the ingredient list, including:

- Brown sugar
- Cane sugar
- Confectioners' sugar
- Corn syrup and high-fructose corn syrup

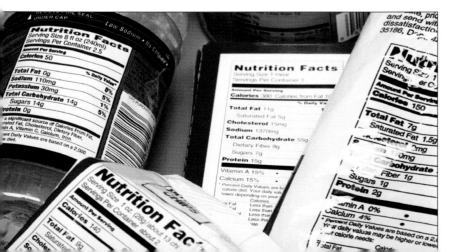

- Crystallized cane sugar or juice
- Date sugar
- Dextrose and dextrin
- Distilled or concentrated fruit sugars
- Fructose
- Glucose and glucose polymers
- Honey
- Invert sugar
- Malt
- Maltose
- Maple syrup
- Molasses
- Raw sugar
- Turbinado sugar

day by day: foods to include

One of the problems with many low-carb regimens is that they recommend limiting or avoiding entire food groups, which can result in nutrient deficiencies that affect your health. No matter what controlled-carbohydrate strategy you choose, here's what you need to include in your diet and why:

- 3 servings low-fat dairy daily
  To provide bone-building calcium and vitamin D, nutrients that reduce your risk for osteoporosis.
- 2–3 servings whole grains daily
  To provide fiber that promotes feelings of fullness. Fortified grains contain folic acid and other B vitamins for heart health, iron, and zinc, and they may provide calcium and vitamin D.
- Daily multivitamin supplement
  Acts as a nutritional safety net, filling in some gaps.

Committing to low-carb living: good for the entire family

Cutting carbs can benefit every family member, as long as their diets are balanced and appropriate for their age. Cutting back on sweets provides the most obvious benefits to everyone. Children may clamor for treats, but they do not need the sugar found in ice cream, cookies, cake, and certain breakfast cereals.

There's no need to go to extremes with kids, however. In fact, keeping bread, potatoes, and cereal off your children's menu may be detrimental to their health because they need carbohydrates for energy. A growing child (excluding infants) requires at least half of his calories from carbohydrate. Offering little ones healthy foods such as meat, poultry, and seafood; whole grains; dairy products; and fruits and vegetables every day and leaving sugary cereals and other foods as special treats will give your child the right idea about eating.

- 2 fish meals a week, at least
  To reduce risk of heart disease.
- No fewer than 3 meals a day
  To reduce the hunger that causes binges and feelings of deprivation.
- 5 or more servings of fruits daily
  To include fiber that promotes feelings of fullness and antioxidant vitamins and minerals that help fight chronic conditions, including heart disease and cancer.

the fat conundrum

The major problem with fat is that it tastes so good you may end up eating more than you need, leading to excess calorie consumption. But some low-carb diets advocate shedding your fear of dietary fat to drop pounds. They argue that dietary fat does not promote weight gain because fat cannot provoke the insulin release that causes it.

Abiding by certain low-carb regimens may mean eating far more fat than you ever have on other weight-loss programs.

In reality, fat contains more than double the calories of protein or carbohydrate (nine versus four). So how do you explain the success of high-fat eating plans such as Dr. Atkins' New Diet Revolution? Skeptics argue that after a short time of being allowed to gorge on steak, cheese, and cream, dieters tire of these foods and decrease their consumption, dropping their calorie intake to levels that promote weight loss.

Regardless of its role in weight gain and weight loss, we need to remember that fat is essential to good health. Fat supplies essential fatty acids, the building blocks of important bodily substances that maintain life and promote

health. And fat is necessary for transporting and storing vitamins A, D, E, and K.

All fat is not created equal, however. In the past, all fat in the diet was perceived as bad news for health. But a growing body of evidence suggests that diets rich in unsaturated fats actually protect against heart disease and may help control blood glucose concentrations and elevated triglyceride levels. The American Heart Association and the U.S. Dietary Guidelines for Americans encourage consumers to replace saturated fat, found in foods such as meat, cream, cheese, and certain processed foods, with unsaturated fat, found in foods including nuts and canola and olive oils. When building your low-carb diet, aim to get 50 to 60 grams of fat per day.

fill up on fiber

Dietary fiber, also know as roughage and bulk, is a complex carbohydrate, found in fruits, vegetables, legumes, nuts, and grains, that cannot be broken down by your body during digestion. If your body cannot process it, why is fiber so important to health? Fiber aids digestion, reducing the chances of constipation and hemorrhoids, and it may help deter heart disease and certain cancers. When whittling your waistline is the goal, fiber is particularly helpful because it makes you feel full and that full feeling lasts longer.

Plus, fiber's capacity to provide bulk in your stomach makes it difficult to overeat fiber-rich foods, as compared to low-fiber, highly refined alternatives. For example, it's a lot easier and quicker to drink 8 ounces of apple juice, which is refined and low in fiber, than it is to eat two whole apples, although the juice and the apples have an equivalent number of calories.

Foods high in fiber are typically low in natural and added sugars, making them perfect choices for low-carb living. In fact, many low-carb diet proponents recommend choosing foods rich in fiber, including whole grains and certain fruits and vegetables, because fiber slows down the release of glucose into the bloodstream, preventing insulin surges that may result in weight gain. Fiber-filled foods are also rich in several vital nutrients, including vitamins, minerals, and phytonutrients, plant substances that may guard against heart disease and cancer.

low-carb eating in the real world

It's easier to prepare and eat lower-carb meals in the comfort of your own kitchen, where you know the ingredients involved and have the ability to measure portions. It's much harder to negotiate a low-carb diet when you leave home. Tempting food is everywhere, whether you're at the movie theater or the ball game, grocery shopping, filling your tank at the gas station, or shopping at the mall.

The first rule of thumb: Don't let yourself get so hungry that you'll eat anything. Before going out, eat a high-protein snack and drink a large glass of water to tide you over until your next meal.

When dining out, take the food you need when your meal arrives and ask for a doggy bag immediately. Ask the wait staff to remove the bread or chip basket from your table, and order extra low-carb vegetables in lieu of potato dishes and rice. Split one dessert between four or more people.

When asked to potluck parties, bring a low-carb dish and fill up on it. It's okay to indulge at times, but curb your carbohydrate consumption to compensate for splurges, and avoid "trigger" foods that could cause you to overeat for days.

sample lower-carb menu
What does a day's worth of low-carb eating look like? Here's a sample menu to give you a sense of it.
BREAKFAST
    ½ cup whole-grain cereal
    4 ounces 1% low-fat milk
    ½ cup sliced strawberries
SNACK
    1 hard-boiled egg
    1 cheese stick (1 ounce reduced-fat mozzarella)

LUNCH

Salad (made of 2 cups mixed salad greens; 1 small tomato, chopped; 6½ ounce can white tuna, drained; 1 tablespoon each balsamic vinegar and olive oil)

1 ounce whole-grain crackers

SNACK

1 ounce almonds

DINNER

Orange chicken (4 ounce serving sautéed with ½ cup mushrooms; ¼ small onion, chopped; ½ tablespoon orange marmalade; small amount of soy sauce and water; and salt and pepper)

1 cup steamed broccoli

1 teaspoon butter or margarine

SNACK

Fruit smoothie

(Combine ½ cup frozen berries with 1 teaspoon vanilla extract, 2 ice cubes, 8 ounces low-fat plain yogurt, and artificial sweetener in blender and whip until frothy.)

what can i have instead?

Boredom and feelings of deprivation can be the end of any well-intentioned eating plan, low-carb or not. By choosing a lower-carb lifestyle, there is little doubt that you will be doing without some of your favorite foods. However, there is no need to sacrifice all in the name of good health. Eating smaller portions of pasta, rice, bread, and potatoes curbs carbohydrate consump-tion without denying you them alto-gether. And taking a new approach to high-carb favorites helps, too. On the following page are some suggestions to start you on the low-carb substitution path.

busting low-carb myths

Some statements about low-carb diet-ing have been repeated so often that they have taken on mythic proportions. Let's dispel these myths before they hamper your weight-loss efforts.

Myth: Americans have been follow-ing the high-carbohydrate, low-fat advice doled out by nutrition profes-sionals, and we are heavier than ever. Clearly, a low-fat diet doesn't work.

Reality: On the whole, Americans have not followed the government's eating recommendations based on the Food Guide Pyramid, which specifies serving sizes and number of portions. Statistics show that we have been eating more of *every* calorie-containing nutrient, not just carbohydrates, and that we are ever more sedentary. As a result, the obesity rate in America has skyrocketed and shows no sign of slowing down anytime soon.

Myth: Low-carb diets work because they are low in carbohydrates.

Reality: Low-carb proponents argue that carbohydrates promote fat stor-age, so curbing their intake whittles your waistline for that very reason. However, for most people, curbing carbohydrates means cutting calories. Each gram of carbohydrate contains four calories, so fewer carbs means a lower calorie intake and may lead to weight loss as long as you don't increase calories from any other source. For example, coffee-lovers who use 2 tablespoons of sugar over the course of a day in their cups of java add 96 calories to their total intake. Eliminating that sugar amounts to a calorie deficit of nearly 35,000 calories a year, the equivalent of more than 10 pounds of body fat.

Myth: It's possible to live off foods such as steak, eggs, butter, and cream and maintain good health.

Reality: Most animal foods pack saturated fat and cholesterol, which contribute to clogged arteries. When arteries that feed the heart become blocked, oxygen-rich blood cannot make it to your heart, and a heart attack occurs. When the same situation takes place in the brain, a stroke happens. Beneficial nutrients that stave off heart disease and stroke go missing on a fat-based diet, making matters worse. For example, fruits and vegetables are packed with antioxidant vitamins and minerals that ward off cell damage leading to heart disease and cancer. Fortified grains provide folic acid, a B vitamin linked to a lower risk of heart disease and stroke.

Instead of:	Try:
Pasta with marinara sauce	Whole-wheat pasta or steamed spaghetti squash sautéed with olive oil and garlic and topped with fresh tomato sauce
Rice CHEX	Whole-Wheat CHEX
Instant oatmeal	Quick cooking (1- or 5-minute) oats
White potatoes, french fries	Baked or roasted sweet potato
Fruit yogurt	Plain yogurt + ½ cup berries + artificial sweetener
Chips	Peanuts or almonds
Hamburger	Open-faced turkey burger (100% ground turkey breast) or grilled portobello mushroom with 1 ounce cheddar cheese, lettuce, tomato slices, onions
Tuna salad sandwich on white bread	Tuna salad rolled up in iceberg or romaine lettuce leaves
Peanut butter	Natural peanut butter
Pepperoni pizza	Pizza on whole-wheat crust prepared with half the cheese and twice the vegetables
Milk chocolate bar	Strawberries dipped in melted dark chocolate
Ice cream frappé	Smoothie prepared with plain yogurt, berries, ice cubes, artificial sweetener, and vanilla extract
Orange juice	Orange
White wine	White wine spritzer: half wine, half soda water
Plain bagel	2 slices oat bran bread
Bottled Italian dressing	Balsamic vinegar and oil

exercise: the universal fitness tool

When it comes to the battle of the bulge, no matter what type of diet you follow, there's no more universally helpful weight-loss tool than exercise. Making exercise a regular habit and learning to simply incorporate more activity into your day can make any diet more powerful. Paired with a low-carb diet, regular physical activity can increase your fat burning and help you reach your goals sooner. Keep it up even after you've lost the pounds, and exercise can help you maintain that weight loss.

the best exercise

Any form of exercise will help you burn extra calories and, therefore, help you control your weight. Aerobic exercises, such as walking, running, swimming, or cycling, are especially good fat burners. For an exercise to be aerobic, it must work the large muscles—those in the legs and buttocks or arms and shoulders—continuously for an extended period. In so doing, it increases your body's demand for oxygen, forcing your breathing and heart rate to speed up. And that's exactly what you want when you're trying to lose weight, because your body needs that extra oxygen in order to release stored body fat and use it as fuel for your working muscles. The longer you keep up the activity, the more stored body fat is released and burned as fuel.

What's the best aerobic exercise to choose to help you lose weight? It's the one that you will enjoy and stick with for the duration—not just during weight loss but for the rest of your life. Legions of dieters who have lost weight and managed to keep it off over the years say that exercise is the key. But an exercise that is too difficult to master, can only be done when the weather cooperates or during certain times of the year, or that you simply don't like doing is an exercise that won't be a very effective weight-loss tool.

Face it, we all know that even when we have the best intentions, it's easy to

find an excuse not to exercise. So why choose an activity that has a lot of requirements and, as a result, a lot of ready-made excuses built in? Better to find something that you can do alone or with someone else, in good weather and bad, without having to drive across town, buy loads of equipment, or block out hours of every day.

That's why, at least at the beginning, as you learn how to make exercising a task that you actually look forward to, we suggest something as simple and versatile as walking. Almost everybody can do it. It doesn't require a big investment in equipment. It can be done outdoors, in the city, suburbs, or rural areas. It can be done indoors, either in a shopping mall or a community center, in a gym, or even at home on a treadmill. It can be done alone, with a friend, or with other regular walkers. It can be done in one chunk or, when your schedule is tight, in smaller increments. It can even be

done when you're on vacation or traveling for business.

To that end, in the following section, we've included a walking program that you can adjust to your current level of fitness. It can provide you with structure and suggestions to get you started toward that trimmer body you desire.

maybe you need spice?

What if walking isn't your style or you're looking to add more excitement or challenge to your exercise routine? Well, they do say variety is the spice of life. And if you prefer to vary your activities to keep exercise enjoyable, go for it. Try jogging, swimming, cycling, or aerobics. Take a country or salsa dancing class, join a recreational volleyball league, or play some pickup basketball. As long as the exercise gets your heart pumping harder, your breath coming quicker, and your muscles moving, it can be a part of your exercise plan—especially if it keeps you committed. If you're a tennis fan, you could schedule a tennis match three times a week, then walk (or cycle or jog) on other days or when your tennis partner cancels. The key is to always have a backup activity for the days when your preferred exercise appointments fall through. So you'll be

Figuring your target zone

Here's an example of how a 35-year-old would determine her target heart-rate zone. To find your own target zone, simply substitute your age for the number "35."
1. To find her maximum heart rate, she would subtract her age from 220 (220−35= 185).
2. She would multiply her maximum heart rate by 0.65 to find the lower end of her target zone (185×0.65=120).
3. She would multiply her maximum by 0.85 to find the upper end of her target zone (185×0.85=157).
   So her target heart-rate zone during exercise is 120–157 beats per minute.

Taking your pulse

When you're exercising, give yourself time to raise your heart rate. Then check your pulse during the routine to see if you're in your target zone.

To check your pulse, place the index and middle finger of one hand on the underside of the wrist of your other hand. You should be able to feel your pulse just below the heel of your hand. (If you don't feel your pulse right away, slide your fingers around the wrist area until you can feel the beats.) Count the beats for 15 seconds. Then multiply that number by four to get the beats per minute. Try to take your pulse while continuing to perform the exercise if possible, or take it as quickly as you can so your heart rate doesn't have a chance to fall.

If your pulse during exercise falls below your target zone, you'll need to exercise a little harder. If your pulse is above your target zone, ease up on the intensity. After some practice, you may even find that you can tell if you're working in your target zone based just on how hard you feel you're working. Even so, it doesn't hurt to check your pulse from time to time to be sure.

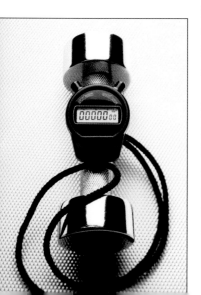

less likely to skip the exercise and just plop yourself on the couch.

the one-two punch against pounds

Wouldn't it be great if you could burn extra calories when you're lying around watching television or surfing the Web? As miraculous as it may seem, you really can. The way to do it is to add strength training to your regular exercise routine.

Strength training—whether it's by lifting free weights, pulling against resistance bands (those giant rubber bands), using weight or resistance machines, or even doing push-ups and sit-ups—builds muscle. By building more muscle, you increase your metabolism. That's because muscle is very active tissue, while fat is not. The more muscle you have, the more calories you burn, even when you're lounging on the sofa or sitting at your desk. So, if you do at least two strength-building sessions a week, you really can burn more calories (and more body fat) during those times when your body isn't in motion. In fact, one study found that women who built muscle by strength training twice a week burned up to 300 more calories a day. For more on strength training, see pages 62–67.

how much is enough?

Moderation is the key. Here's what you need to know:

frequency: Exercising aerobically three times a week is the minimum. If you're really serious about losing body fat, however, shoot for five times a week or even every day. Build up to that frequency gradually, though, especially if you've been relatively inactive lately. You should also engage in at least two strength-training sessions each week. Schedule your strength training for alternate days to give your muscles needed recovery time between workouts—time to repair and build themselves up. Or, if you would like to do some strength training every day, alternate the muscle groups that you work. For instance, you might do leg and lower back work on Monday, do arm and chest exercises on Tuesday, then go back to the leg and back exercises on Wednesday.

intensity: If exercise feels "light to somewhat hard," it's probably about right. You should be able to carry on a conversation while you exercise, but if you can easily belt out a tune, you need to pick up the pace a bit.

A more exact way to measure intensity is by monitoring your heart rate during exercise. You'll get the best results by working in what's called your "target heart-rate zone." Your target zone is 65 to 85 percent of your maximum heart rate per minute. Your maximum heart rate can be determined through a stress test given by a physician. But if you're in good health, you can get a reasonably accurate idea of your maximum heart rate by subtracting your age from 220. Once you know your maximum heart rate, multiply it by 0.65 and 0.85 to find the lower and upper ends of your target zone, respectively. (You'll find an example of how to calculate your target zone in the box on page 51.) Then, as you exercise, check your pulse (see the box on page 52) occasionally to be sure that you are working in your target zone.

time: Twenty minutes in your target zone is the minimum, but 30 minutes is a good goal for most people. Of course, if you can stretch that to 40, 50, or even 60 minutes a day, you'll burn even more body fat. Again,

though, if you have been sedentary, start with shorter workouts and increase the time gradually.

If you have a week when you are extremely busy, instead of just skipping exercise altogether, you can break your 30 minutes a day into two or three shorter workouts. For instance, you might ride an exercise bike for 10 to 15 minutes before work, then get in 10 to 15 minutes of walking during your lunch or after dinner. Try to make these shorter sessions more intense by working at the higher end of your target zone if you can. You may not get the same fat-burning effect as you would by exercising for a continuous 30 or 40 minutes, but you will burn calories and, more importantly, you'll keep up your exercise habit. Aim for consistency. Your body reaps rewards whenever you get moving.

commitment: If you truly want to lose weight without lowering your calorie intake to dangerous levels, you must exercise. There's no two ways about it. You must commit yourself to exercising and getting more physical. One way to help yourself fulfill that commitment is to actually schedule your exercise

Fat-burning tip

A moderate pace allows you to exercise longer than a more intense one. But if you have limited time to exercise, you can burn more body fat—without burning yourself out—by picking up the pace for one- to three-minute intervals during your workout. For example, try alternating five or ten minutes of moderate effort with three minutes of more-intense effort throughout the exercise session.

sessions into your day. If you use any type of planner or calendar, mark down the times you will allot to exercise in your weekly schedule. Consider it a commitment like any other. If you have an important meeting or event to attend or a task that must be done, you probably write it down. Your exercise sessions should have the same importance. Scheduling—and keeping—your exercise appointments also helps bring a sense of accomplishment when you can look back over your week and see that you met your exercise goals.

safety check

Most healthy adults can start a sensible exercise program without elaborate medical testing. But if you have any chronic medical problems, are pregnant, or are greatly overweight, it's best to consult your doctor before beginning a regular exercise program. If you have been inactive for a long time, have never exercised regularly before, or are very overweight, be sure to start out slowly.

To give your heart and muscles time to adjust, start each aerobic exercise session with a few minutes of activity at a slower pace, and end each session with a few minutes at that slower pace. For example, if you intend to go jogging, spend about five minutes walking or jogging at a slow pace to get warmed up, then jog at your normal pace for 20 minutes or more, and

finally, cool down by ending your session with five more minutes of slow jogging or walking.

And no matter what type of exercise you're doing, if the activity hurts, slow down until it doesn't or just stop the activity. Exercise should be challenging and should make demands on your body, but it should not be painful. Likewise, be sure to move into a new exercise program gradually, no matter what shape you're in. Increase the intensity of the movement or the heaviness of the weight by steps, and over time. Barreling head-on into a new activity, without giving your body a chance to gradually work up its tolerance, will set you up for injury. And there's nothing that can put the kibosh on an exercise program, on a weight-loss program, and on your motivation like injury can. So don't go for broke.

finishing touches

If you really want to lose weight and keep it off for good, your goal should be to get and stay active, not just through regular exercise, but throughout your daily routine. You may be wondering how you can, when it seems you can barely find time to exercise as it is. Well, sometimes the solutions to our problems are staring us right in the face and we just don't recognize them. That may very well be the case when it comes to living a more active lifestyle.

To illustrate, think about how many times you've gone to the mall or the grocery store and spent five, even ten minutes driving around looking or waiting for that spot by the door to open up. Chances are there were plenty of open spots at the farther reaches of the parking lot, but of course, they were *so far.* And you'd *have to walk* all that way. But if you turned that "have to" into "be able to," and spent that same five or ten minutes walking instead of waiting, you'd have burned extra calories and spent no "extra" time at all.

In everyday life there are plenty of situations in which we spend as much or more time taking the less active—but supposedly more convenient—route, only to complain about the time and inconvenience of having to exercise. If we just start looking at those situations as calorie-burning opportunities, chances to get our muscles moving and our blood pumping, living an active life becomes as easy as putting one foot in front of the other.

So to put the finishing touches on your "active" pursuit of weight loss, try to start tuning in to these seemingly small opportunities to move closer to your weight-loss goals. Here are some other suggestions you might try:

- Use the stairs instead of the elevator.
- Get off the bus a stop early and walk the rest of the way.
- Avoid driving distances of less than

½ mile; walk or ride or even strap on your inline skates and roll there instead.

- Walk around while you talk on the phone.
- Walk your dog instead of just letting him do his duty in the yard.
- Deliver messages in person instead of calling or e-mailing.
- Take a short exercise break instead of a coffee break.
- At work, use the restroom farthest from your desk.
- Ride a stationary bike, walk a treadmill, march in place, or do push-ups while you watch television.
- Use a rake instead of a leaf blower to clean the yard.
- Wash the car by hand.
- Take a walk instead of lingering over leftovers.
- Bring the groceries from the car into the house one bag at a time.

It honestly is fairly simple to find ways to boost your calorie burning and live a more active life all around. And once you discover them, living a more active life will become second nature. Just go out and try it and you'll see for yourself. And go ahead and give a friendly wave as you walk swiftly and proudly by that poor person still waiting for that closer parking space.

walk off pounds!

These days, all you have to do is a little channel surfing and you'll see a handful of advertisements for products claiming to be the best new thing for weight loss. Take it off; keep it off; trim it down; firm it up; get stronger; improve your looks, personality, and social life in 15 minutes a day. What's a consumer to believe?

While it is virtually impossible to choose a "best" weight-loss activity for everyone, any activity vying for the title would need to be totally adaptable to all fitness levels, convenient, relatively inexpensive, functional in a way that makes us stronger and better prepared for the demands of everyday life, and an outstanding calorie burner.

Walking is one activity that can meet this challenge. Because of its versatility, it has stepped to the forefront of popularity among U.S. exercisers. For most people, a more convenient activity cannot be found. It's easy to adjust walking to your personal fitness level by changing speed, duration, or terrain. It's a weight-bearing activity, so it can help strengthen bones. And, best of all, walking makes it very easy to burn loads of calories.

You can expect to burn 100 to 200 calories during a moderately paced 30-minute walk. Using the program here, you can go from casual walker to power walker and more than double your calorie-burning rate.

If weight loss is your goal, you'll want to burn at least 300 extra calories a day, or about 1,500 extra calories a week. That can lead to half a pound of weight loss a week even if you don't trim carbs or calories from your diet. If you also cut just 400 empty carb calories from your daily food intake, you could lose five pounds in a month.

go for the (calorie) burn

Engaging in long, slow exercise sessions has been touted as the best way to lose fat, because you burn more fat calories at a low intensity. Research suggests, however, that low-intensity training does not result in faster weight loss. Renowned weight-loss researcher Jack Wilmore, Ph.D., of Texas A & M University, explains, "It is misleading because the lower intensity does burn a higher *percentage* of fat versus carbohydrate. However, high-intensity exercise burns more total calories, and even though the percentage of fat burned is lower, the total fat burned is greater at high intensity." In other words, if you compare an hour's worth of low-intensity exercise to an hour's worth of high-intensity exercise, you'll actually burn more total fat and calories working at the higher intensity. And that can be an important consideration, since many of us have to struggle to find time to exercise.

"The American way is to try to pack more into less time. It makes sense to increase your fitness because you maximize your time by increasing the number of calories you can burn in a workout," says Peggy Norwood Keating, former fitness director at the Duke University Diet and Fitness Center in Durham, North Carolina. By improving your fitness, you can fit more calorie burning into a shorter period of time.

Here's how it works. The number of calories you burn per mile is fairly constant, regardless of whether you walk that distance or run it. It's affected primarily by your own body weight. A 140-pound person burns approximately 80 calories per mile (to figure out how many calories you burn, add or subtract five calories per mile for

S-t-r-e-t-c-h!

To increase your flexibility and help prevent injury, spend several minutes at the end of your workout stretching the muscles in the following areas (hold each stretch for 20 to 60 seconds):

Ankles: Rotate each ankle through a full range of motion by tracing large circles with your toes, first in a clockwise direction and then counterclockwise.

Shins: Sit down with your legs extended and your heels on the ground, and gently point your toes toward the ground.

Calves: Lean forward against a wall, with your palms on the wall and your fingers pointing up, and step back with one leg. Keep your back leg straight and gently press the heel into the floor. Switch leg positions and repeat.

Quadriceps (front of thigh): Stand with your right hand on a wall or chair for balance. Bend your left knee and, grasping the left ankle with your left hand, pull your left foot toward your buttocks. Repeat with the opposite leg.

Hamstrings (back of thigh): Lie faceup on the floor with your right leg bent, your right foot flat on the floor, and your left leg extended. Grasping the back of your left knee, bend your left knee and pull your left leg toward your chest. Then gently straighten the left knee and push your left heel toward the ceiling. Release and repeat with the right leg.

Lower back: Lie on your back and pull both legs to your chest until your hips lift from the floor.

every ten pounds over or under 140). At 140 pounds, walking 2.5 miles per hour (a mile in 24 minutes), you will burn 100 calories during a 30-minute walk. If you increase your fitness level and walk at four miles per hour (a mile in 15 minutes), you will burn 160 calories in the same amount of time. Add short intervals of running within that half hour, and the number of calories you burn could top 300, because you will end up covering more miles in the same amount of time.

for the health of it

The benefits of a walking routine go beyond weight loss to improvements in physical health and mental attitude. And the more you exercise, the more benefits you gain. (There is a qualifier, however: The more you exercise, the greater your risk of injury or burnout. So as with any habit, use common sense and don't go overboard.)

In general, you can rack up most of the health benefits of physical activity—including controlling blood pressure and blood sugar and decreasing the risk of heart disease—by burning an extra 800 to 1,000 calories a week. In simpler terms, you'll help improve your health profile by getting a total of 30 minutes of noncontinuous exercise each day—say a ten-minute walk in the morning, a ten-minute walk at lunch, and a ten-minute walk after work. Unlike weight loss, these health benefits are affected more by increasing the *amount* of exercise rather than the *intensity*.

gauging your intensity

Since the number of calories you burn in a specific period of time depends in part on the intensity of your workout, you need to be able to measure how hard your body is working. You'll find instructions for calculating what's called your target heart-rate zone in Exercise: The Universal Fitness Tool, on pages 50–55. During your walking workouts, aim for a training range between 65 and 85 percent of your maximum heart rate; what part of that range you work in will depend on which level of walking workout you choose. You can also use your own sense of how hard you are working.

sneak up on your training zone

When you begin a walking workout session, you can't just jump right into your training zone. You need to sneak up on that zone with five to ten minutes of easy walking first. By gradually increasing the pace, you slowly bring your effort and heart rate into your training zone. It also warms up your muscles, ligaments, and tendons. The result is that your muscles are ready to use more oxygen, you move more easily, and you are less susceptible to injury.

It's important to back out of a workout the same way. At the end of the workout, do another five to ten minutes of easy walking to bring your heart rate back down near your resting level. The movement of the muscles will keep the blood from pooling in your hands and feet, which could lead to lightheadedness or fainting. The end of the workout, when your muscles are very warm, is the best time to stretch (see the stretches on page 57).

time to play

It would be impractical to propose one walking program for every schedule, fitness level, and degree of motivation. So this program has three levels. It's not necessary to "graduate" from one level to the next if you are satisfied with the calorie-burning and fitness results you are already getting from the level that you are on. On the other hand, you might find that stepping up your intensity helps keep you challenged or gives you the boost you need to get over a weight-loss plateau, when the pounds don't seem to be budging.

level I—lifestyle walking

This program is for beginning exercisers who want the tremendous health benefits that even 30 minutes of daily

Form is everything

Practice these posture pointers as you walk:
- Keep your body stacked like a column, with your ears, shoulders, hips, knees, and ankles aligned directly over one another.
- Hold your pelvis in a position that maintains the natural curve in your lower back without excessive arching (lordosis) or flattening (tucking the buttocks too far underneath you). Try squeezing a towel between your upper thighs to help bring your pelvis into a good position. Then drop the towel but maintain that position. Relax your buttocks, but contract your abdominals lightly to hold your pelvis in this position as you walk.
- To help determine if you are aligning your head over your shoulders, try this exercise: Put your fingers to your lips as if you were smoking a cigarette (make-believe only, please). Leaving your fingers exactly where they are, gently lean your head directly backward until you feel resistance in the neck muscles, then relax forward just until the pressure disappears. The distance between your face and your fingers is how much out of line you typically hold your head.
- Walk tall without leaning forward at the waist. Don't slouch or stare at the ground as you walk; this restricts your breathing.
- Do not overstride. Your stride should be a comfortable length and you should glide without bouncing.
- Push off fully with the rear leg to work the entire leg and the buttocks.

activity can bring but are not ready for a more time-consuming workout program. You literally squeeze activity into your life by fitting walking into your day's activities. Aim for at least 30 minutes of moderate- to brisk-paced walking a day. A good place to start is your daily commute. If you can't walk the entire distance, you can walk to the subway or bus stop or get on or off one stop early. Get off the elevator one floor early and take the stairs. Never use an escalator or one of those moving sidewalks in airports; we call them energy savers, but you should start

thinking of them as calorie-storage aids.

Once you master these, you can begin getting off of the bus and the elevator two, three, or four stops early. Also, add very short walking breaks during the day. Relax, clear your head, and add five minutes to your daily activity total at the same time.

level II—walking for a workout

This level makes structured exercise a part of your daily routine. The extra time allotted to exercise makes it possible to safely achieve the level of exertion necessary to significantly improve your fitness and burn more calories.

Your first goal is to walk at a comfortable pace for 15 to 20 minutes. Increase the total time of your daily walks by no more than five minutes each week until you reach 30 to 45 minutes per walk.

Next, increase your pace during the training phase of your workout, which is the 20- to 30-minute period between warmup and cooldown. The amount of effort you expend should be challenging, but you should still be able to hold a conversation while you exercise. (If you're walking alone and aren't afraid to look a little silly, try singing a song, reciting a poem, or going over your daily schedule out loud.) In terms of your heart-rate zone, aim for 60 to 75 percent of your maximum.

level III—interval training

This phase is for walkers who want an extra challenge in their workouts and who want to maximize their calorie-burning potential. The basis of this phase is interval training, which is simply alternating periods of high-intensity work with rest intervals of easy walking.

The benefits include even greater improvement in cardiovascular fitness; extra work for the muscles, which helps make them stronger; and more calories burned per minute. It also provides a challenge, which, for some folks, could be the difference between staying on the exercise bandwagon or falling off.

One possible drawback is an increased chance of injury, and this makes attention to proper rest, stretching, and form even more important. In addition, it's advisable that you successfully complete at least six weeks of the level II workout, with your heart rate in the target zone for at least 20 minutes of each workout session, before attempting the level III workout.

Many types of activities can be used to increase your workout intensity. Intervals of very brisk walking may be enough, especially when you first start at this level. But you may also want to try intervals of running, walking stairs, "bench stepping" on an aerobic step, or climbing rolling hills on an outdoor walk. These activities require that you "lift" the body weight more than you do when walking on level ground and can greatly increase the calories burned per mile. During a 60-minute walk, you could potentially increase your calorie burning by 20 percent if you spend five or six intervals climbing a long hill (or hills) with a 9- to 10-percent grade.

Begin your interval program by interspersing three 3- to 5-minute high-intensity intervals ("high intensity" meaning an effort that pushes your heart rate up to about 80 percent of your maximum). This effort should be hard but controlled, and you should not be exhausted at the end of the interval. Recover for an equal amount of time with easy walking.

If you want the variety of interval training but are not yet up to the rigors of the really high intensities, try making the transition more gradually. Increase your effort so that your heart rate is at least 75 percent of your maximum for three to five minutes, and rest for only one minute in between. Your intense intervals won't be quite as strenuous, but the shorter rests will make the overall workout more demanding.

To increase your calorie burning even more, decrease the length of the high-intensity intervals and increase the length of the rest periods in between. Sound like the opposite of what you want to do? Well, the reason you increase the length of the rest interval is so that you can work even harder during the high-intensity intervals. Do one to two minutes at a heart rate of 85 percent, or even a bit more, of your maximum (but never above your maximum). This effort should feel "hard to very hard." Then spend twice as much time in your rest interval, walking at an easy pace. In other words, after one minute of working at 85 percent of your maximum, you spend two minutes walking at 65 to 70 percent of your maximum. (Due to the cardiovascular demands of such high-intensity work, it's important to get your doctor's approval before increasing your workout intensity to this level.)

Even after you begin this interval program, don't forget to include walks from levels I and II in your weekly routine. Lifestyle walking is especially important in keeping you more active, and it actually becomes easier after you have gotten more fit through structured, high-intensity exercise. On days when time is especially tight and five to ten minutes is all you have, take advantage of it with a short "moving break" to get away from it all. It will help reduce stress and it will keep you on track so that you won't be tempted to skip exercising altogether. Have fun and enjoy being active!

Fat-burning tip

To increase your energy expenditure—and the amount of fat that you burn—during workouts, get your upper body in on the act, too. You can increase the calories you burn by as much as ten percent by pumping your arms vigorously as you walk. Joggers and step-aerobicizers can also boost their calorie burning by adding arm movements. If you use a stair-climbing machine or stationary bicycle at the gym or are thinking of buying one, opt for a model with movable handlebars that you pump with your arms.

strengthening exercises to burn more fat

You may have worn holes in the soles of your sneakers from walking, chlorine-bleached your hair from swimming laps, or ridden your bicycle to the point of needing a good tune-up. But if you're doing only aerobic exercise, your exercise program is not complete. A weight-loss regimen that relies on a low-carb diet and aerobic exercise is like a car that has enough gas and fully inflated wheels but was built with too small an engine.

Your muscles are your body's engine, and developing them through strength training is your way of burning fuel (calories). The more muscle you build, the more fuel you will burn (and the stronger you'll become). And that muscular engine will keep burning fuel even when the car is idling at the drive-in movie or parked in the garage for the night.

what's in it for me?

It's easy to overlook the benefits of strength training. After all, you can see how jogging or walking the treadmill can expend lots of calories and help you lose weight. But, though the benefits of strength training aren't as obvious, they are actually even more plentiful.

Building your lean muscle tissue will give you:

- Greater strength in performing everyday activities, such as carrying the groceries
- A higher metabolism, so you burn more calories even at rest
- Stronger bones
- An increased ability to do aerobic exercise
- Better body composition (an improved ratio of lean tissue to fat)
- A more toned and slim-looking physique
- Protection against injury

looking gooood!

Let's talk for a minute about how good you're going to look. After all, that's one of the main reasons you're dieting and exercising, isn't it? And when you get discouraged, isn't it looking better, along with feeling better, that keeps you motivated?

Strength training several times a week will firm you up, so you're going to look slimmer even if you don't lose weight. Although muscle tissue is more dense than fat, meaning it weighs more than fat, it actually takes up about 20 percent less room. As a result, your waistline, your arms, and your legs will shrink as you strengthen those muscles, even if the number on your scale stays the same or even increases a bit. Your clothes will fit differently, and you'll have a leaner look. The change in appearance can be dramatic.

One more thing: Strength training helps the parts of your body that tend to be the most affected by gravity's pull. Those parts will stay firmer, longer, as a result of your strength-training efforts. So you can add looking younger to the list of strength-training benefits.

getting started

It can be confusing, but the terms *strength training, weight training, weight lifting,* and *resistance training* all refer to the same thing: exercises that build and tone muscle. When you do a strength-training exercise, your muscle contracts against resistance.

That resistance can be the weight of your own body (as when you do sit-ups or push-ups), a hand weight (also called a free weight or dumbbell), a resistance band (a long elastic loop), wrist and/or ankle weights (anchored to wrist or ankle with Velcro closures), or a weight machine (either at the gym or at home).

Some other words you need to know before you begin are *repetition* and *set.* A repetition, or *rep,* is the number of times you actually do a particular exercise. A *set* is the amount of times you complete a group of repetitions. For example, if you're to do three sets of push-ups at 12 reps each, you do 12 push-ups, rest, do 12 more, rest, do 12 more, and you're done.

general guidelines

Before using any kind of weights, you first need to figure out how much weight to start with. A general guideline is that you should be able to com-

Don't bulk me up!

Some people, especially women, avoid strength training because they think they'll end up looking like a bodybuilder. Nothing could be further from the truth. When you strength train, you'll be building a lean, toned look, not a bulky one.

The truth is, bodybuilders have to work very, very hard to achieve that bulky look, and they do it by working their muscles using very heavy weights lifted through only a few repetitions. The amount of weight is increased as soon as the muscle can withstand it.

You, on the other hand, will do a strength-training routine that involves lighter weights lifted through many repetitions. As your muscles get stronger and gain stamina, more repetitions will be added. Weight is increased very slowly.

Make your own weights

If you don't want to spring for a set of weights, especially when you're just starting out, you can make weights from items you have on hand in the kitchen. Some people like to use cans of soup in the beginning. Just weigh them before you start so you know how much weight you're lifting. You can also make your weights. One method is to pour a pound or more of beans or rice into an old sock and tie it securely. Another method is to fill small plastic milk or juice jugs with the amount of beans or rice you want to lift.

plete at least two sets of at least eight controlled repetitions with the weight you choose. If you can't, it's too heavy. On the other hand, if you can comfortably do more than three sets of 12 repetitions, it's time to move up to a heavier weight. You may need different weights for different exercises.

It's important to give your muscles a day of rest in between workouts. But that doesn't mean you can't strength train every day if you want. All you need to do is work the upper body one day and the lower body the next day. If you prefer to skip a day, however, you can strength train your whole body at one session, then take the following day off.

Always exhale as you contract the muscle or lift the weight. Then inhale as you relax the muscle or lower the weight.

Proper form is very important when you're strength training. To avoid injury and to get the most out of your routine, you need to keep your body properly aligned, breathe correctly, and contract and release your muscles slowly and smoothly. It may be worth the expense to hire a personal trainer for one session to get you going safely. A trainer can also design a strength-training program unique to your physique, your abilities, and your lifestyle. Instructors can be found at local YMCAs, community centers, community colleges, athletic clubs, and gyms. If you do go that

route, just be sure to check the trainer's credentials. A certified trainer will be happy to oblige.

a sample workout

If you want to start a strength-training routine but aren't sure what exercises to include, try the ones we describe below. They're basic to any strength-training program.

exercises for the upper body

The following exercises should be performed for two to three sets of 8 to 12 repetitions.

1. **BICEPS CURL** *(tones the front of the upper arms)*
   Sit on the edge of a stool or bench or stand with your knees slightly bent, about hip-distance apart. Hold one weight in each hand and extend the arms down the front of your thighs, with the inner forearms facing outward. Without moving the upper arms, slowly lift the weights, for four counts, until they are almost touching your upper arms. At the peak of the movement, flex the biceps and hold for two counts. Slowly lower the weights to the starting position, to the count of four.

2. **TRICEPS KICKBACK** *(tones the back of the upper arms)*
   Stand with your knees bent, feet about hip-distance apart. Lean slightly forward, take a weight in each hand, and hold them right next to your hips. Elbows should be

bent and held closely to your sides. Without moving your upper arms or your elbows, straighten the arms and extend the weights as high as you can in back of you, to the count of four. Flex the triceps and hold for two counts. Slowly lower the weights to the starting position to the count of four.

3. **TRICEPS EXTENSION** *(tones the back of the upper arms)*
Sit erect in a low-backed chair or on a stool or exercise bench. Hold the weight in your right hand. Raise your right arm straight above your right shoulder.

Keep your elbow pointed up (towards the ceiling) as you slowly lower the weight behind your head. Then slowly press the weight back up to the starting position. Alternate arms after completing each set.

4. **SIDE RAISE** *(tones the middle deltoid muscle, at the side of the shoulder)*
Hold a weight in each hand, with the arms extended down the sides of the thighs, wrists facing outward. Slowly raise the weights to shoulder level, to a count of four. Hold for two counts, then slowly lower them to the starting position, also to the count of four.

5. **CHEST FLY** *(tones the pectoralis major muscles)*
Lie on a weight bench, aerobics step (if you have one), or the floor. Hold a weight in each hand, arms

extended out to the sides at chest level, the insides of the forearms facing up toward the ceiling. Your arms should remain rigid throughout the exercise, although the elbows should be slightly bent (not locked). Slowly bring the weights together directly above your chest, to the count of four. Hold for two counts, then slowly lower to the starting position, to the count of four.

exercises for the lower body
The following exercises should be performed for three sets of 8 to 12 repetitions. These exercises can be done

with or without wearing ankle weights. Wearing ankle weights will increase the intensity of the exercises. *Do not perform these exercises to the point of discomfort, and skip the exercise if you feel pain.*

1. **OUTER THIGH LIFT** *(tones the outer thigh and butt muscles)*
Lie on your side with your head resting on your extended arm. Bend your bottom knee to increase your base of support. Make sure your hips are stacked one above the other and perpendicular to the floor.

   Lift your top leg about two feet, with your foot parallel to the ceiling and your toe pointing out.

   Continue with the training progression that follows, completing all repetitions. Then switch to the other side.

   - Complete three sets of eight repetitions—two counts up, hold for two counts, then down in two counts.
   - Complete two sets of eight repetitions—small pulses up, down in one count.
   - Complete one set of eight small pulses.

2. **INNER THIGH LIFT** *(tones and develops the inner thigh)*
Lie on your left side, propping yourself up on your left elbow and forearm. Cross the right leg over the left, placing the right foot on the floor next to your left knee, right knee pointed toward the ceiling. Check to be sure your left leg is aligned with your hip, waist, and shoulder.

   Extend the left leg, with the inner thigh facing the ceiling and the foot flexed. Lift the left leg toward the ceiling. At the peak of the movement, tighten the inner thigh muscle. Lower.

   Follow the training progression below. Don't worry if you can't do the whole routine at first. Simply do as many sets as you can and gradually work up to completing the whole progression.

   - Complete three sets of eight repetitions—two counts up, hold for two counts, down in two counts.

- Complete two sets of eight repetitions—three small pulses up, down in one count.
- Complete three sets of eight small pulses

When you've completed all repetitions, switch to the other side. To increase intensity, add extra sets of pulses.

3. **QUADRICEPS EXTENSION** *(strengthens the muscles in the front of your thighs)*

Lie on your back with your knees bent, feet flat on the floor, and arms resting alongside your body. Your shoulders, arms, and neck should stay relaxed.

Slowly straighten your right knee, keeping the thigh aligned with the thigh of your left leg. Do not lock the knee. Slowly return to the starting position. Alternate legs after each set.

4. **BUTT-BUSTERS** *(tones the butt and back of your thighs)*

Get down on all fours, with your right knee bent and aligned under your hip. Extend your left leg behind you, with the toe touching the floor. Bend your elbows so that your forearms and hands rest on the floor. Make sure your elbows are aligned under your shoulders and that your head, with eyes downward, is aligned with your spine.

Slowly lift your left leg so the thigh is parallel to the floor, while simultaneously tightening the buttocks. Do not lift any higher, or you will place strain on the lower back. Do not arch your back and do not lock your knee. Lower almost to the floor, without touching down. After you've done three sets with one leg, repeat with the other leg.

5. **PARALLEL SQUAT** *(tones the front and back of your thighs and the butt muscles)*

*Note: You may find it easier to squat if you do so against a wall. As you continue to perform this exercise, your quadriceps will lengthen, allowing you to remain in this position longer. Do not perform this exercise if you feel any pain in your knees.

Take a dumbbell in each hand. Stand with feet a little closer than hip distance apart, knees slightly bent. Hold the weights at your sides. Squat down by sitting back as though you were lowering yourself into a chair. Keep your back straight. To avoid knee stress, make sure your weight is firmly on your heels.

Lower yourself until your thighs are parallel to the floor, no lower, to a count of four. Do not let your knees bend so far that they extend forward beyond your toes. Tighten your buttocks, and press back up to the starting position, for a count of four.

get to know the glycemic index

When you're following a low-carbohydrate diet, you want to make the best choices on your limited carbohydrate budget. That typically means choosing carbohydrates that are digested slowly and, therefore, raise your blood sugar slowly. The slower your blood sugar rises, the theory goes, the less insulin will be released. Since insulin puts glucose into storage and eventually converts excess glucose to body fat, the less of it released the better.

How do you know which carbohydrates cause your blood sugar to spike and which raise it more slowly? Well, there are some general guidelines. Whole-grain foods, for instance, are digested more slowly than foods that are highly refined. Foods with lots of added sugar are more likely to raise your blood sugar level quickly than are foods with less sugar or only naturally occurring sugars.

using glycemic index values

There's another, much more precise, way to determine how a particular food will affect your blood sugar level. You can use the glycemic index, which is a ranking of foods by the amount that they raise blood sugar levels.

There are two different types of rankings: One assigns a glycemic index (GI) value of 100 to white bread and then compares all other foods to it. Foods that are converted to sugar more slowly than white bread have lower GI values, while foods that are converted faster have higher values. Another method of ranking GI values is to assign glucose a GI of 100. In that case, foods are compared to the effect glucose has on blood sugar.

No matter which method is used, the idea is the same. The GI value of a food lets you compare its effect on your blood sugar relative to other foods. That can help you make wiser food choices.

To get the values for each individual food listed in the glycemic index, researchers had a group of healthy people eat the food and then tested their blood for glucose levels two to three hours later. The food was then assigned a GI number based on the rapidity with which it raised blood sugar levels compared to either white bread or glucose.

High Glycemic Index Foods		Moderate Glycemic Index Foods		Low Glycemic Index Foods	
Glucose	100	Orange Juice	57	Apple	36
Baked Potato	85	White Rice	56	Pear	36
Corn Flakes	84	Popcorn	55	Skim Milk	32
Cheerios	74	Corn	55	Green Beans	30
Graham Crackers	74	Brown Rice	55	Lentils	29
Honey	73	Sweet Potato	54	Kidney Beans	27
Watermelon	72	(Ripe) Banana	50	Grapefruit	25
White Bread/Bagel	70–72	Orange	43	Barley	25
Table Sugar	65	Apple Juice	41		
Raisins	64				

Reprinted by permission of www.healthchecksystems.com.

highs and lows

Foods that caused a rapid and marked increase in blood sugar levels were assigned a high glycemic index (GI) value (more than 70), while those that had slower and less dramatic effects on blood sugar levels were assigned low glycemic index values (less than 55).

There are only a few nutrition research groups in the world that have tested the glycemic response and compiled GI values. We've included a sample chart, above, to give you some idea of the comparative glycemic value of some common foods. For further information about the glycemic index and a searchable database of foods, visit the University of Sydney's Web site at *www.glycemicindex.com.*

A caveat: The way a food is prepared can affect its GI. Pasta cooked al dente (firm) is absorbed more slowly than pasta that is cooked longer. Adding fat (butter to a potato, for instance) will decrease the GI of a food because it slows its effect on blood sugar. The same is true of adding protein or foods with organic acids, such as yogurt and pickles, to a meal. All of these slow down the conversion of carbohydrates into sugars.

pay attention to portion size

A basic premise of low-carb dieting is that we eat too much carbohydrate. But most weight-control experts believe there is a yet more important reason behind our ever-expanding waistlines: We eat too much, period. Even when we are trying to lose weight, we tend to underestimate the total amount of food we eat. Researchers have discovered, for example, that dieters who thought they weren't losing weight because they had a "slow metabolism" were actually eating double the amount of food they thought they were consuming. Just because you're eating foods with fewer carbs doesn't mean you can overeat them. In order to lose weight, you must take in fewer calories than your body needs so it is forced to burn fat for fuel. So no matter which low-carb program you follow—indeed, no matter what type of weight-loss plan you use—you must pay attention to portion size.

How do you know if the bran muffin you ate or the bowl of cereal you poured is a single serving or five servings? You have to keep tabs on how much you eat by measuring and weighing for a while until your eyes get used to true portion sizes.

Start out by measuring and weighing the foods you eat most frequently. A food scale for weighing portions and a set of measuring cups and spoons will provide the information you need. Read food labels and use the serving and portion information here to find out how much of a food is in a standard serving. (You may be surprised to discover how much smaller a standard serving of steak is compared to the steak portions generally served in restaurants.) This may all seem tedious at first. But once you become familiar with what a serving looks like, you'll be able to judge food on sight with minimum effort, even at parties and restaurants. Eventually, you will only have to weigh or measure foods from time to time to spot-check for accuracy.

If you find that your helpings are not always standard serving sizes, gradu-

Standard servings

Bread, Cereal, Rice, and Pasta (Grains)
1 slice bread
1 ounce ready-to-eat cereal
½ cup cooked cereal, rice, or pasta

Fruit
1 medium piece raw fruit (an apple, banana, or peach, for example)
½ cup cut-up raw fruit
½ cup canned fruit
¾ cup fruit juice

Vegetables
1 cup raw, leafy vegetables
½ cup cut-up raw vegetables
½ cup cooked vegetables
¾ cup vegetable juice

Meat, Poultry, Fish, Dry Beans, Eggs, and Nuts
2–3 ounces cooked, lean meat, poultry, or fish
½ cup cooked dry beans (equal to 1 ounce of meat)
1 egg (equal to 1 ounce of meat)
2 tablespoons peanut butter (equal to 1 ounce of meat)

Milk, Yogurt, and Cheese
1 cup milk or yogurt
1½ ounces natural cheese
2 ounces processed cheese

ally cut back. For example, if you normally have three slices of bacon, try two instead. Also, try to serve your foods in standard portion sizes by dividing larger servings into two or more standard portions on your plate, to develop an eye for what a standard portion really is. For example, pour only one ounce of cereal to familiarize yourself with how much that is. And be honest. If you're not sure about your portion, overestimate its size and, if necessary, reduce the amount you eat.

Here are more suggestions for satisfying yourself with smaller portions:

- Remove serving dishes and bowls from the table during meals. If the food's right there, it's easy to take a few more bites. Measure out portions before bringing food to the table.
- Use smaller plates, bowls, and glasses to make your portions look larger. For example, put your entree on a salad plate instead of a dinner plate. Eat cereal from a cup rather than a bowl. One study showed that 70 percent of the people in a weight-reduction program were more satisfied with less food when it was served on a salad plate than when it was served on a dinner plate.
- Serve fiber-rich, high-bulk foods at the beginning of the meal. Try a hearty salad, fresh fruit, or crunchy raw vegetables for starters. This may help you feel satisfied with far fewer calories and minimize that famished feeling so you have better control during the rest of the meal.
- Take small bites and chew each thoroughly. Swallow what is in your mouth before preparing the next bite.
- Set some food aside at each meal—a few peas, a spoonful of rice, a bite of meat—to break the "clean plate" habit.
- Get rid of leftovers immediately. Many dieters eat more calories after the meal is over. The best way to prevent nibbling is to pack up or toss out leftovers quickly. When you focus too much on not letting food go to waste, it usually ends up going to your waist.

An eye for portions

When dining or snacking away from home, weighing or measuring your food isn't very practical, so use these handy visuals to estimate the size of portions:

Your clenched fist = 1 serving fruit, 1 cup uncooked vegetables, or 1 cup cooked pasta

Pair of dice = 1½ ounces natural cheese

Domino = 2 ounces processed cheese

Golf ball = 1 ounce cooked meat

Deck of cards = 3 ounces cooked meat or poultry

Your hand minus your thumb = 3 ounces cooked fish

Matchbook = 1 ounce cooked meat

measure your success

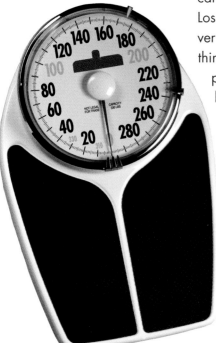

As you progress on your diet plan, you'll no doubt want to measure your progress toward your weight-loss goal. But it's important to include more than a regular trip to your bathroom scale in that evaluation.

get real

The first step is to make sure the expectations you begin with are realistic and good for you physically and mentally. We would all love to drop all our extra pounds in a week, of course. But you have to remember you didn't put the extra pounds on overnight, so you can't expect to lose them overnight. Losing a large amount of weight in a very short time generally means something is wrong—either with your diet plan, your health, or both. A weight loss of between a half pound and two pounds a week is the most you should aim for. Go beyond that and you not only put your health at risk, but you lower your chances of keeping that weight off in the long run.

When setting your goal, you need to know what a healthy weight is for you and how far you are from that goal. That's true even if your main motivation for losing weight is your appearance. People who are at a healthy weight tend to look good. Besides, it simply makes no sense to risk vitamin deficiencies, bone loss, dehydration, eating disorders, and other health troubles for the sake of achieving some model-thin physique. Face it, for the vast majority of us, that waiflike look isn't feasible or healthy, nor is it necessarily all that attractive, despite what advertisers might have us believe. Achieving a healthy weight, on the other hand, brings with it a lowered risk of high blood pressure, diabetes, heart disease, and other health problems.

figure your BMI

How do you determine what healthy weight to aim for? One of the most widely accepted methods is the Body Mass Index, or BMI. The BMI reflects the amount of body fat better than the weight on the scale alone does. It is also a better gauge of the effect your weight has on your health.

Here's how to calculate your BMI:
1) Weigh yourself first thing in the morning, without clothes.
2) Confirm your height, in inches.

3) Multiply your weight in pounds by 700.
4) Divide the result in step 3 by your height in inches.
5) Divide the result in step 4 by your height in inches again. The resulting number is your BMI.

A BMI between 19 and 25 is in the healthy range; it's associated with the least risk of disease. A BMI more than 25 and less than 30 indicates that you are overweight, while a BMI over 30 means that you're obese and have a much greater risk of disease.

To then find out if your goal weight—the weight that you would like to get down to—is a healthy one, do the equation again, substituting your goal weight for your current weight. If the resulting BMI for your goal weight falls within the 19–25 range, then it's a healthy one. If it falls below or above that range, adjust your goal weight until it's in the healthy range. Once you've determined what healthy weight to shoot for, subtract it from your current weight, and you'll know how many pounds you need to lose.

use more than the scale

You can use your bathroom scale once a week to track your movement toward your goal weight—as long as you do not obsess over what it says. There's no sense in weighing yourself every day. The weight on the scale can go up or down by a pound or two in response to water retention and other factors, and the daily changes you may see on the scale may not indicate a loss (or gain) of body fat. In addition, as you build muscle through exercise, that will be reflected on the scale. Some weeks, the number on the scale may not budge much, but you may still be exchanging pounds of fat for pounds of muscle—a success indeed and one that will make it easier to continue burning calories. It's important, therefore, to be aware of other signs of progress. For example, you may notice that your jeans don't feel as tight or that your watchband is looser on your arm. Look in the mirror and enjoy how much fitter you're beginning to look. And celebrate the extra energy that comes with more muscle and less fat.

If you're not noticing a difference in these areas, double-check your efforts. This is where a food and exercise diary can be extremely helpful. Look back at the past couple of weeks to make sure that the reason you aren't losing weight isn't because you've actually slipped back to eating larger portions or more empty carbs. If that's the case, don't get down on yourself. Use what you've learned to rededicate yourself to your diet and exercise program. Stick with it. Soon, you'll start losing again. And rest assured that these "plateaus" are simply natural and temporary pauses on the path to healthy weight loss.

the nutrient counter

Variety is key to a healthy diet. Variety in the foods you eat helps ensure you get a full range of the vitamins, minerals, and other nutrients so important for health. Variety can also be the difference between a successful weight-loss plan and one that is too boring to be tolerated for long.

How do you make eating a pleasure when you're on a diet that restricts carbohydrates? At first, it may seem easy, because you get to have higher-fat foods—steaks and such—that are often discouraged in traditional weight-loss plans. But after awhile, even these foods can lose their allure. What you need is to expand your food horizons. You need to go beyond processed foods and empty carbs and explore the abundance of whole foods out there.

That's where this nutrient counter comes in. The counter lists nutrient values for hundreds of foods with varying amounts of carbs, so you can compare foods side-by-side to decide which fit best in your weight-loss plan.

For each food item, the counter lists the calories and the number of grams of total carbohydrate, fiber, protein, total fat, and saturated fat in a portion. (While the total carbohydrate value for a food includes its fiber content, we've broken out the number of fiber grams where available so you can see how many of a food's carb grams come from beneficial, indigestible fiber.) Values have been rounded to the nearest whole number. If "Tr" (which stands for trace) appears in a column, it means there's less than half a gram of that nutrient in a single portion of that food. If "na" appears, that means the value was not available to us. When comparing foods, remember to check the portion sizes listed to be sure you're looking at equal portions of each food.

The counter can also help you deal with reality. Despite your best intentions, there may be times when your food choices are not exactly low carb. Instead of giving up on your diet because you simply couldn't pass up that fresh-baked Vienna bread or you just didn't want to say no to a slice of your surprise birthday cake, you can account for it. Use the counter to get an idea of how many extra grams of carbohydrate you took in, then look for lower-carb foods for the rest of the meal or the next few meals to help balance it out and get back on track.

Thank you, uncle sam

This nutrient counter was adapted from: U.S. Department of Agriculture, Agricultural Research Service. 2000. USDA Nutrient Database for Standard Reference, Release 16. Nutrient Data Laboratory Home Page, http://www.nal.usda.gov/fnic/foodcomp

Food, portion	Cal	Total Carb (g)	Fiber (g)	Protein (g)	Total Fat (g)	Sat Fat (g)
Baked Products						
Bagels, egg, 1 medium	292	56	2	11	2	Tr
Bagels, plain (includes onion, poppy, sesame), 1 medium	289	56	2	11	2	Tr
Biscuits, plain or buttermilk, 1 medium	186	25	1	3	8	1
Bread, cornbread, made with low-fat (2%) milk, 1 piece	173	28	na	4	5	1
Bread crumbs, dry, grated, plain, 1 cup	427	78	5	14	6	1
Bread, French or Vienna (includes sourdough), 1 slice, medium	175	33	2	6	2	Tr
Bread, Italian, 1 slice, medium	54	10	1	2	1	Tr
Bread, mixed-grain (includes whole-grain, 7-grain), 1 slice	65	12	2	3	1	Tr
Bread, oat bran, 1 slice	71	12	1	3	1	Tr
Bread, pita, white, 1 small	77	16	1	3	Tr	Tr
Bread, pita, whole-wheat, 1 small	74	15	2	3	1	Tr
Bread, pumpernickel, 1 slice	65	12	2	2	1	Tr
Bread, raisin, 1 slice	71	14	1	2	1	Tr
Bread, rye, 1 slice	83	15	2	3	1	Tr
Bread sticks, plain, 1 small stick	21	3	Tr	1	Tr	Tr
Bread stuffing, from dry mix, 1 oz	50	6	1	1	2	Tr
Bread, white, 1 slice	67	13	1	2	1	Tr
Bread, whole-wheat, 1 slice	69	13	2	3	1	Tr
Brownies, 1 large square	227	36	1	3	9	2

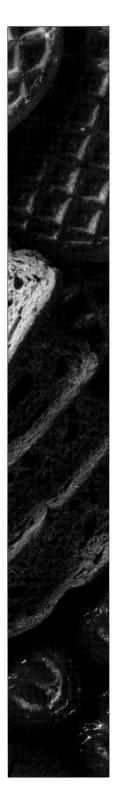

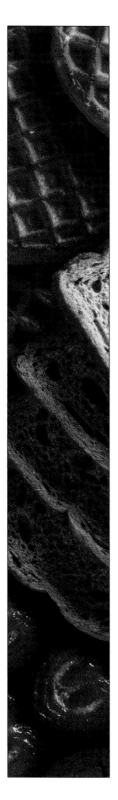

Food, portion	Cal	Total Carb (g)	Fiber (g)	Protein (g)	Total Fat (g)	Sat Fat (g)
Baked Products *(cont.)*						
Cake, angel food, ¹⁄₁₂ of 12 oz	72	16	Tr	2	Tr	Tr
Cake, chocolate, without frosting, ¹⁄₁₂ of 9″ dia	340	51	2	5	14	5
Cake, pound, ¹⁄₁₂ of 12 oz	109	14	Tr	2	6	3
Cake, sponge, ¹⁄₁₂ of 16 oz	110	23	Tr	2	1	Tr
Cake, white, ¹⁄₁₂ of 9″ dia	264	42	1	4	9	2
Cake, yellow, ¹⁄₁₂ of 8″ dia	245	36	Tr	4	10	3
Cheesecake, ⅙ of 17 oz	257	20	Tr	4	18	8
Coffeecake, cheese, ⅙ of 16 oz	258	34	1	5	12	4
Cookies, butter, 1 cookie	23	3	Tr	Tr	1	1
Cookies, chocolate chip, 1 medium cookie	48	7	Tr	1	2	1
Cookies, chocolate sandwich, with creme filling, 1 cookie	47	7	Tr	Tr	2	Tr
Cookies, fortune, 1 cookie	30	7	Tr	Tr	Tr	Tr
Cookies, gingersnaps, 1 cookie	29	5	Tr	Tr	1	Tr
Cookies, oatmeal, 1 cookie	61	10	Tr	1	2	1
Cookies, peanut butter, 1 cookie	72	9	Tr	1	4	1
Cookies, raisin, 1 cookie	60	10	Tr	1	2	1
Cookies, sugar, 1 cookie	66	8	Tr	1	3	1
Cookies, sugar wafers with creme filling, 1 small wafer	18	2	Tr	Tr	1	Tr
Crackers, cheese, 1 cracker (1″ square)	5	1	Tr	Tr	Tr	Tr
Crackers, cheese, sandwich with peanut butter filling, 1 sandwich	32	4	Tr	1	2	Tr
Crackers, crispbread, rye, 1 crispbread	37	8	2	1	Tr	Tr

Food, portion	Cal	Total Carb (g)	Fiber (g)	Protein (g)	Total Fat (g)	Sat Fat (g)
Crackers, matzo, plain, 1 matzo	111	23	1	3	Tr	Tr
Crackers, matzo, whole-wheat, 1 matzo	98	22	3	4	Tr	Tr
Crackers, melba toast, 1 round	12	2	Tr	Tr	Tr	Tr
Crackers, saltines, 1 cracker	13	2	Tr	Tr	Tr	Tr
Crackers, wheat, 1 thin square	9	1	Tr	Tr	Tr	Tr
Crackers, whole-wheat, 1 cracker	18	3	Tr	Tr	1	Tr
Croissants, butter, 1 croissant	231	26	1	5	12	7
Croutons, fast food, 1 package	47	6	1	1	2	1
Danish pastry, fruit, 1 pastry	263	34	1	4	13	3
Doughnuts, cake, plain, frosted, or chocolate-coated, 1 doughnut	204	21	1	2	13	3
Doughnuts, yeast-leavened, glazed, 1 doughnut	242	27	1	4	14	3
English muffins, plain, enriched (includes sourdough), 1 muffin	134	26	2	4	1	Tr
English muffins, whole-wheat, 1 muffin	134	27	4	6	1	Tr
Fig bars, 1 cookie	56	11	1	1	1	Tr
French toast, made with low-fat (2%) milk, 1 slice	149	16	na	5	7	2
Graham crackers, 2½" square	30	5	Tr	Tr	1	Tr
Ice cream cones, wafer, 1 cone	17	3	Tr	Tr	Tr	Tr
Ice cream cones, sugar, 1 cone	40	8	Tr	1	Tr	Tr
Muffins, blueberry, 1 medium	313	54	3	6	7	2
Muffins, corn, 1 medium	345	58	4	7	9	2
Muffins, oat bran, 1 medium	305	55	5	8	8	1
Pancakes, 1 pancake (4" dia)	74	14	Tr	2	1	Tr

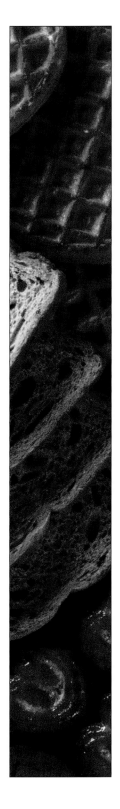

Food, portion	Cal	Total Carb (g)	Fiber (g)	Protein (g)	Total Fat (g)	Sat Fat (g)
Baked Products *(cont.)*						
Phyllo dough, 1 sheet dough	57	10	Tr	1	1	Tr
Pie, apple, ⅙ of 8″ dia	277	40	2	2	13	4
Pie crust, cookie-type, graham cracker, baked, ⅛ of 9″ crust	148	20	Tr	1	7	2
Pie crust, standard-type, dry mix, prepared, baked, ⅛ of 9″ crust	100	10	Tr	1	6	2
Pie, pecan, ⅛ of 9″ dia	503	64	na	6	27	5
Pie, pumpkin, ⅙ of 8″ dia	229	30	3	4	10	2
Rolls, dinner, plain, 1 roll	84	14	1	2	2	Tr
Rolls, dinner, whole-wheat, 1 roll	96	18	3	3	2	Tr
Rolls, french, 1 roll	105	19	1	3	2	Tr
Rolls, burger or hotdog, 1 roll	120	21	1	4	2	Tr
Rolls, hard, 1 roll	167	30	1	6	2	Tr
Sweet rolls, cinnamon, with raisins, 1 roll	223	31	1	4	10	2
Taco shells, baked, 1 medium	62	8	1	1	3	Tr
Toaster pastries, fruit, 1 pastry	204	37	1	2	5	1
Tortillas, corn, 1 tortilla	53	11	1	1	1	Tr
Tortillas, flour, 1 tortilla	150	26	2	4	3	1
Waffles, plain, frozen, ready-to-heat, 1 waffle square	98	15	1	2	3	1
Wonton and egg roll wrappers, 1 wrapper	93	19	1	3	Tr	Tr
Beef Products						
Beef, ground, 85% lean/15% fat, broiled, 1 patty (¼ lb raw)	193	0	0	20	12	5
Beef, ground, 95% lean/5% fat, broiled, 1 patty (¼ lb raw)	140	0	0	22	5	3

FOOD, PORTION	CAL	TOTAL CARB (G)	FIBER (G)	PROTEIN (G)	TOTAL FAT (G)	SAT FAT (G)
Bottom round, braised, 3 oz	234	0	0	24	14	5
Bottom sirloin butt, broiled, 3 oz	213	0	0	26	11	4
Brisket, whole, braised, 3 oz	327	0	0	20	27	11
Chuck, arm roast, braised, 3 oz	282	0	0	23	20	8
Corned beef, brisket, cured, cooked, 3 oz	213	Tr	0	15	16	5
Eye of round, roasted, 3 oz	195	0	0	23	11	4
Liver, pan-fried, 1 slice	142	4	0	21	4	1
Rib, eye, broiled, 3 oz	174	0	0	25	8	3
Rib, prime, roasted, 3 oz	361	0	0	18	31	13
Shank crosscuts, simmered, 3 oz	224	0	0	26	12	5
Short loin, porterhouse steak, broiled, 3 oz	280	0	0	19	22	9
Short loin, T-bone, broiled, 3 oz	274	0	0	19	21	8
Skirt steak, broiled, 3 oz	174	0	0	23	9	3
Tenderloin, broiled, 3 oz	247	0	0	21	17	7
Top round, broiled, 3 oz	195	0	0	26	9	3
Top sirloin, broiled, 3 oz	219	0	0	24	13	5
BEVERAGES						
Beer, light, 12 fl oz	99	5	0	1	0	0
Beer, regular, 12 fl oz	117	6	Tr	1	Tr	0
Carbonated beverage, low-calorie, other than cola or pepper, with aspartame, 12 fl oz	0	0	0	Tr	0	0
Chocolate syrup, 2 tbsp	109	25	1	1	Tr	Tr
Chocolate-flavor beverage mix for milk, powder, 1 serving	80	21	1	1	1	Tr
Chocolate-flavor soda, 12 fl oz	155	39	0	0	0	0

Food, portion	Cal	Total Carb (g)	Fiber (g)	Protein (g)	Total Fat (g)	Sat Fat (g)
Beverages *(cont.)*						
Citrus fruit juice drink, frozen concentrate, prepared with water, 8 fl oz	124	30	Tr	Tr	Tr	0
Clam and tomato juice, 5.5 oz	80	18	Tr	1	Tr	Tr
Club soda, 12 fl oz	0	0	0	0	0	0
Cocoa mix, no sugar added, powder, 1 envelope	56	10	1	2	Tr	Tr
Cocoa mix, powder, 3 heaping tsp	111	24	1	2	1	1
Coffee, brewed from grounds, 8 fl oz	9	0	0	Tr	2	0
Coffee, instant, regular, prepared with water, 6 fl oz	4	1	0	Tr	0	Tr
Coffee, instant, with sugar, cappuccino-flavor powder, 1 serving envelope	107	20	Tr	1	2	1
Coffee substitute, cereal grain beverage, prepared with water, 8 fl oz	12	2	1	Tr	Tr	Tr
Cola, carbonated, 12 fl oz	155	40	0	Tr	0	0
Cola, carbonated, low-calorie, with aspartame, 12 fl oz	4	Tr	0	Tr	0	0
Cola or pepper-type beverage, carbonated, low-calorie, with sodium saccharin, 12 fl oz	0	Tr	0	0	0	0
Cranberry juice cocktail, 8 fl oz	144	36	Tr	0	Tr	Tr
Cranberry-apple juice drink, 8 fl oz	174	44	Tr	Tr	Tr	0
Cranberry-grape juice drink, 8 fl oz	137	34	Tr	Tr	Tr	Tr

Food, portion	Cal	Total Carb (g)	Fiber (g)	Protein (g)	Total Fat (g)	Sat Fat (g)
Cream soda, 12 fl oz	189	49	0	0	0	0
Fruit punch drink, frozen concentrate, prepared, 8 fl oz	114	29	Tr	Tr	0	Tr
Ginger ale, 12 fl oz	124	32	0	0	0	0
Grape juice drink, 8 fl oz	125	32	na	Tr	0	0
Grape soda, 12 fl oz	160	42	0	0	0	0
Hard liquor (gin, rum, vodka, whiskey), distilled, 80 proof, 1 jigger (1.5 fl oz)	97	0	0	0	0	0
Lemon-lime soda, 12 fl oz	147	38	0	0	0	0
Lemonade, low-calorie, powder, prepared, 8 fl oz	5	1	0	Tr	0	0
Lemonade, frozen concentrate, prepared, 8 fl oz	131	34	Tr	Tr	Tr	Tr
Liqueur, coffee, 53 proof, 1 jigger (1.5 fl oz)	175	24	0	Tr	Tr	Tr
Orange carbonated beverage, 12 fl oz	179	46	0	0	0	0
Pepper-type beverage, carbonated, 12 fl oz	151	38	0	0	Tr	Tr
Pineapple and grapefruit juice drink, canned, 8 fl oz	118	29	Tr	1	Tr	Tr
Pineapple and orange juice drink, canned, 8 fl oz	125	30	Tr	3	0	0
Rice beverage, RICE DREAM, canned, 1 cup	120	25	0	Tr	2	Tr
Root beer, 12 fl oz	152	39	0	0	0	0
TABASCO Tomato Cocktail, mild, ready-to-drink, 8 fl oz	56	12	1	2	0	0
Tea, brewed, 8 fl oz	2	1	0	0	0	Tr

FOOD, PORTION	CAL	TOTAL CARB (G)	FIBER (G)	PROTEIN (G)	TOTAL FAT (G)	SAT FAT (G)
BEVERAGES (CONT.)						
Tea, chamomile, brewed, 6 fl oz	2	Tr	0	0	0	Tr
Tea, herb, other than chamomile, brewed, 6 fl oz	2	Tr	0	0	0	Tr
Tea, instant, unsweetened, powder, prepared, 8 fl oz	2	Tr	0	Tr	0	0
Tonic water, 12 fl oz	124	32	na	0	0	0
Water, 8 fl oz	0	0	0	0	0	0
Wine, dessert, sweet, 3.5 fl oz	165	14	0	Tr	0	0
Wine, table, 3.5 fl oz	79	3	0	Tr	0	0
BREAKFAST CEREALS						
ALL-BRAN Original, ½ cup	78	22	10	4	1	Tr
ALL-BRAN WITH EXTRA FIBER, ½ cup	58	23	15	3	1	Tr
Bran flakes, ¾ cup	96	24	5	3	1	Tr
CHEERIOS, 1 cup	111	22	3	3	2	Tr
Corn CHEX, 1 cup	112	26	1	2	Tr	Tr
Corn grits, white, cooked with water, 1 cup	143	31	1	3	Tr	Tr
CRACKLIN' OAT BRAN, ¾ cup	225	39	6	5	8	2
CREAM OF RICE, cooked with water, 1 cup	127	28	Tr	2	Tr	Tr
CREAM OF WHEAT, regular, cooked with water, 1 cup	126	27	1	4	Tr	Tr
CRISPIX, 1 cup	109	25	Tr	2	Tr	Tr
Farina, enriched, cooked with water, ¾ cup	84	18	1	2	Tr	Tr
FIBER ONE, ½ cup	59	24	14	2	1	Tr
GOLDEN GRAHAMS, ¾ cup	112	25	1	2	1	Tr

FOOD, PORTION	CAL	TOTAL CARB (G)	FIBER (G)	PROTEIN (G)	TOTAL FAT (G)	SAT FAT (G)
GRAPE-NUTS, ½ cup	208	47	5	6	1	Tr
GREAT GRAINS Raisin, Date & Pecan Cereal, ⅔ cup	204	40	4	4	5	1
HEALTHY CHOICE, Almond Crunch with Raisins, 1 cup	198	43	5	5	3	Tr
HONEY BUNCHES OF OATS, ¾ cup	118	25	1	2	2	Tr
HONEY BUNCHES OF OATS with Almonds, ¾ cup	126	24	1	2	3	Tr
HONEY NUT CHEERIOS, 1 cup	112	24	2	3	1	Tr
KELLOGG'S Corn Flakes, 1 cup	101	24	1	2	Tr	Tr
KELLOGG'S FROSTED MINI-WHEATS, bite size, 1 cup	189	45	6	6	1	Tr
KELLOGG'S Raisin Bran, 1 cup	195	47	7	5	2	Tr
MALT-O-MEAL, chocolate, cooked with water, 1 cup	122	26	1	4	Tr	Tr
Multi-Bran CHEX, 1 cup	166	41	6	3	1	Tr
NATURE VALLEY LOW FAT FRUIT GRANOLA, ⅔ cup	212	44	3	4	3	Tr
Oats, instant, plain, prepared with water, cooked, 1 cup	129	22	4	5	2	Tr
POST BANANA NUT CRUNCH, 1 cup	249	44	4	5	6	1
POST Bran Flakes, ¾ cup	96	24	5	3	1	Tr
POST FRUIT & FIBRE Dates, Raisins & Walnuts Cereal, 1 cup	212	42	5	4	3	Tr
PRODUCT 19, 1 cup	100	25	1	2	Tr	Tr
QUAKER Low Fat 100% Natural Granola with Raisins, ½ cup	195	41	3	4	3	1
Rice CHEX, 1¼ cups	117	27	Tr	2	Tr	Tr

Food, portion	Cal	Total Carb (g)	Fiber (g)	Protein (g)	Total Fat (g)	Sat Fat (g)
Breakfast Cereals (CONT.)						
RICE KRISPIES, 1¼ cups	119	29	Tr	2	Tr	Tr
SMART START, 1 cup	182	43	2	3	1	Tr
SPECIAL K, 1 cup	117	22	1	7	Tr	Tr
Wheat CHEX, 1 cup	104	24	3	3	1	Tr
Wheat germ, toasted, 1 cup	432	56	17	33	12	2
WHEATIES, 1 cup	107	24	3	3	1	Tr
Whole Grain TOTAL, ¾ cup	97	23	2	2	1	Tr
Cereal Grains and Pasta						
Amaranth, 1 cup	729	129	30	28	13	3
Barley, pearled, cooked, 1 cup	193	44	6	4	1	Tr
Buckwheat groats, roasted, cooked, 1 cup	155	33	5	6	1	Tr
Bulgur, cooked, 1 cup	151	34	8	6	Tr	Tr
Corn flour, whole-grain, yellow, 1 cup	422	90	16	8	5	1
Cornmeal, self-rising, bolted, plain, enriched, yellow, 1 cup	407	86	8	10	4	1
Cornstarch, 1 cup	488	117	1	Tr	Tr	Tr
Couscous, cooked, 1 cup	176	36	2	6	Tr	Tr
Hominy, canned, white, 1 cup	119	24	4	2	1	Tr
Macaroni, cooked, enriched, 1 cup elbow-shaped	197	40	2	7	1	Tr
Macaroni, cooked, enriched, 1 cup small shells	162	33	1	5	1	Tr
Macaroni, whole-wheat, cooked, 1 cup elbow-shaped	174	37	4	7	1	Tr
Millet, cooked, 1 cup	207	41	2	6	2	Tr

Food, portion	Cal	Total Carb (g)	Fiber (g)	Protein (g)	Total Fat (g)	Sat Fat (g)
Noodles, chow mein, 1 cup	237	26	2	4	14	2
Noodles, egg, cooked, 1 cup	213	40	2	8	2	Tr
Noodles, soba, cooked, 1 cup	113	24	na	6	Tr	Tr
Oat bran, cooked, 1 cup	88	25	6	7	2	Tr
Oats, 1 cup	607	103	17	26	11	2
Quinoa, 1 cup	636	117	10	22	10	1
Rice, brown, long-grain, cooked, 1 cup	216	45	4	5	2	Tr
Rice noodles, cooked, 1 cup	192	44	2	2	Tr	Tr
Rice, white, long-grain, cooked, 1 cup	205	45	1	4	Tr	Tr
Rye flour, medium, 1 cup	361	79	15	10	2	Tr
Semolina, enriched, 1 cup	601	122	7	21	2	Tr
Spaghetti, cooked, 1 cup	197	40	2	7	1	Tr
Triticale, 1 cup	645	138	na	25	4	1
Wheat flour, white, bread, enriched, 1 cup	495	99	3	16	2	Tr
Wheat flour, white, cake, enriched, 1 cup unsifted	496	107	2	11	1	Tr
Wheat flour, whole-grain, 1 cup	407	87	15	16	2	Tr
Wild rice, cooked, 1 cup	166	35	3	7	1	Tr
Dairy Products						
Cheese, blue, 1 oz	100	1	0	6	8	5
Cheese, brie, 1 oz	95	Tr	0	6	8	5
Cheese, cheddar, 1 oz	114	Tr	0	7	9	6
Cheese, colby, 1 oz	112	1	0	7	9	6
Cheese, cottage, creamed, 1 cup (not packed)	232	6	0	28	10	6

Food, portion	Cal	Total Carb (g)	Fiber (g)	Protein (g)	Total Fat (g)	Sat Fat (g)
Dairy Products (cont.)						
Cheese, cottage, low-fat, 2% milkfat, 1 cup (not packed)	203	8	0	31	4	3
Cheese, cream, 1 tbsp	51	Tr	0	1	5	3
Cheese, feta, crumbled, 1 cup	396	6	0	21	32	22
Cheese food, pasteurized process, American, 1 oz	94	2	0	5	7	4
Cheese, low-fat, cheddar or colby, 1 oz	49	1	0	7	2	1
Cheese, mozzarella, part skim, 1 oz	72	1	0	7	5	3
Cheese, parmesan, grated, 1 tbsp	22	Tr	0	2	1	1
Cheese, provolone, 1 oz	98	1	0	7	7	5
Cheese, ricotta, part skim, ½ cup	171	6	0	14	10	6
Cheese, swiss, 1 oz	108	2	0	8	8	5
Cream, half-and-half, 1 tbsp	20	1	0	Tr	2	1
Cream, half-and-half, fat free, 1 individual (.5 fl oz) container	9	1	0	Tr	Tr	Tr
Cream, heavy whipping, 1 cup, whipped	414	3	0	2	44	28
Cream, light (coffee or table), 1 individual container	22	Tr	0	Tr	2	1
Cream, sour, 1 tbsp	26	1	0	Tr	3	2
Cream, sour, reduced-fat, 1 tbsp	20	1	0	Tr	2	1
Cream, whipped, topping, pressurized, 1 tbsp	8	Tr	0	Tr	1	Tr
Egg substitute, liquid, 1 cup	211	2	0	30	8	2
Egg, whole, fried, 1 large	92	Tr	0	6	7	2

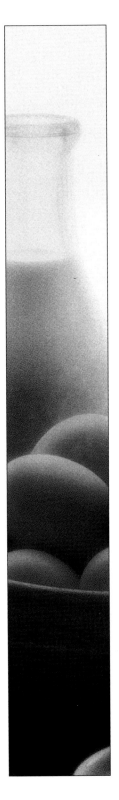

Food, portion	Cal	Total Carb (g)	Fiber (g)	Protein (g)	Total Fat (g)	Sat Fat (g)
Egg, whole, hard-boiled, chopped, 1 cup	211	2	0	17	14	4
Egg, whole, omelet, 1 large	93	Tr	0	6	7	2
Egg, whole, raw, fresh, 1 large	74	Tr	0	6	5	2
Egg, whole, scrambled, 1 large	101	1	0	7	7	2
Eggnog, 1 cup	343	34	0	10	19	11
Milk, 2%, 1 cup	122	11	0	8	5	2
Milk, buttermilk, low-fat, 1 cup	98	12	0	8	2	1
Milk, canned, condensed, sweetened, 1 cup	982	166	0	24	27	17
Milk, canned, evaporated, 1 cup	338	25	0	17	19	12
Milk, canned, evaporated, nonfat, 1 cup	200	29	0	19	1	Tr
Milk, chocolate, lower-fat, 1 cup	180	26	1	8	5	3
Milk, fat-free or skim, 1 cup	83	12	0	8	Tr	Tr
Milk shakes, chocolate, 10.6 oz	357	63	1	9	8	5
Milk shakes, vanilla, 11 oz	351	56	0	12	9	6
Milk, whole, 3.25%, 1 cup	146	11	0	8	8	5
Yogurt, fruit, low-fat, 8 fl oz	243	46	0	10	3	2
Yogurt, plain, low-fat, 8 fl oz	154	17	0	13	4	2
Yogurt, plain, nonfat, 8 fl oz	137	19	0	14	Tr	Tr
Yogurt, plain, whole milk, 8 fl oz	149	11	0	9	8	5
Yogurt, vanilla, low-fat, 8 fl oz	208	34	0	12	3	2
Fast Foods						
Biscuit, egg and ham, 1 biscuit	442	30	1	20	27	6
Biscuit, egg, cheese, and bacon, 1 biscuit	477	33	na	16	31	11

Food, portion	Cal	Total Carb (g)	Fiber (g)	Protein (g)	Total Fat (g)	Sat Fat (g)
Fast Foods (cont.)						
Cheeseburger, large, double patty, with condiments and vegetables, 1 sandwich	704	40	na	38	44	18
Cheeseburger, large, single patty, with bacon and condiments, 1 sandwich	608	37	na	32	37	16
Cheeseburger, double patty, with condiments and vegetables, 1 sandwich	417	35	na	21	21	9
Cheeseburger, single patty, with condiments, 1 sandwich	295	27	na	16	14	6
Chicken, breaded and fried, boneless pieces, with bbq sauce, 6 pieces	330	25	0	17	18	6
Chicken, breaded and fried, dark meat, 2 pieces	431	16	na	30	27	7
Chicken, breaded and fried, light meat, 2 pieces	494	20	na	36	30	8
Chicken fillet sandwich, plain, 1 sandwich	515	39	na	24	29	9
Chili con carne, 8 fl oz	256	22	na	25	8	3
Chimichanga, beef and cheese, 1 chimichanga	443	39	na	20	23	11
Coleslaw, ¾ cup	147	13	na	1	11	2
Crab cake, 1 cake	160	5	Tr	11	10	2
Croissant, egg and cheese, 1 croissant	368	24	na	13	25	14
Enchilada, cheese and beef, 1 enchilada	323	30	na	12	18	9
English muffin, egg, cheese, and sausage, 1 muffin	487	31	na	22	31	12

Food, portion	Cal	Total Carb (g)	Fiber (g)	Protein (g)	Total Fat (g)	Sat Fat (g)
Fish fillet, battered or breaded, fried, 1 fillet	211	15	Tr	13	11	3
Fish sandwich, with tartar sauce, 1 sandwich	431	41	na	17	23	5
French toast sticks, 5 pieces	513	58	3	8	29	5
Frijoles with cheese, 1 cup	225	29	na	11	8	4
Ham, egg, and cheese sandwich, 1 sandwich	347	31	na	19	16	7
Hamburger, large, single patty, with condiments and vegetables, 1 sandwich	512	40	na	26	27	10
Hamburger, double patty, with condiments, 1 sandwich	576	39	na	32	32	12
Hamburger, single patty, with condiments, 1 sandwich	272	34	2	12	10	4
Hotdog, plain, 1 sandwich	242	18	na	10	15	5
Hotdog, with chili, 1 sandwich	296	31	na	14	13	5
Hotdog, with corn flour coating (corndog), 1 sandwich	460	56	na	17	19	5
Hush puppies, 5 pieces	257	35	na	5	12	3
Ice milk, vanilla, soft-serve, with cone, 1 cone	164	24	Tr	4	6	4
Nachos, with cheese, 1 portion (6–8 nachos)	346	36	na	9	19	8
Nachos, with cheese, beans, ground beef, and peppers, 1 portion (6–8 nachos)	569	56	na	20	31	12
Onion rings, breaded and fried, 1 portion (8–9 onion rings)	276	31	na	4	16	7
Pizza with cheese, 1 slice	140	21	na	8	3	2

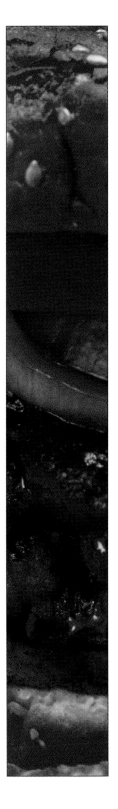

FOOD, PORTION	CAL	TOTAL CARB (G)	FIBER (G)	PROTEIN (G)	TOTAL FAT (G)	SAT FAT (G)
FAST FOODS (CONT.)						
Pizza with cheese, meat, and vegetables, 1 slice	184	21	na	13	5	2
Pizza with pepperoni, 1 slice	181	20	na	10	7	2
Potato, baked, with cheese sauce and bacon, 1 serving	451	44	na	18	26	10
Potato, baked, with cheese sauce and broccoli, 1 serving	403	47	na	14	21	9
Potato, baked, with sour cream and chives, 1 serving	393	50	na	7	22	10
Potato, french fried in vegetable oil, 1 small order	291	34	3	4	16	3
Potato salad, ⅓ cup	108	13	na	1	6	1
Roast beef sandwich, plain, 1 sandwich	346	33	na	22	14	4
Roast beef sandwich with cheese, 1 sandwich	473	45	na	32	18	9
Salad, vegetable, tossed, without dressing, ¾ cup	17	3	na	1	Tr	Tr
Salad, vegetable, tossed, without dressing, with cheese and egg, 1½ cups	102	5	na	9	6	3
Salad, vegetable, tossed, without dressing, with chicken, 1½ cups	105	4	na	17	2	1
Salad, vegetable, tossed, without dressing, with pasta and seafood, 2½ cups	379	32	na	16	21	3
Salad, vegetables tossed, without dressing, with turkey, ham and cheese, 1½ cups	267	5	na	26	16	8
Shrimp, breaded and fried, 1 portion (6–8 shrimp)	454	40	na	19	25	5

Food, portion	Cal	Total Carb (g)	Fiber (g)	Protein (g)	Total Fat (g)	Sat Fat (g)
Submarine sandwich, with cold cuts, 1 submarine	456	51	na	22	19	7
Submarine sandwich, with roast beef, 1 submarine	410	44	na	29	13	7
Submarine sandwich, with tuna salad, 1 submarine	584	55	na	30	28	5
Taco, 1 small	369	27	na	21	21	11
Taco salad, 1½ cups	279	24	na	13	15	7
Fats and Oils						
Butter, salted, 1 tbsp	102	Tr	0	Tr	12	6
Lard, 1 tbsp	115	0	0	0	13	5
Margarine, stick, 80% fat, 1 tbsp	100	Tr	0	Tr	11	2
Margarine, tub, 80% fat, 1 tbsp	102	Tr	0	Tr	11	2
Margarine spread, fat-free, tub, 1 tbsp	6	1	0	Tr	Tr	Tr
Margarine, vegetable oil spread, stick/tub/bottle, 60% fat, 1 tbsp	75	0	0	Tr	8	1
Margarine-butter blend, 60% corn oil margarine and 40% butter, 1 tsp	36	Tr	0	Tr	4	1
Margarine-like spread, approx 40% fat, corn, 1 tsp	17	Tr	0	Tr	2	Tr
Margarine-like spread, 60% fat, tub, soybean/cottonseed, 1 tsp	26	0	0	Tr	3	1
Oil, olive, 1 tbsp	119	0	0	0	14	2
Oil, peanut, 1 tbsp	119	0	0	0	14	2
Oil, sesame, 1 tbsp	120	0	0	0	14	2
Oil, soybean, 1 tbsp	120	0	0	0	14	2

FOOD, PORTION	CAL	TOTAL CARB (G)	FIBER (G)	PROTEIN (G)	TOTAL FAT (G)	SAT FAT (G)
FATS AND OILS (CONT.)						
Oil, vegetable, canola, 1 tsp	40	0	0	0	5	Tr
Oil, vegetable, corn, 1 tsp	40	0	0	0	5	1
Oil, vegetable, safflower, 1 tsp	40	0	0	0	5	Tr
Oil, vegetable, sunflower, 1 tsp	40	0	0	0	5	Tr
Salad dressing, French, 1 tbsp	73	2	0	Tr	7	1
Salad dressing, French, reduced-fat, 1 tbsp	37	5	Tr	Tr	2	Tr
Salad dressing, Italian, 1 tbsp	43	2	0	Tr	4	1
Salad dressing, Italian, reduced-fat, 1 tbsp	11	1	0	Tr	1	Tr
Salad dressing, ranch, 2 tbsp	148	1	Tr	Tr	16	2
Salad dressing, thousand island, 1 tbsp	59	2	Tr	Tr	6	1
Salad dressing, thousand island, reduced-fat, 1 tbsp	31	3	Tr	Tr	2	Tr
Salad dressing, vinegar and oil, 1 tbsp	72	Tr	0	0	8	1
FINFISH AND SHELLFISH PRODUCTS						
Anchovy, European, canned in oil, drained, 1 anchovy	8	0	0	1	Tr	Tr
Bass, striped, cooked, 3 oz	105	0	0	19	3	1
Catfish, cooked, 3 oz	89	0	0	16	2	1
Clam, raw, 1 medium	11	Tr	0	2	Tr	Tr
Cod, Atlantic, cooked, 3 oz	70	0	0	15	1	Tr
Crab, Alaska king, cooked, 1 leg	130	0	0	26	2	Tr
Crab, Alaska king, imitation, made from surimi, 3 oz	87	9	0	10	1	Tr

Food, portion	Cal	Total Carb (g)	Fiber (g)	Protein (g)	Total Fat (g)	Sat Fat (g)
Crab, dungeness, cooked, moist heat, 1 crab	140	1	0	28	2	Tr
Crayfish, wild, cooked, moist heat, 3 oz	70	0	0	14	1	Tr
Dolphinfish, cooked, 3 oz	93	0	0	20	1	Tr
Fish sticks, frozen, preheated, 1 stick (4"×1"×½")	76	7	Tr	4	3	1
Flatfish (flounder and sole), cooked, 1 fillet	149	0	0	31	2	Tr
Gefiltefish, sweet recipe, 1 piece	35	3	0	4	1	Tr
Halibut, cooked, 3 oz	119	0	0	23	2	Tr
Herring, Atlantic, cooked, 3 oz	173	0	0	20	10	2
Lobster, 1 lobster	135	1	0	28	1	Tr
Mackerel, Atlantic, cooked, 3 oz	223	0	0	20	15	4
Mussel, blue, raw, 1 medium	14	1	0	2	Tr	Tr
Orange roughy, 3 oz	59	0	0	12	1	Tr
Oyster, Eastern, breaded/fried, 6 medium	173	10	0	8	11	3
Perch, cooked, 3 oz	99	0	0	21	1	Tr
Pike, Northern, cooked, 3 oz	96	0	0	21	1	Tr
Salmon, smoked (lox), 1 oz	33	0	0	5	1	Tr
Salmon, pink, canned, solids with bone and liquid, 3 oz	118	0	0	17	5	1
Salmon, sockeye, cooked, 3 oz	184	0	0	23	9	2
Sardine, Atlantic, canned in oil, drained, with bone, 1 small	25	0	0	3	1	Tr
Scallops, breaded/fried, 2 large	67	3	0	6	3	1
Sea bass, cooked, 3 oz	105	0	0	20	2	1
Shrimp, 1 medium	6	Tr	0	1	Tr	Tr

Food, portion	Cal	Total Carb (g)	Fiber (g)	Protein (g)	Total Fat (g)	Sat Fat (g)
Finfish and Shellfish Products *(cont.)*						
Snapper, cooked, 3 oz	109	0	0	22	1	Tr
Squid, fried, 3 oz	149	7	0	15	6	2
Surimi, 3 oz	84	6	0	13	1	Tr
Swordfish, cooked, 3 oz	132	0	0	22	4	1
Trout, rainbow, wild, cooked, 3 oz	128	0	0	19	5	1
Tuna, fresh, bluefin, cooked, 3 oz	156	0	0	25	5	1
Tuna, light, canned in water, drained, 1 can	191	0	0	42	1	Tr
Tuna, white, canned in water, drained, 1 can	220	0	0	41	5	1
Walleye, cooked, 3 oz	101	0	0	21	1	Tr
Whitefish, smoked, 3 oz	92	0	0	20	1	Tr
Fruits and Fruit Juices						
Apple juice, unsweetened, 1 cup	117	29	Tr	Tr	Tr	Tr
Apples, raw, with skin, 1 medium (3 per lb.)	72	19	3	Tr	Tr	Tr
Applesauce, sweetened, 1 cup	194	51	3	Tr	Tr	Tr
Apricots, juice pack, with skin, halves, 1 cup	117	30	4	2	Tr	Tr
Apricots, dried, stewed, without added sugar, halves, 1 cup	213	55	7	3	Tr	Tr
Apricots, raw, 1 apricot	17	4	1	Tr	Tr	Tr
Avocados, raw, 1 cup, puréed	368	20	15	5	34	5
Bananas, raw, 1 medium	105	27	3	1	Tr	Tr
Blackberries, raw, 1 cup	62	14	8	2	1	Tr
Blueberries, raw, 1 cup	83	21	3	1	Tr	Tr

Food, portion	Cal	Total Carb (g)	Fiber (g)	Protein (g)	Total Fat (g)	Sat Fat (g)
Cantaloupe, raw, ⅛ melon	23	6	1	1	Tr	Tr
Casaba melon, raw, 1 melon	459	108	15	18	2	Tr
Cherries, sweet, raw, 1 cherry	4	1	Tr	Tr	Tr	Tr
Cranberry sauce, canned, sweetened, 1 slice (½″ thick)	86	22	1	Tr	Tr	Tr
Dates, deglet noor, 1 date	23	6	1	Tr	Tr	Tr
Dates, medjool, pitted, 1 date	66	18	2	Tr	Tr	0
Figs, raw, 1 medium (2¼″ dia)	37	10	1	Tr	Tr	Tr
Fruit cocktail, juice pack, 1 cup	109	28	2	1	Tr	Tr
Grape juice, sweetened, 1 cup	128	32	Tr	Tr	Tr	Tr
Grapefruit juice, white, canned, sweetened, 1 cup	115	28	Tr	1	Tr	Tr
Grapefruit, raw, ½ medium	41	10	1	1	Tr	Tr
Grapes, red or green, raw, seedless, 1 grape	3	1	Tr	Tr	Tr	Tr
Honeydew, ⅛ of 5¼″ dia melon	45	11	1	1	Tr	Tr
Kiwi fruit, skinless, 1 medium	46	11	2	1	Tr	Tr
Kumquats, raw, 1 fruit	13	3	1	Tr	Tr	Tr
Lemon juice, 1 lemon's yield	12	4	Tr	Tr	0	0
Lime juice, 1 lime's yield	10	3	Tr	Tr	Tr	Tr
Mangos, raw, 1 fruit	135	35	4	1	1	Tr
Nectarines, raw, 1 fruit	60	14	2	1	Tr	Tr
Olives, ripe, canned, 1 large	5	Tr	Tr	Tr	Tr	Tr
Orange juice, canned, unsweetened, 1 cup	105	25	Tr	1	Tr	Tr
Orange-grapefruit juice, canned, unsweetened, 1 cup	106	25	Tr	1	Tr	Tr
Oranges, raw, 1 fruit	62	15	3	1	Tr	Tr

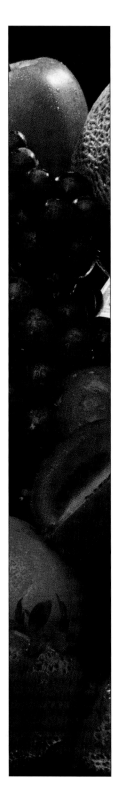

Food, portion	Cal	Total Carb (g)	Fiber (g)	Protein (g)	Total Fat (g)	Sat Fat (g)
Fruits and Fruit Juices *(cont.)*						
Papayas, raw, 1 medium	119	30	5	2	Tr	Tr
Passion-fruit, purple, raw, 1 fruit	17	4	2	Tr	Tr	Tr
Peach nectar, canned, 1 cup	134	35	1	1	Tr	Tr
Peaches, canned, juice pack, halves or slices, 1 cup	109	29	3	2	Tr	Tr
Peaches, raw, 1 medium	38	9	1	1	Tr	Tr
Pears, canned, juice pack, 1 half, with liquid	38	10	1	Tr	Tr	Tr
Pears, raw, 1 medium pear	96	26	5	1	Tr	Tr
Pineapple, canned, juice pack, 1 cup, crushed, sliced, or chunks	149	39	2	1	Tr	Tr
Pineapple juice, canned, unsweetened, 1 cup	140	34	1	1	Tr	Tr
Pineapple, raw, 1 slice	40	11	1	Tr	Tr	Tr
Plantains, raw, 1 medium	218	57	4	2	1	Tr
Plums, canned, purple, juice pack, 1 plum with liquid	27	7	Tr	Tr	Tr	Tr
Plums, raw, 1 fruit (2⅛″ dia)	30	8	1	Tr	Tr	Tr
Pomegranates, raw, 1 fruit	105	26	1	1	Tr	Tr
Prune juice, canned, 1 cup	182	45	3	2	Tr	Tr
Quinces, raw, 1 fruit	52	14	2	Tr	Tr	Tr
Raisins, seedless, 1 box (.5 oz)	42	11	1	Tr	Tr	Tr
Raspberries, raw, 10 raspberries	10	2	1	Tr	Tr	Tr
Rhubarb, raw, diced, 1 cup	26	6	2	1	Tr	Tr
Strawberries, raw, 1 large	6	1	Tr	Tr	Tr	Tr
Tangerines, raw, 1 medium	37	9	2	1	Tr	Tr
Watermelon, raw, ¹⁄₁₆ of melon	86	22	1	2	Tr	Tr

Food, portion	Cal	Total Carb (g)	Fiber (g)	Protein (g)	Total Fat (g)	Sat Fat (g)
Lamb and Veal						
Lamb, ground, broiled, 3 oz	241	0	0	21	17	7
Lamb, leg (shank and sirloin), roasted, 3 oz	219	0	0	22	14	6
Lamb, loin, roasted, 3 oz	263	0	0	19	20	9
Lamb, shoulder (arm and blade), roasted, 3 oz	235	0	0	19	17	7
Veal, boneless breast, braised, 3 oz	226	0	0	23	14	6
Veal, ground, broiled, 3 oz	146	0	0	21	6	3
Veal, loin, roasted, 3 oz	184	0	0	21	10	4
Veal, shoulder, roasted, 3 oz	156	0	0	22	7	3
Legumes and Legume Products						
Bacon, meatless, 1 strip	16	Tr	Tr	1	1	Tr
Beans, adzuki, boiled, 1 cup	294	57	17	17	Tr	Tr
Beans, baked, canned, plain or vegetarian, 1 cup	236	52	13	12	1	Tr
Beans, baked, canned, with pork and sweet sauce, 1 cup	281	53	13	13	4	1
Beans, black, boiled, 1 cup	227	41	15	15	1	Tr
Beans, great Northern, boiled, 1 cup	209	37	12	15	1	Tr
Beans, kidney, boiled, 1 cup	225	40	11	15	1	Tr
Beans, navy, boiled, 1 cup	258	48	12	16	1	Tr
Beans, pinto, boiled, 1 cup	234	44	15	14	1	Tr
Beans, white, boiled, 1 cup	254	46	19	16	1	Tr
Broadbeans, boiled, 1 cup	187	33	9	13	1	Tr
Chickpeas (garbanzo beans), boiled, 1 cup	269	45	12	15	4	Tr

Food, portion	Cal	Total Carb (g)	Fiber (g)	Protein (g)	Total Fat (g)	Sat Fat (g)
Legumes and Legume Products *(cont.)*						
Chili with beans, canned, 1 cup	287	30	11	15	14	6
Cowpeas (blackeyes, crowder, Southern), boiled, 1 cup	198	35	11	13	1	Tr
Falafel, home-prepared, 1 patty	57	5	na	2	3	Tr
HARVEST BURGER, Original Flavor, All Vegetable Protein Patties, 1 patty	138	7	6	18	4	1
Hummus, 1 tbsp	27	3	1	1	1	Tr
Lentils, boiled, 1 cup	230	40	16	18	1	Tr
Lima beans, large, boiled, 1 cup	216	39	13	15	1	Tr
BIG FRANKS, meatless franks, 1 serving	118	2	2	12	7	1
Miso, 1 cup	567	77	15	32	17	2
Noodles, Chinese, cellophane or long rice (mung beans), dehydrated, 1 cup	491	121	1	Tr	Tr	Tr
Peanut butter, chunky, 2 tbsp	188	7	2	8	16	3
Peanut butter, smooth, 2 tbsp	192	6	2	8	17	3
Peanuts, dry-roasted, without salt, 1 cup	854	31	12	35	73	10
Peanuts, raw, 1 cup	828	24	12	38	72	10
Peas, split, boiled, 1 cup	231	41	16	16	1	Tr
Refried beans, canned, 1 cup	237	39	13	14	3	1
Sausage, meatless, 1 link	64	2	1	5	5	1
Soy flour, full-fat, raw, 1 cup	366	30	8	29	17	3
Soy milk, fluid, 1 cup	120	11	3	9	5	1
Soy sauce (tamari), 1 tbsp	11	1	Tr	2	Tr	Tr
Soybeans, mature, raw, 1 cup	774	56	17	68	37	5

Food, portion	Cal	Total Carb (g)	Fiber (g)	Protein (g)	Total Fat (g)	Sat Fat (g)
Tempeh, 1 cup	320	16	na	31	18	4
Tofu, firm, prepared with calcium sulfate and magnesium chloride (nigari), ¼ block	62	2	Tr	7	4	1
Tofu, salted and fermented (fuyu), 1 block	13	1	na	1	1	Tr
Tofu, soft, prepared with calcium sulfate and magnesium chloride (nigari), ¼ block	71	2	Tr	8	4	1
Nut and Seed Products						
Almonds, 1 cup, whole	827	28	17	30	72	6
Brazilnuts, dried, unblanched, 1 cup shelled (32 kernels)	918	17	11	20	93	21
Cashew nuts, dry-roasted, with salt added, 1 cup	786	45	4	21	63	13
Coconut meat, dried, sweetened, flaked, packaged, 1 cup	351	35	3	2	24	21
Hazelnuts or filberts, 10 nuts	88	2	1	2	9	1
Macadamia nuts, dry-roasted, 1 oz (10–12 kernels)	203	4	2	2	22	3
Mixed nuts, oil-roasted, with peanuts, with salt added, 1 cup	876	30	13	24	80	12
Pecans, 1 oz (20 halves)	196	4	3	3	20	2
Pine nuts, dried, 10 nuts	11	Tr	Tr	Tr	1	Tr
Pistachio nuts, dry-roasted, without salt added, 1 cup	702	34	13	26	57	7
Pumpkin and squash seed kernels, dried, 1 cup	747	25	5	34	63	12
Sesame butter, tahini, 1 tbsp	89	3	1	3	8	1
Sesame seeds, whole, dried, 1 tbsp	52	2	1	2	4	1

FOOD, PORTION	CAL	TOTAL CARB (G)	FIBER (G)	PROTEIN (G)	TOTAL FAT (G)	SAT FAT (G)
NUT AND SEED PRODUCTS (*CONT.*)						
Sunflower seeds, dried, 1 cup	262	9	5	10	23	2
Sunflower seed kernels, dried, without hulls, 1 cup	821	27	15	33	71	7
Walnuts, English, 7 nuts	183	4	2	4	18	2
Watermelon seed kernels, dried, 1 cup	602	17	na	31	51	11
PORK PRODUCTS						
Backribs, fresh, roasted, 1 piece	810	0	0	53	65	24
Bacon, cured, pan-fried, 1 slice	42	Tr	0	3	3	1
Canadian-style bacon, cured, grilled, 2 slices (6 per 6-oz pkg)	87	1	0	11	4	1
Ground pork, cooked, 3 oz	252	0	0	22	18	7
Ham, cured, boneless, extra-lean (approx 5% fat), roasted, 3 oz	123	1	0	18	5	2
Ham, cured, regular (approx 13% fat), canned, roasted, 3 oz	192	Tr	0	17	13	4
Ham shank, fresh, roasted, 3 oz	246	0	0	22	17	6
Loin, blade (chops), fresh, bone-in, pan-fried, 1 chop	284	0	0	18	23	8
Loin, country-style ribs, fresh, braised, 1 piece	696	0	0	56	51	19
Loin, fresh, sirloin (roasts), boneless, roasted, 3 oz	176	0	0	24	8	3
Spareribs, braised, 1 piece	703	0	0	51	54	20
POULTRY PRODUCTS						
Chicken, breast, meat and skin, batter-fried, ½ breast	364	13	Tr	35	18	5
Chicken, breast, meat and skin, roasted, ½ breast	193	0	0	29	8	2

Food, portion	Cal	Total Carb (g)	Fiber (g)	Protein (g)	Total Fat (g)	Sat Fat (g)
Chicken, canned, no broth, 5 oz can	230	1	0	32	10	3
Chicken, drumstick, meat and skin, batter-fried, 1 drumstick	193	6	Tr	16	11	3
Chicken, drumstick, meat and skin, roasted, 1 drumstick	112	0	0	14	6	2
Chicken, leg, meat and skin, batter-fried, 1 leg	431	14	Tr	34	26	7
Chicken, leg, meat and skin, roasted, 1 leg	264	0	0	30	15	4
Chicken, roasting, light meat only, roasted, 1 cup chopped	214	0	0	38	6	2
Chicken, thigh, meat and skin, batter-fried, 1 thigh	238	8	Tr	19	14	4
Chicken, thigh, meat and skin, roasted, 1 thigh	153	0	0	16	10	3
Chicken, wing, meat and skin, batter-fried, 1 wing	159	5	Tr	10	11	3
Chicken, wing, meat and skin, roasted, 1 wing	99	0	0	9	7	2
Cornish game hens, meat and skin, roasted, 1 whole bird	668	0	0	57	47	13
Duck, roasted, ½ duck	1287	0	0	73	108	37
Turkey, breast, meat and skin, roasted, ½ breast	1633	0	0	248	64	18
Turkey, ground, cooked, 1 patty (4 oz raw)	193	0	0	22	11	3
Turkey, leg, meat and skin, roasted, 1 leg	1136	0	0	152	54	17

Food, portion	Cal	Total Carb (g)	Fiber (g)	Protein (g)	Total Fat (g)	Sat Fat (g)
Sausages and Luncheon Meats						
Beef, cured, sausage, cooked, smoked, 1 sausage	134	1	0	6	12	5
Beef, thin sliced, 5 slices	37	1	0	6	1	Tr
Bologna, beef, 1 slice	87	1	0	3	8	3
Bologna, turkey, 1 slice	59	1	Tr	3	4	1
Bratwurst, pork, cooked, 1 link	281	2	0	12	25	9
Frankfurter, beef, 1 frankfurter	149	2	0	5	13	5
Ham, sliced, extra-lean (approx 5% fat), 1 slice	37	Tr	0	5	1	Tr
Ham, sliced, regular, 1 slice	46	1	Tr	5	2	1
LOUIS RICH, Turkey Bacon, 1 serving	35	Tr	0	2	3	1
Pastrami, beef, 98% fat-free, 6 slices	54	1	0	11	1	0
Pastrami, cured, 1 slice (1 oz)	98	1	0	5	8	3
Pepperoni, pork/beef, 15 slices	135	1	Tr	6	12	5
Salami, cooked, beef, 1 slice	67	Tr	0	3	6	3
Salami, dry or hard, pork, 1 slice (3⅛″ dia×1/16″ thick)	41	Tr	0	2	3	1
Sausage, Italian, pork, cooked, 1 link (4 links per lb)	268	1	0	17	21	8
Sausage, pork, cooked, 1 link	81	0	0	5	7	2
Sausage, smoked link, pork and beef, 1 piece (4″ long×1⅛″ dia)	218	2	0	8	20	7
Sausage, turkey, reduced-fat, brown and serve, cooked, 1 cup	256	14	Tr	22	13	4
Turkey breast meat, 1 slice	27	4	1	2	Tr	Tr

FOOD, PORTION	CAL	TOTAL CARB (G)	FIBER (G)	PROTEIN (G)	TOTAL FAT (G)	SAT FAT (G)
SNACKS						
Banana chips, 1 oz	147	17	2	1	10	8
Beef jerky, 1 piece, large	82	2	Tr	7	5	2
Beef sticks, smoked, 1 stick	110	1	0	4	10	4
BETTY CROCKER Fruit Roll Ups, berry flavored, 2 rolls	104	24	na	Tr	1	Tr
CHEX mix, 1 oz (approx ⅔ cup)	120	18	2	3	5	2
Corn chips, plain, 1 bag (7 oz)	1067	113	10	13	66	9
Granola bar, hard, peanut, 1 oz	136	18	1	3	6	1
Granola bar, soft, uncoated, nut and raisin, 1 bar (1 oz)	127	18	2	2	6	3
Popcorn, air-popped, 1 cup	31	6	1	1	Tr	Tr
Popcorn, caramel-coated, with peanuts, 1 oz (approx ⅔ cup)	113	23	1	2	2	Tr
Popcorn, cheese-flavor, 1 cup	58	6	1	1	4	1
Pork skins, plain, ½ oz	77	0	0	9	4	2
Potato chips, plain, salted, 8 oz	1217	120	10	16	79	25
Pretzels, hard, salted, 10 twists	229	48	2	5	2	Tr
Tortilla chips, plain, 1 oz	142	18	2	2	7	1
Trail mix, 1 cup	693	67	na	21	44	8
SOUPS, SAUCES, AND GRAVIES						
Gravy, beef or brown, 1 serving	25	4	Tr	1	1	Tr
Gravy, turkey, canned, 1 tbsp	8	1	Tr	Tr	Tr	Tr
Sauce, barbecue, 8 fl oz	188	32	3	5	5	1
Sauce, cheese, ¼ cup	110	4	Tr	4	8	4
Sauce, hoisin, 1 tbsp	35	7	Tr	1	1	Tr
Sauce, NESTLÉ, LJ MINOR Sweet N' Sour Sauce, 1 serving	40	8	Tr	Tr	1	Tr

Food, portion	Cal	Total Carb (g)	Fiber (g)	Protein (g)	Total Fat (g)	Sat Fat (g)
Soups, Sauces, and Gravies *(cont.)*						
Sauce, pasta, spaghetti/ marinara, 1 cup	143	21	4	4	5	1
Sauce, pepper or hot, 1 tsp	1	Tr	Tr	Tr	Tr	Tr
Sauce, salsa, ½ cup	36	8	2	2	Tr	Tr
Sauce, teriyaki, 1 tbsp	15	3	Tr	1	0	0
Sauce, Worcestershire, 1 tbsp	11	3	0	0	0	0
Soup, bean with ham, canned, chunky, ready-to-serve, 8 fl oz	231	27	11	13	9	3
Soup, beef broth, 8 fl oz	29	2	0	5	0	0
Soup, beef broth or bouillon, canned, ready-to-serve, 1 cup	17	Tr	0	3	1	Tr
Soup, beef noodle, canned, prepared with equal volume water, 8 fl oz	83	9	1	5	3	1
Soup, black bean, canned, prepared with equal volume water, 1 cup	116	20	4	6	2	Tr
Soup, chicken noodle, canned, prepared with equal volume water, 8 fl oz	75	9	1	4	2	1
Soup, chicken vegetable, chunky, ready-to-serve, 8 fl oz	166	19	na	12	5	1
Soup, chicken with rice, canned, prepared with equal volume water, 8 fl oz	60	7	1	4	2	Tr
Soup, clam chowder, New England, canned, prepared with equal volume milk, 1 cup	164	17	1	9	7	3
Soup, cream of chicken, canned, prepared with equal volume milk, 8 fl oz	191	15	Tr	7	11	5

Food, portion	Cal	Total Carb (g)	Fiber (g)	Protein (g)	Total Fat (g)	Sat Fat (g)
Soup, cream of mushroom, canned, prepared with equal volume milk, 8 fl oz	203	15	Tr	6	14	5
Soup, lentil with ham, ready-to-serve, 8 fl oz	139	20	na	9	3	1
Soup, minestrone, canned, prepared with equal volume water, 8 fl oz	82	11	1	4	3	1
Soup, split pea with ham, chunky, ready-to-serve, 1 cup	185	27	4	11	4	2
Soup, split pea with ham, chunky, reduced fat and sodium, ready-to-serve, 1 serving	185	27	na	13	3	1
Soup, tomato, canned, prepared with equal volume water, 8 fl oz	85	17	Tr	2	2	Tr
Soup, vegetable beef, canned, prepared with equal volume water, 8 fl oz	78	10	Tr	6	2	1
Sweets						
100 GRAND Bar, 1 bar (1.5 oz)	192	31	Tr	1	8	5
AFTER EIGHT Mints, 1 piece	29	6	Tr	Tr	1	1
BABY RUTH Bar, 1 bar (0.75 oz)	97	13	1	1	5	3
BRACH'S STAR BRITES Peppermint Mints, 3 pieces	59	15	0	0	Tr	0
Butterscotch candies, 3 pieces	63	14	0	Tr	1	Tr
Caramels, 1 piece	39	8	Tr	Tr	1	1
Chewing gum, 1 stick	7	2	Tr	0	Tr	Tr
Frostings, chocolate, creamy, ready-to-eat, 2 tbsp	163	26	Tr	Tr	7	2
Frozen juice novelties, fruit and juice bars, 1 bar (2.5 fl oz)	63	16	1	1	Tr	0

Food, portion	Cal	Total Carb (g)	Fiber (g)	Protein (g)	Total Fat (g)	Sat Fat (g)
Sweets *(cont.)*						
Frozen yogurts, chocolate, soft-serve, ½ cup (4 fl oz)	115	18	2	3	4	3
Frozen yogurts, vanilla, soft-serve, ½ cup (4 fl oz)	117	17	0	3	4	2
Gelatin desserts, dry mix, prepared with water, ½ cup	84	19	0	2	0	0
Gelatin desserts, dry mix, reduced-calorie, with aspartame, prepared with water, ½ cup	23	5	0	1	0	0
Gumdrops, 10 gummy bears	87	22	Tr	0	0	0
Honey, 1 tbsp	64	17	Tr	Tr	0	0
Ice creams, chocolate, ½ cup	143	19	1	3	7	4
Ice creams, strawberry, ½ cup	127	18	1	2	6	3
Ice creams, vanilla, ½ cup	145	17	1	3	8	5
Ice novelties, Italian ice, ½ cup	61	16	0	Tr	Tr	0
Jams and preserves, 1 tbsp	56	14	Tr	Tr	Tr	Tr
Jellies, 1 tbsp	56	15	Tr	Tr	Tr	Tr
Jellybeans, 10 small	41	10	Tr	0	Tr	0
"M&M's" Milk Chocolate Candies, 10 pieces	34	5	Tr	Tr	1	1
"M&M's" Peanut Chocolate Candies, 10 pieces	103	12	1	2	5	2
Marshmallows, 1 regular	23	6	Tr	Tr	Tr	Tr
Milk chocolate, 1 bar (1.55 oz)	235	26	1	3	13	6
Milk chocolate, 10 kisses	246	27	2	4	14	7
Milk chocolate, with almonds, 1 bar (1.45 oz)	216	22	3	4	14	7
MILKY WAY Bar, 1 bar (.8 oz)	97	16	Tr	1	4	2

Food, portion	Cal	Total Carb (g)	Fiber (g)	Protein (g)	Total Fat (g)	Sat Fat (g)
Molasses, blackstrap, 1 tbsp	47	12	0	0	0	0
NESTLÉ CRUNCH, 1.4 oz	209	26	1	2	11	6
Peanut bar, 1 bar (1.4 oz)	209	19	2	6	13	2
Puddings, banana, 1 oz	36	6	Tr	1	1	Tr
Puddings, chocolate, ready-to-eat, 1 can (5 oz)	197	33	1	4	6	1
Puddings, JELL-O Brand Fat-Free Sugar-Free Instant Reduced-Calorie Pudding & Pie Filling, chocolate, powder, 1 serving	34	8	1	1	Tr	Tr
Puddings, rice, ready-to-eat, 1 can (5 oz)	231	31	Tr	3	11	2
Puddings, tapioca, ready-to-eat, 1 snack size (4 oz)	134	22	Tr	2	4	1
Puddings, vanilla, ready-to-eat, 1 snack size (4 oz)	146	25	0	3	4	1
RAISINETS, 10 pieces	41	7	1	Tr	2	1
REESE'S Peanut Butter Cups, 2 cups (1.6 oz package)	232	25	2	5	14	5
Semisweet chocolate chips, 1 cup (6 oz package)	805	106	10	7	50	30
Sherbet, orange, ½ cup (4 fl oz)	107	22	2	1	1	1
SKITTLES, 10 pieces	43	10	0	Tr	Tr	Tr
STARBURST Fruit Chews, 1 piece	20	4	0	Tr	Tr	Tr
Sugars, brown, 1 cup, packed	829	214	0	0	0	0
Sugars, granulated, 1 tsp	16	4	0	0	0	0
Sugars, granulated, 1 cup	774	200	0	0	0	0
Sugars, powdered, 1 tbsp	31	8	0	0	Tr	Tr
Syrups, chocolate, fudge, 2 tbsp	133	24	1	2	3	2

Food, portion	Cal	Total Carb (g)	Fiber (g)	Protein (g)	Total Fat (g)	Sat Fat (g)
Sweets (cont.)						
Syrups, corn, light, 1 tbsp	59	16	0	0	Tr	0
Syrups, pancake, 1 tbsp	47	12	Tr	0	0	0
Toppings, strawberry, 2 tbsp	107	28	Tr	Tr	Tr	Tr
TWIZZLERS Strawberry Twists, 4 pieces from 5-oz package	133	30	0	1	1	0
YORK Peppermint Pattie, 1 patty (1.5 oz)	165	35	1	1	3	2
Vegetables and Vegetable Products						
Alfalfa sprouts, raw, 1 cup	10	1	1	1	Tr	Tr
Amaranth leaves, boiled, 1 cup	28	5	0	3	Tr	Tr
Artichoke hearts, boiled, ½ cup	42	9	5	3	Tr	Tr
Artichokes, raw, 1 medium	60	13	7	4	Tr	Tr
Arugula, raw, 1 leaf	1	Tr	Tr	Tr	Tr	Tr
Asparagus, boiled, 4 spears	13	2	1	1	Tr	Tr
Bamboo shoots, boiled, 1 cup	14	2	1	2	Tr	Tr
Beans, fava, in pod, raw, 1 cup	111	22	na	10	1	Tr
Beans, lima, canned, ½ cup	88	17	4	5	Tr	Tr
Beans, pinto, frozen, boiled, ⅓ 10-oz package	152	29	8	9	Tr	Tr
Beans, snap, green, boiled, 1 cup	44	10	4	2	Tr	Tr
Beet greens, boiled, ½ cup	19	4	2	2	Tr	Tr
Beets, boiled, slices, ½ cup	37	8	2	1	Tr	Tr
Broccoli, raw, 1 cup chopped	30	6	2	2	Tr	Tr
Brussels sprouts, boiled, 1 sprout	8	1	1	1	Tr	Tr
Cabbage, Chinese (pak choi), boiled, shredded, 1 cup	20	3	2	3	Tr	Tr

Food, portion	Cal	Total Carb (g)	Fiber (g)	Protein (g)	Total Fat (g)	Sat Fat (g)
Cabbage, Chinese (pe-tsai), boiled, shredded, 1 cup	17	3	2	2	Tr	Tr
Cabbage, raw, shredded, 1 cup	17	4	2	1	Tr	Tr
Cabbage, red, boiled, shredded, ½ cup	22	5	2	1	Tr	Tr
Carrot juice, canned, 1 cup	94	22	2	2	Tr	Tr
Carrots, baby, raw, 1 medium	4	1	Tr	Tr	Tr	Tr
Carrots, boiled, slices, ½ cup	27	6	2	1	Tr	Tr
Carrots, raw, 1 medium	25	6	2	1	Tr	Tr
Catsup, 1 tbsp	14	4	Tr	Tr	Tr	Tr
Cauliflower, boiled, ½ cup	14	3	2	1	Tr	Tr
Cauliflower, raw, 1 floweret	3	1	Tr	Tr	Tr	Tr
Celery, raw, 1 medium stalk	6	1	1	Tr	Tr	Tr
Chard, Swiss, raw, 1 cup	7	1	1	1	Tr	Tr
Chives, raw, chopped, 1 tbsp	1	Tr	Tr	Tr	Tr	Tr
Coleslaw, ½ cup	41	7	1	1	2	Tr
Collards, boiled, chopped, 1 cup	49	9	5	4	1	Tr
Corn pudding, 1 cup	273	32	na	11	13	6
Corn, sweet, boiled, 1 ear	83	19	2	3	1	Tr
Corn, sweet, canned, whole kernel, 1 cup	133	30	3	4	2	Tr
Cowpeas, boiled, 1 cup	160	34	8	5	1	Tr
Cucumber, ½ cup slices	8	2	Tr	Tr	Tr	Tr
Eggplant, boiled, 1 cup cubes	35	9	2	1	Tr	Tr
Endive, raw, chopped, ½ cup	4	1	1	Tr	Tr	Tr
Garlic, raw, 1 clove	4	1	Tr	Tr	Tr	Tr

Food, portion	Cal	Total Carb (g)	Fiber (g)	Protein (g)	Total Fat (g)	Sat Fat (g)
Vegetables and Vegetable Products *(cont.)*						
Gourd, white-flowered (calabash), boiled, 1 cup cubes	22	5	na	1	Tr	Tr
Grape leaves, canned, 1 leaf	3	Tr	na	Tr	Tr	Tr
Hearts of palm, canned, 1 piece	9	2	1	1	Tr	Tr
Kale, cooked, chopped, 1 cup	36	7	3	2	1	Tr
Kohlrabi, raw, 1 cup	36	8	5	2	Tr	Tr
Leeks, bulb and lower leaf-portion, raw, 1 leek	54	13	2	1	Tr	Tr
Lettuce, butterhead or iceberg, 1 leaf	1	Tr	Tr	Tr	Tr	Tr
Lettuce, cos or romaine, 1 leaf	2	Tr	Tr	Tr	Tr	Tr
Mung beans, sprouted, stir-fried, 1 cup	62	13	2	5	Tr	Tr
Mushrooms, boiled, ½ cup pieces	22	4	2	2	Tr	Tr
Mushrooms, raw, 1 medium	4	1	Tr	1	Tr	Tr
Mustard greens, boiled, chopped, 1 cup	21	3	3	3	Tr	Tr
Okra, boiled, ½ cup slices	18	4	2	1	Tr	Tr
Onion rings, breaded, par-fried, frozen, heated in oven, 10 rings	244	23	1	3	16	5
Onions, boiled, 1 cup	92	21	3	3	Tr	Tr
Onions, raw, 1 tbsp, chopped	4	1	Tr	Tr	Tr	Tr
Onions, raw, 1 slice (⅛" thick)	6	1	Tr	Tr	Tr	Tr
Onions, spring, or scallions (tops and bulb), raw, 1 tbsp chopped	2	Tr	Tr	Tr	Tr	Tr
Parsnips, boiled, slices, ½ cup	55	13	3	1	Tr	Tr
Peas and carrots, boiled, ½ cup	38	8	2	2	Tr	Tr

Food, portion	Cal	Total Carb (g)	Fiber (g)	Protein (g)	Total Fat (g)	Sat Fat (g)
Peas, green, boiled, 1 cup	134	25	9	9	Tr	Tr
Pepper, serrano, raw, 1 pepper	2	Tr	Tr	Tr	Tr	Tr
Peppers, hot chili, green, 1 pepper	18	4	1	1	Tr	Tr
Peppers, jalapeno, 1 pepper	4	1	Tr	Tr	Tr	Tr
Peppers, sweet, green, raw, 1 medium	24	6	2	1	Tr	Tr
Peppers, sweet, yellow, raw, 10 strips	14	3	Tr	1	Tr	Tr
Pickle, dill, 1 medium	12	3	1	Tr	Tr	Tr
Pickle, sour, 1 slice	1	Tr	Tr	Tr	Tr	Tr
Pickle, sweet, 1 midget gherkin	7	2	Tr	Tr	Tr	Tr
Pickle, sweet, 1 slice	8	2	Tr	Tr	Tr	Tr
Pickle relish, hotdog, 1 tbsp	14	4	Tr	Tr	Tr	Tr
Pickle relish, sweet, 1 tbsp	20	5	Tr	Tr	Tr	Tr
Pimento, canned, 1 tbsp	3	1	Tr	Tr	Tr	Tr
Potato pancakes, 1 pancake	207	22	2	5	12	2
Potato salad, 1 cup	358	28	3	7	21	4
Potatoes, au gratin, 1 cup	323	28	4	12	19	12
Potatoes, baked, flesh, 1 potato	145	34	2	3	Tr	Tr
Potatoes, baked, flesh and skin, 1 potato	161	37	4	4	Tr	Tr
Potatoes, french fried, frozen, oven-heated, 10 strips	100	16	2	2	4	1
Potatoes, hashed brown, 1 cup	413	55	5	5	20	2
Potatoes, mashed, dehydrated flakes, whole milk and butter added, 1 cup	204	23	2	4	11	6

Food, portion	Cal	Total Carb (g)	Fiber (g)	Protein (g)	Total Fat (g)	Sat Fat (g)
VEGETABLES AND VEGETABLE PRODUCTS (*CONT.*)						
Potatoes, mashed, whole milk added, 1 cup	174	37	3	4	1	1
Potatoes, red, flesh and skin, baked, 1 medium potato	154	34	3	4	Tr	Tr
Pumpkin, canned, 1 cup	83	20	7	3	1	Tr
Radicchio, raw, 1 leaf	2	Tr	Tr	Tr	Tr	Tr
Radishes, raw, 1 medium	1	Tr	Tr	Tr	Tr	Tr
Rutabagas, cooked, boiled, 1 cup cubes	66	15	3	2	Tr	Tr
Sauerkraut, canned, 1 cup	27	6	4	1	Tr	Tr
Shallots, raw, chopped, 1 tbsp	7	2	na	Tr	Tr	Tr
Soybeans, mature seeds, sprouted, steamed, 1 cup	76	6	1	8	4	1
Spinach, frozen, chopped or leaf, boiled, ½ cup	30	5	4	4	Tr	Tr
Spinach, raw, 1 leaf	2	Tr	Tr	Tr	Tr	Tr
Squash, summer, all varieties, raw, sliced, 1 cup	18	4	1	1	Tr	Tr
Squash, summer, crookneck, boiled, sliced, 1 cup	36	8	3	2	1	Tr
Squash, summer, zucchini, with skin, boiled, sliced, 1 cup	29	7	3	1	Tr	Tr
Squash, winter, acorn, baked, cubes, 1 cup	115	30	9	2	Tr	Tr
Squash, winter, butternut, baked, cubes, 1 cup	82	22	na	2	Tr	Tr
Succotash, boiled, 1 cup	221	47	9	10	2	Tr
Sweet potato, baked in skin, 1 medium	103	24	4	2	Tr	Tr

Food, portion	Cal	Total Carb (g)	Fiber (g)	Protein (g)	Total Fat (g)	Sat Fat (g)
Sweet potato, candied, 1 piece	144	29	3	1	3	1
Tomatillos, raw, 1 medium	11	2	1	Tr	Tr	Tr
Tomato juice, canned, with salt added, 1 cup	41	10	1	2	Tr	Tr
Tomato paste, canned, 1 cup	215	50	12	11	1	Tr
Tomato sauce, with herbs and cheese, canned, ½ cup	72	12	3	3	2	1
Tomato sauce, with mushrooms, canned, 1 cup	86	21	4	4	Tr	Tr
Tomato sauce, with onions, green peppers, and celery, canned, 1 cup	103	22	4	2	2	Tr
Tomatoes, stewed, 1 cup	66	16	3	2	Tr	Tr
Tomatoes, raw, 1 cup cherry	27	6	2	1	Tr	Tr
Tomatoes, raw, 1 cup, chopped	32	7	2	2	Tr	Tr
Tomatoes, raw, 1 medium	22	5	1	1	Tr	Tr
Tomatoes, sun-dried, packed in oil, drained, 1 cup	234	26	6	6	15	2
Turnip greens, boiled, 1 cup	48	8	6	5	1	Tr
Turnips, boiled, cubes, 1 cup	34	8	3	1	Tr	Tr
Vegetable juice cocktail, 1 cup	46	11	2	2	Tr	Tr
Vegetables, mixed, frozen, boiled, ½ cup	59	12	4	3	Tr	Tr
Wasabi, root, raw, 1 cup, sliced	142	31	10	6	1	0
Waterchestnuts, Chinese (matai), raw, slices, ½ cup slices	60	15	2	1	Tr	Tr
Watercress, raw, chopped, 1 cup	4	Tr	Tr	1	Tr	Tr
Yam, baked, cubes, 1 cup	158	38	5	2	Tr	Tr

enjoy low-carb recipes

You'll love eating low carb with the scrumptious recipes in this section. They're light on carbs but packed with flavor. And with the nutritional information provided with each one, you'll know how each dish fits in your low-carb plan. The preparation times are based on the approximate amount of time that is needed to assemble the recipe before cooking, baking, chilling, or serving. They include prep steps, such as measuring, mixing, and chopping. (If some preparation and cooking can be done simultaneously, that's taken into account.) Preparation of optional ingredients and serving suggestions is not included.

great-start breakfasts

ham & cheddar frittata

nutrients per serving:

Calories: 210
Carbohydrate: 5 g
Calories From Fat: 56%
Total Fat: 13 g
Saturated Fat: 6 g
Cholesterol: 201 mg
Sodium: 995 mg
Dietary Fiber: 1 g
Protein: 19 g

      3 eggs
      3 egg whites
    ½ teaspoon salt
    ½ teaspoon freshly ground black pepper
 1 ½ cups (4 ounces) frozen broccoli florets, thawed
      6 ounces deli smoked ham, cut into ½-inch cubes (1 ¼ cups)
    ⅓ cup drained bottled roasted red bell peppers, cut into thin strips
      1 tablespoon butter
    ½ cup (2 ounces) shredded sharp Cheddar cheese

1. Preheat broiler.

2. Beat eggs, egg whites, salt and pepper in large bowl until blended. Stir in broccoli, ham and pepper strips.

3. Melt butter over medium heat in 10-inch ovenproof skillet with sloping side. Pour egg mixture into skillet; cover. Cook 5 to 6 minutes or until eggs are set around edge. (Center will be wet.)

4. Uncover; sprinkle cheese over frittata. Transfer skillet to broiler; broil, 5 inches from heat source, 2 minutes or until eggs are set in center and cheese is melted. Let stand 5 minutes; cut into wedges.   *Makes 4 servings*

baked eggs

nutrients per serving:

Calories: 79
Carbohydrate: 2 g
Calories From Fat: 8%
Total Fat: 1 g
Saturated Fat: <1 g
Cholesterol: 3 mg
Sodium: 248 mg
Dietary Fiber: 0 g
Protein: 15 g

      4 eggs
      4 teaspoons milk
        Salt and black pepper to taste

1. Preheat oven to 375°F. Grease 4 small baking dishes or custard cups.

2. Break 1 egg into each dish. Add 1 teaspoon milk to each dish. Sprinkle with salt and pepper.

3. Bake about 15 minutes or until set.   *Makes 4 servings*

Baked Egg Options: Top eggs with desired amount of one or more of the following before baking; half-and-half, salsa, shredded cheese, chopped ham, minced chives or minced fresh herbs. Bake as directed above.

ham & cheddar frittata

triple-decker vegetable omelet

1 cup finely chopped broccoli
½ cup diced red bell pepper
½ cup shredded carrot
⅓ cup sliced green onions
1 clove garlic, minced
2½ teaspoons FLEISCHMANN'S® Original Margarine, divided
¾ cup low-fat cottage cheese (1% milkfat), divided
1 tablespoon plain dry bread crumbs
1 tablespoon grated Parmesan cheese
½ teaspoon Italian seasoning
1½ cups EGG BEATERS® Healthy Real Egg Product, divided
⅓ cup chopped tomato
Chopped fresh parsley, for garnish

In 8-inch nonstick skillet, over medium-high heat, sauté broccoli, bell pepper, carrot, green onions and garlic in 1 teaspoon margarine until tender. Remove from skillet; stir in ½ cup cottage cheese. Keep warm. Combine bread crumbs, Parmesan cheese and Italian seasoning; set aside.

In same skillet, over medium heat, melt ½ teaspoon margarine. Pour ½ cup Egg Beaters into skillet. Cook, lifting edges to allow uncooked portion to flow underneath. When almost set, slide unfolded omelet onto ovenproof serving platter. Top with half each of the vegetable mixture and bread crumb mixture; set aside.

Prepare 2 more omelets with remaining Egg Beaters and margarine. Layer 1 omelet onto serving platter over vegetable and bread crumb mixture; top with remaining vegetable mixture and bread crumb mixture. Layer with remaining omelet. Top omelet with remaining cottage cheese and tomato. Bake at 425°F for 5 to 7 minutes or until heated through. Garnish with parsley. Cut into wedges to serve.

Makes 4 servings

Prep Time: 20 minutes
Cook Time: 30 minutes

triple-decker vegetable omelet

vegetable strata

2 slices white bread, cubed
¼ cup shredded reduced-fat Swiss cheese
½ cup sliced carrots
½ cup sliced mushrooms
¼ cup chopped onion
1 clove garlic, crushed
1 teaspoon FLEISCHMANN'S® Original Margarine
½ cup chopped tomato
½ cup snow peas
1 cup EGG BEATERS® Healthy Real Egg Product
¾ cup skim milk

Place bread cubes evenly on bottom of greased 1½-quart casserole dish. Sprinkle with cheese; set aside.

In medium nonstick skillet, over medium heat, sauté carrots, mushrooms, onion and garlic in margarine until tender. Stir in tomato and snow peas; cook 1 to 2 minutes more. Spoon over cheese. In small bowl, combine Egg Beaters® and milk; pour over vegetable mixture. Bake at 375°F for 45 to 50 minutes or until knife inserted in center comes out clean. Let stand 10 minutes before serving. *Makes 6 servings*

Prep Time: 15 minutes
Cook Time: 55 minutes

vegetable strata

brunch eggs olé

8 eggs
½ cup all-purpose flour
1 teaspoon baking powder
¾ teaspoon salt
2 cups (8 ounces) shredded Monterey Jack cheese with jalapeño peppers
1½ cups (12 ounces) small curd cottage cheese
1 cup (4 ounces) shredded sharp Cheddar cheese
1 jalapeño pepper,* seeded and chopped
½ teaspoon hot pepper sauce
Fresh Salsa (recipe follows)

*Jalapeño peppers can sting and irritate the skin; wear rubber gloves when handling peppers and do not touch eyes. Wash hands after handling.

1. Preheat oven to 350°F. Grease 9-inch square baking pan.

2. Beat eggs in large bowl at high speed with electric mixer 4 to 5 minutes or until slightly thickened and lemon colored.

3. Combine flour, baking powder and salt in small bowl. Stir flour mixture into eggs until blended.

4. Combine Monterey Jack cheese, cottage cheese, Cheddar cheese, jalapeño and hot pepper sauce in medium bowl; mix well. Fold into egg mixture until well blended. Pour into prepared pan.

5. Bake 45 to 50 minutes or until golden brown and firm in center. Let stand 10 minutes before cutting into squares to serve. Serve with Fresh Salsa. Garnish as desired. *Makes 8 servings*

fresh salsa

3 medium plum tomatoes, seeded and chopped
2 tablespoons chopped onion
1 small jalapeño pepper,* stemmed, seeded and minced
1 tablespoon chopped fresh cilantro
1 tablespoon lime juice
¼ teaspoon salt
⅛ teaspoon black pepper

*Jalapeño peppers can sting and irritate the skin; wear rubber gloves when handling peppers and do not touch eyes. Wash hands after handling.

Stir together tomatoes, onion, jalapeño pepper, cilantro, lime juice, salt and black pepper in small bowl. Refrigerate until ready to serve. *Makes 1 cup*

brunch eggs olé

apple and brie omelet

nutrients per serving:

Calories: 334
Carbohydrate: 11 g
Calories From Fat: 65%
Total Fat: 24 g
Cholesterol: 469 mg
Sodium: 362 mg
Dietary Fiber: 1 g
Protein: 19 g

2 large Golden Delicious apples
2 tablespoons butter or margarine, divided
½ teaspoon ground nutmeg
4 ounces Brie cheese
8 large eggs, lightly beaten
2 green onions, thinly sliced

1. Place large serving platter in oven and preheat to 200°F. Peel, core and slice apples; place in microwavable container. Top with 1 tablespoon butter and nutmeg. Cover and microwave at HIGH (100% power) 3 minutes. Set aside. While apples cook, trim rind from cheese; thinly slice cheese.

2. Melt 1½ teaspoons butter in medium nonstick skillet over medium heat; rotate skillet to coat bottom. Place eggs in medium bowl and whisk until blended. Pour half of eggs into skillet. Let cook, without stirring, 1 to 2 minutes, or until set on bottom. With rubber spatula, lift side of omelet and slightly tilt pan to allow uncooked portion of egg flow underneath. Cover pan and cook 2 to 3 minutes, until eggs are set but still moist on top. Remove platter from oven and slide omelet into center. Spread apples evenly over entire omelet, reserving a few slices for garnish, if desired. Evenly space cheese slices over apples. Sprinkle with onion, reserving some for garnish. Return platter to oven.

3. Cook remaining beaten eggs in remaining 1½ teaspoons butter as directed above. When cooked, slide spatula around edge to be certain omelet is loose. Carefully place second omelet over cheese, apple and onion mixture. Top with reserved apple and onion slices. Cut into wedges to serve. *Makes 4 servings*

apple and brie omelet

deep south ham and redeye gravy

1 tablespoon butter
1 ham steak (about 1⅓ pounds)
1 cup strong coffee
¾ teaspoon sugar
¼ teaspoon hot pepper sauce

1. Heat large skillet over medium-high heat until hot. Add butter; tilt skillet to coat bottom. Add ham steak; cook 3 minutes. Turn; cook 2 minutes longer or until lightly browned. Remove ham to serving platter; set aside and keep warm.

2. Add coffee, sugar and pepper sauce to same skillet. Bring to a boil over high heat; boil 2 to 3 minutes or until liquid is reduced to ¼ cup liquid, scraping up any brown bits. Serve gravy over ham.   *Makes 4 servings*

Serving Suggestion: Serve ham steak with sautéed greens and poached eggs.

mushroom-herb omelet

1 cup EGG BEATERS® Healthy Real Egg Product
1 tablespoon chopped fresh parsley
1 teaspoon finely chopped oregano, basil or thyme (*or* ¼ teaspoon dried)
2 cups sliced fresh mushrooms
2 teaspoons FLEISCHMANN'S® Original Margarine, divided

In small bowl, combine Egg Beaters®, parsley and oregano, basil or thyme; set aside.

In 8-inch nonstick skillet, over medium heat, sauté mushrooms in 1 teaspoon margarine until tender; set aside. In same skillet, over medium heat, melt ½ teaspoon margarine. Pour half the egg mixture into skillet. Cook, lifting edges to allow uncooked portion to flow underneath. When almost set, spoon half of mushrooms over half of omelet. Fold other half over mushrooms; slide onto serving plate. Repeat with remaining margarine, egg mixture and mushrooms.   *Makes 2 servings*

Prep Time: 10 minutes
Cook Time: 20 minutes

deep south ham and redeye gravy

greek isles omelet

nutrients per serving:

½ of omelet

Calories: 111
Carbohydrate: 7 g
Calories From Fat: 26%
Total Fat: 3 g
Saturated Fat: <1 g
Cholesterol: 0 mg
Sodium: 538 mg
Dietary Fiber: 1 g
Protein: 13 g

Nonstick cooking spray
¼ cup chopped onion
¼ cup canned artichoke hearts, rinsed and drained
¼ cup washed and torn spinach leaves
¼ cup chopped plum tomato
1 cup cholesterol-free egg substitute
2 tablespoons sliced pitted ripe olives, rinsed and drained
Dash black pepper

1. Spray small nonstick skillet with cooking spray; heat over medium heat until hot. Cook and stir onion 2 minutes or until crisp-tender.

2. Add artichoke hearts. Cook and stir until heated through. Add spinach and tomato; toss briefly. Remove from heat. Transfer vegetables to small bowl. Wipe out skillet and spray with cooking spray.

3. Combine egg substitute, olives and pepper in medium bowl. Heat skillet over medium heat until hot. Pour egg mixture into skillet. Cook over medium heat 5 to 7 minutes; as eggs begin to set, gently lift edges of omelet with spatula and tilt skillet so that uncooked portion flows underneath.

4. When egg mixture is set, spoon vegetable mixture over half of omelet. Loosen omelet with spatula and fold in half. Slide omelet onto serving plate.

Makes 2 servings

greek isles omelet

chile scramble

nutrients per serving:

Calories: 112
Carbohydrate: 13 g
Calories From Fat: 12%
Total Fat: 2 g
Saturated Fat: <1 g
Cholesterol: 0 mg
Sodium: 427 mg
Dietary Fiber: 3 g
Protein: 13 g

2 tablespoons minced onion
1 teaspoon FLEISCHMANN'S® Original Margarine
1 cup EGG BEATERS® Healthy Real Egg Product
1 (4-ounce) can diced green chiles, drained
¼ cup whole kernel corn
2 tablespoons diced pimientos

In 10-inch nonstick skillet, over medium-high heat, sauté onion in margarine for 2 to 3 minutes or until onion is translucent. Pour Egg Beaters® into skillet; cook, stirring occasionally, until mixture is set. Stir in chiles, corn and pimientos; cook 1 minute more or until heated through.   *Makes 2 servings*

Prep Time: 5 minutes
Cook Time: 10 minutes

scrambled eggs with chicken and sun-dried tomatoes

nutrients per serving:

Calories: 247
Carbohydrate: 4 g
Calories From Fat: 53%
Total Fat: 14 g
Saturated Fat: 6 g
Cholesterol: 337 mg
Sodium: 211 mg
Dietary Fiber: 1 g
Protein: 24 g

4 eggs
2 tablespoons milk
1 teaspoon dried basil leaves
   Ground black pepper
5 ounces cooked chicken, chopped
¼ cup oil-packed sun-dried tomatoes, drained and cut into thin strips
2 tablespoons chopped green onion
1 tablespoon butter
1 tablespoon grated BELGIOIOSO® Romano Cheese

In medium bowl, beat together eggs, milk, basil and pepper to taste. Stir in chicken, tomatoes and onion. In large skillet, melt butter over medium heat; pour in egg mixture. Cook, without stirring, until mixture begins to set on bottom and around edges. Using large spoon or spatula, lift and fold partially cooked eggs so uncooked portion flows underneath. Continue cooking over medium heat 2 to 3 minutes. Remove from heat. Sprinkle with BelGioioso Romano Cheese and serve immediately.

Makes 3 servings

chile scramble

spinach & egg casserole

1 box (10 ounces) BIRDS EYE® frozen Chopped Spinach
1 can (15 ounces) Cheddar cheese soup
1 tablespoon mustard
½ pound deli ham, cut into ¼-inch cubes
4 hard-boiled eggs, chopped or sliced

- Preheat oven to 350°F.
- In large saucepan, cook spinach according to package directions; drain well.
- Stir in soup, mustard and ham.
- Pour into 9×9-inch baking pan. Top with eggs.
- Bake 15 to 20 minutes or until heated through.   *Makes 4 servings*

Serving Suggestion: Sprinkle with paprika for added color.

Birds Eye Idea: Cook eggs the day before and refrigerate. They will be much easier to peel.

Prep Time: 10 minutes
Cook Time: 15 to 20 minutes

country ham omelets

2 tablespoons butter or margarine
3 slices HILLSHIRE FARM® Ham, chopped
½ cup finely chopped potato
¼ cup chopped green bell pepper
¼ cup chopped onion
½ cup sliced fresh mushrooms
8 to 12 eggs, beaten
½ cup (2 ounces) shredded sharp Cheddar cheese

Melt butter in medium skillet over medium heat; sauté Ham, potato, pepper and onion 3 to 4 minutes. Add mushrooms; stir and heat through.

Prepare four 2 or 3 egg omelets. Fill each with 2 tablespoons cheese and ¼ cup ham mixture. Use remaining ham mixture as omelet topping.   *Makes 4 servings*

spinach & egg casserole

crunchy ranch-style eggs

nutrients per serving:
Calories: 245
Carbohydrate: 9 g
Calories From Fat: 66%
Total Fat: 18 g
Saturated Fat: 7 g
Cholesterol: 232 mg
Sodium: 606 mg
Dietary Fiber: 1 g
Protein: 12 g

    2 cans (10 ounces each) tomatoes and green chilies, drained
1⅓ cups *French's*® French Fried Onions, divided
    2 tablespoons *Frank's*® *RedHot*® Original Cayenne Pepper Sauce
    2 tablespoons *French's*® Worcestershire Sauce
    6 eggs
    1 cup (4 ounces) shredded Cheddar cheese

Preheat oven to 400°F. Grease 2-quart shallow baking dish. Combine tomatoes, ⅔ cup French Fried Onions, **Frank's RedHot** Sauce and Worcestershire in prepared dish. Make 6 indentations in mixture. Break 1 egg into each indentation.

Bake, uncovered, 15 to 20 minutes or until eggs are set. Top with cheese and remaining ⅔ cup onions. Bake 1 minute or until onions are golden.

Makes 6 servings

Tip: Recipe may be prepared in individual ramekin dishes. Bake until eggs are set.

Prep Time: 5 minutes
Cook Time: 16 minutes

sunrise squares

nutrients per serving:
Calories: 389
Carbohydrate: 9 g
Calories From Fat: 64%
Total Fat: 27 g
Saturated Fat: 10 g
Cholesterol: 294 mg
Sodium: 843 mg
Dietary Fiber: <1 g
Protein: 26 g

    1 pound BOB EVANS® Original Recipe Roll Sausage
    2 slices bread, cut into ½-inch cubes (about 2 cups)
    1 cup (4 ounces) shredded sharp Cheddar cheese
    6 eggs
    2 cups milk
    ½ teaspoon salt
    ½ teaspoon dry mustard

Preheat oven to 350°F. Crumble sausage into medium skillet. Cook over medium heat until browned, stirring occasionally. Drain off any drippings. Spread bread cubes in greased 11×7-inch baking dish; top with sausage and cheese. Whisk eggs, milk, salt and mustard until well blended; pour over cheese. Bake 30 to 40 minutes or until set. Let stand 5 minutes before cutting into squares; serve hot. Refrigerate leftovers.

Makes 6 servings

Tip: You can make this tasty meal ahead and refrigerate overnight before baking.

crunchy ranch-style egg

nutrients per serving:

Calories: 254
Carbohydrate: 15 g
Calories From Fat: 50%
Total Fat: 14 g
Saturated Fat: 7 g
Cholesterol: 246 mg
Sodium: 1163 mg
Dietary Fiber: 3 g
Protein: 21 g

baked eggs florentine

2 packages (10 ounces each) frozen creamed spinach
4 slices (1/8 inch thick) deli ham, about 5 to 6 ounces
4 eggs
    Salt and black pepper
1/8 teaspoon ground nutmeg
1/2 cup (2 ounces) shredded provolone cheese
2 tablespoons chopped roasted red pepper

1. Preheat oven to 450°F. Make small cut in each package of spinach. Microwave at HIGH 5 to 6 minutes, turning packages halfway through cooking time.

2. Meanwhile, grease 8-inch square baking pan. Place ham slices on bottom of prepared pan, overlapping slightly. Spread spinach mixture over ham slices.

3. Make 4 indentations in spinach. Carefully break 1 egg in each. Season to taste with salt and black pepper. Sprinkle with nutmeg.

4. Bake 16 to 19 minutes or until eggs are set. Remove from oven. Sprinkle cheese and red pepper over top. Return to oven and bake 1 to 2 minutes longer or until cheese is melted. Serve immediately.   *Makes 4 servings*

Serving Suggestion: Serve with fresh pineapple pieces.

Prep & Cook Time: 28 minutes

baked egg florentine

chile cheese puff

¾ **cup all-purpose flour**
1½ **teaspoons baking powder**
9 **eggs**
4 **cups (16 ounces) shredded Monterey Jack cheese**
2 **cups (16 ounces) low-fat (1%) cottage cheese**
2 **cans (4 ounces each) diced green chilies, drained**
1½ **teaspoons sugar**
¼ **teaspoon salt**
⅛ **teaspoon hot pepper sauce**
1 **cup salsa**

1. Preheat oven to 350°F. Spray 13×9-inch baking dish with nonstick cooking spray.

2. Combine flour and baking powder in small bowl.

3. Whisk eggs in large bowl until blended; stir in Monterey Jack, cottage cheese, chilies, sugar, salt and hot pepper sauce. Add flour mixture; stir just until combined. Pour into prepared dish.

4. Bake, uncovered, 45 minutes or until egg mixture is set. Let stand 5 minutes before serving. Serve with salsa. *Makes 8 servings*

three-egg omelet

1 **tablespoon butter or margarine**
3 **eggs, lightly beaten**
  Salt and black pepper
¼ **cup (1 ounce) shredded Cheddar cheese**
¼ **cup chopped cooked ham**

1. Melt butter in 10-inch skillet over medium heat. Add eggs; lift cooked edge with spatula to allow uncooked eggs to flow under cooked portion. Season with salt and black pepper to taste. Shake pan to loosen omelet. Cook until set.

2. Place cheese and ham on ½ of omelet. Fold omelet in half. Transfer to serving plate. Serve immediately. *Makes 1 serving*

chile cheese puff

easy brunch frittata

nutrients per serving:

Calories: 102
Carbohydrate: 11 g
Calories From Fat: 20%
Total Fat: 2 g
Saturated Fat: 1 g
Cholesterol: 7 mg
Sodium: 627 mg
Dietary Fiber: 1 g
Protein: 9 g

Nonstick cooking spray
1 cup small broccoli florets
2½ cups (12 ounces) frozen hash brown potatoes with onions and peppers (O'Brien style), thawed
1½ cups cholesterol-free egg substitute, thawed
2 tablespoons reduced-fat (2%) milk
¾ teaspoon salt
¼ teaspoon black pepper
½ cup (2 ounces) shredded reduced-fat Cheddar cheese

1. Preheat oven to 450°F. Coat medium nonstick ovenproof skillet with nonstick cooking spray. Heat skillet over medium heat until hot. Add broccoli; cook and stir 2 minutes. Add potatoes; cook and stir 5 minutes.

2. Beat together egg substitute, milk, salt and pepper in small bowl; pour over potato mixture. Cook 5 minutes or until edge is set (center will still be wet).

3. Transfer skillet to oven; bake 6 minutes or until center is set. Sprinkle with cheese; let stand 2 to 3 minutes or until cheese is melted.

4. Cut into wedges; serve with sour cream, if desired. *Makes 6 servings*

fluffy scrambled eggs with fresh herbs

nutrients per serving:

Calories: 351
Carbohydrate: 6 g
Calories From Fat: 69%
Total Fat: 27 g
Saturated Fat: 7 g
Cholesterol: 640 mg
Sodium: 649 mg
Dietary Fiber: 1 g
Protein: 20 g

6 large eggs
¼ cup milk, half-and-half or light cream
¼ teaspoon salt
⅛ teaspoon ground white pepper
2 tablespoons I CAN'T BELIEVE IT'S NOT BUTTER!® Spread
⅓ cup finely chopped onion or shallots
1 teaspoon finely chopped fresh tarragon, parsley, chive, basil, marjoram or oregano leaves

In medium bowl, with wire whisk, blend eggs, milk, salt and pepper.

In 12-inch nonstick skillet, melt I Can't Believe It's Not Butter!® Spread over medium-high heat and cook onion, stirring occasionally, 3 minutes or until onion is tender. Reduce heat to medium and stir in egg mixture until eggs and onions are combined. Stir in herbs and cook, stirring frequently, until eggs are set. *Makes 2 servings*

easy brunch frittata

satisfying main dishes

rosemary steak

nutrients per serving:

Calories: 328
Carbohydrate: 1 g
Calories From Fat: 44%
Total Fat: 16 g
Saturated Fat: 6 g
Cholesterol: 110 mg
Sodium: 392 mg
Dietary Fiber: 0 g
Protein: 42 g

4 boneless beef top loin (New York strip) steaks (about 6 ounces each)
2 tablespoons minced fresh rosemary
2 cloves garlic, minced
1 tablespoon extra-virgin olive oil
1 teaspoon grated lemon peel
1 teaspoon coarsely ground black pepper
½ teaspoon salt
Fresh rosemary sprigs

Score steaks in diamond pattern on both sides. Combine minced rosemary, garlic, oil, lemon peel, pepper and salt in small bowl; rub mixture onto surface of meat. Cover and refrigerate at least 15 minutes. Grill steaks over medium-hot KINGSFORD® Briquets about 4 minutes per side until medium-rare or to desired doneness. Cut steaks diagonally into ½-inch-thick slices. Garnish with rosemary sprigs.

Makes 4 servings

august moon korean ribs

nutrients per serving:

Calories: 331
Carbohydrate: 3 g
Calories From Fat: 68%
Total Fat: 25 g
Saturated Fat: 11 g
Cholesterol: 94 mg
Sodium: 111 mg
Dietary Fiber: 1 g
Protein: 23 g

⅓ cup water
⅓ cup soy sauce
¼ cup thinly sliced green onions
3 tablespoons dark sesame oil
3 tablespoons honey
2 tablespoons minced garlic
2 tablespoons sesame seeds
1 tablespoon grated fresh ginger
1 teaspoon black pepper
3½ pounds pork back ribs

To prepare marinade, combine all ingredients except ribs in small bowl. Place ribs in large resealable plastic food storage bag. Pour marinade over ribs, turning to coat. Seal bag. Marinate in refrigerator overnight. Arrange medium KINGSFORD® Briquets on each side of rectangular metal or foil drip pan. Grill ribs in center of grid on covered grill 35 to 45 minutes or until ribs are browned and cooked through, turning once.

Makes 8 servings

rosemary steak

chunky chicken and vegetable soup

nutrients per serving:

Calories: 130
Carbohydrate: 5 g
Calories From Fat: 57%
Total Fat: 8 g
Saturated Fat: 3 g
Cholesterol: 27 mg
Sodium: 895 mg
Dietary Fiber: 1 g
Protein: 9 g

1 tablespoon vegetable oil
1 boneless skinless chicken breast (4 ounces), diced
½ cup chopped green bell pepper
½ cup thinly sliced celery
2 green onions, sliced
2 cans (14½ ounces each) chicken broth
1 cup water
½ cup sliced carrots
2 tablespoons cream
1 tablespoon finely chopped parsley
¼ teaspoon dried thyme leaves
⅛ teaspoon black pepper

1. Heat oil in large saucepan over medium heat. Add chicken; cook and stir 4 to 5 minutes or until no longer pink. Add bell pepper, celery and onions. Cook and stir 7 minutes or until vegetables are tender.

2. Add broth, water, carrots, cream, parsley, thyme and black pepper. Simmer 10 minutes or until carrots are tender. *Makes 4 servings*

peppercorn steaks

nutrients per serving:

Calories: 413
Carbohydrate: <1 g
Calories From Fat: 50%
Total Fat: 23 g
Saturated Fat: 7 g
Cholesterol: 129 mg
Sodium: 249 mg
Dietary Fiber: <1g
Protein: 49 g

2 tablespoons olive oil
1 to 2 teaspoons cracked red or black peppercorns or freshly ground pepper
1 teaspoon minced garlic
1 teaspoon dried herbs, such as rosemary or parsley
4 boneless beef top loin (strip) or ribeye steaks (6 ounces each)
¼ teaspoon salt

1. Combine oil, peppercorns, garlic and herbs in small bowl. Rub mixture on both sides of each steak. Cover and refrigerate.

2. Prepare grill for direct cooking.

3. Place steaks on grid over medium heat. Grill, uncovered, 10 to 12 minutes for medium-rare to medium or to desired doneness, turning occasionally. Season with salt after cooking. *Makes 4 servings*

chunky chicken and vegetable soup

nutrients per serving:

Calories: 249
Carbohydrate: 10 g
Calories From Fat: 33%
Total Fat: 9 g
Saturated Fat: g
Cholesterol: 147 mg
Sodium: 960 mg
Dietary Fiber: 7 g
Protein: 31 g

szechwan seafood stir-fry

1 package (10 ounces) fresh spinach leaves
4 teaspoons dark sesame oil, divided
4 cloves garlic, minced and divided
¼ cup reduced-sodium soy sauce
1 tablespoon cornstarch
1 tablespoon dry sherry or sake
1 medium red bell pepper, cut in thin 1-inch-long strips
1½ teaspoons minced fresh or bottled gingerroot
¾ pound peeled, deveined large shrimp, thawed if frozen
½ pound fresh bay scallops
2 teaspoons sesame seeds, toasted

1. Rinse spinach in cold water; drain. Heat 2 teaspoons oil in large saucepan over medium heat. Add 2 cloves garlic; stir-fry 1 minute. Add spinach; cover and steam 4 to 5 minutes or until spinach is wilted, turning with tongs after 3 minutes. Remove from heat; keep covered.

2. Meanwhile, combine soy sauce, cornstarch and sherry; stir until smooth. Set aside. Heat remaining 2 teaspoons oil in large nonstick skillet over medium-high heat. Add bell pepper; stir-fry 2 minutes. Add remaining 2 cloves garlic and ginger; stir-fry 1 minute. Add shrimp; stir-fry 2 minutes. Add scallops; stir-fry 1 minute or until shrimp and scallops are opaque. Add soy sauce mixture; stir-fry 1 minute or until sauce thickens.

3. Stir spinach mixture and transfer to 4 individual plates; top with seafood mixture and sesame seeds. *Makes 4 servings*

Tip: Substitute one large head bok choy, thinly sliced, for spinach. Increase steaming time to 8 minutes or until bok choy is tender. You may also substitute the larger and less expensive sea scallops for the bay scallops; simply cut them in quarters.

szechwan seafood stir-fry

jalapeño-lime chicken

8 chicken thighs
3 tablespoons jalapeño jelly
1 tablespoon olive oil
1 tablespoon lime juice
1 clove garlic, minced
1 teaspoon chili powder
½ teaspoon black pepper
⅛ teaspoon salt
Lime wedges (optional)

1. Preheat oven to 400°F. Line 15×10-inch jelly-roll pan with foil; spray with nonstick cooking spray.

2. Arrange chicken in single layer in prepared pan. Bake 15 minutes; drain off juices. Combine jelly, oil, lime juice, garlic, chili powder, pepper and salt in small bowl. Turn chicken; brush with half of jelly mixture. Bake 20 minutes. Turn chicken; brush with remaining jelly mixture. Bake 10 to 15 minutes or until juices run clear (180°F).

3. Garnish chicken with lime wedges, if desired.   *Makes 8 servings*

jalapeño-lime chicken

nutrients per serving:

1 wedge (⅙ of total recipe) without garnish

Calories: 70
Carbohydrate: 5 g
Calories From Fat: 16%
Total Fat: 1 g
Saturated Fat: 1 g
Cholesterol: 5 mg
Sodium: 316 mg
Dietary Fiber: 1 g
Protein: 9 g

zucchini mushroom frittata

1½ cups EGG BEATERS® Healthy Real Egg Product
½ cup (2 ounces) shredded reduced-fat Swiss cheese
¼ cup fat-free (skim) milk
½ teaspoon garlic powder
¼ teaspoon seasoned pepper
  Nonstick cooking spray
1 medium zucchini, shredded (1 cup)
1 medium tomato, chopped
1 (4-ounce) can sliced mushrooms, drained
  Tomato slices and fresh basil leaves, for garnish

In medium bowl, combine Egg Beaters®, cheese, milk, garlic powder and seasoned pepper; set aside.

Spray 10-inch ovenproof nonstick skillet lightly with nonstick cooking spray. Over medium-high heat, sauté zucchini, tomato and mushrooms in skillet until tender. Pour egg mixture into skillet, stirring well. Cover; cook over low heat for 15 minutes or until cooked on bottom and almost set on top. Remove lid and place skillet under broiler for 2 to 3 minutes or until desired doneness. Slide onto serving platter; cut into wedges to serve. Garnish with tomato slices and basil. *Makes 6 servings*

Prep Time: 20 minutes
Cook Time: 20 minutes

zucchini mushroom frittata

steaks with zesty merlot sauce

½ cup merlot wine
2 tablespoons Worcestershire sauce
1 tablespoon balsamic vinegar
1 teaspoon sugar
1 teaspoon beef bouillon granules
½ teaspoon dried thyme leaves
2 beef ribeye steaks (8 ounces each)
2 tablespoons finely chopped parsley

1. Combine wine, Worcestershire sauce, vinegar, sugar, bouillon granules and thyme; set aside.

2. Heat large nonstick skillet over high heat until hot. Add steaks; cook 3 minutes on each side. Turn steaks again and cook 3 to 6 minutes longer over medium heat or until desired doneness.

3. Cut steaks in half; arrange on serving platter. Place in oven to keep warm.

4. Add wine mixture to same skillet. Bring to a boil; cook and stir 1 minute, scraping up any brown bits. Spoon over steaks. Sprinkle with parsley; serve immediately.

Makes 4 servings

steaks with mushroom onion sauce

1½ pounds boneless beef sirloin steak
2 cups sliced fresh mushrooms
1 medium onion, thinly sliced
1 jar (12 ounces) HEINZ® Fat Free Savory Beef Gravy
1 tablespoon HEINZ® Tomato Ketchup
1 teaspoon HEINZ® Worcestershire Sauce
Dash pepper

Cut steak into 6 portions. Spray a large skillet with nonstick cooking spray. Cook steak over medium high heat to desired doneness, about 5 minutes per side for medium-rare. Remove and keep warm. In same skillet, cook mushrooms and onion until liquid evaporates. Stir in gravy, ketchup, Worcestershire sauce and pepper; simmer 1 minute, stirring occasionally. Serve sauce over steak.

Makes 6 servings (about 2 cups sauce)

steaks with zesty merlot sauce

nutrients per serving:
Calories: 200
Carbohydrate: 13 g
Calories From Fat: 32%
Total Fat: 7 g
Saturated Fat: 1 g
Cholesterol: 78 mg
Sodium: 900 mg
Dietary Fiber: 2 g
Protein: 23 g

thai noodle soup

1 package (3 ounces) ramen noodles
¾ pound chicken tenders
2 cans (about 14 ounces each) chicken broth
¼ cup shredded carrot
¼ cup frozen snow peas
2 tablespoons thinly sliced green onion tops
½ teaspoon minced garlic
¼ teaspoon ground ginger
3 tablespoons chopped fresh cilantro
½ lime, cut into 4 wedges

1. Break noodles into pieces. Cook noodles according to package directions, discarding flavor packet. Drain and set aside.

2. Cut chicken tenders into ½-inch pieces. Combine chicken broth and chicken tenders in large saucepan or Dutch oven; bring to a boil over medium heat. Cook 2 minutes.

3. Add carrot, snow peas, green onion tops, garlic and ginger. Reduce heat to low; simmer 3 minutes. Add cooked noodles and cilantro; heat through. Serve soup with lime wedges. *Makes 4 servings*

Prep and Cook Time: 15 minutes

thai noodle soup

nutrients per serving:

Calories: 221
Carbohydrate: 5 g
Calories From Fat: 37%
Total Fat: 9 g
Saturated Fat: <1 g
Cholesterol: 51 mg
Sodium: 559 mg
Dietary Fiber: 2 g
Protein: 30 g

grilled red snapper with avocado-papaya salsa

1 teaspoon ground coriander
1 teaspoon paprika
¾ teaspoon salt
⅛ to ¼ teaspoon ground red pepper
1 tablespoon olive oil
4 skinless red snapper or halibut fish fillets (5 to 7 ounces each)
½ cup diced ripe avocado
½ cup diced ripe papaya
2 tablespoons chopped cilantro
1 tablespoon fresh lime juice
4 lime wedges

1. Prepare grill for direct grilling. Combine coriander, paprika, salt and red pepper in small bowl or cup; mix well.

2. Brush oil over fish. Sprinkle 2½ teaspoons spice mixture over fish fillets; set aside remaining spice mixture. Place fish, skin side down, on oiled grid over medium-hot heat. Grill 5 minutes per side or until fish is opaque.

3. Meanwhile, combine avocado, papaya, cilantro, lime juice and reserved spice mixture in medium bowl; mix well. Serve fish with salsa and garnish with lime wedges.

Makes 4 servings

grilled red snapper with avocado-papaya salsa

roast turkey breast with spinach-blue cheese stuffing

1 frozen whole boneless turkey breast, thawed (3½ to 4 pounds)
1 package (10 ounces) frozen chopped spinach, thawed and squeezed dry
2 ounces blue cheese or feta cheese
2 ounces reduced-fat cream cheese
½ cup finely chopped green onions
4½ teaspoons Dijon mustard
4½ teaspoons dried basil leaves
2 teaspoons dried oregano leaves
Black pepper to taste
Paprika

1. Preheat oven to 350°F. Coat roasting pan and rack with nonstick cooking spray.

2. Unroll turkey breast; rinse and pat dry. Place between 2 sheets of plastic wrap. Pound turkey breast with flat side of meat mallet to about 1 inch thick. Remove and discard skin from one half of turkey breast; turn meat over so skin side (on other half) faces down.

3. Combine spinach, blue cheese, cream cheese, green onions, mustard, basil and oregano in medium bowl; mix well. Spread evenly over turkey breast. Roll up turkey so skin is on top.

4. Carefully place turkey breast on rack; sprinkle with pepper and paprika. Roast 1½ hours or until no longer pink in center of breast. Remove from oven and let stand 10 minutes before removing skin and slicing. Cut into ¼-inch slices.

Makes 14 servings (3 ounces each)

roast turkey breast with spinach-blue cheese stuffing

nutrients per serving:

Calories: 116
Carbohydrate: 15 g
Calories From Fat: 39%
Total Fat: 5 g
Saturated Fat: 1 g
Cholesterol: 4 mg
Sodium: 396 mg
Dietary Fiber: 5 g
Protein: 5 g

spaghetti squash primavera

1 teaspoon olive oil
¼ cup diced green bell pepper
¼ cup diced zucchini
¼ cup sliced mushrooms
¼ cup diced carrot
¼ cup sliced green onions
2 cloves garlic, minced
1 plum tomato, diced
1 tablespoon red wine or water
½ teaspoon dried basil leaves
¼ teaspoon salt
⅛ teaspoon black pepper
2 cups cooked spaghetti squash
2 tablespoons grated Parmesan cheese

1. Heat oil in medium skillet over low heat. Add bell pepper, zucchini, mushrooms, carrot, green onions and garlic; cook 10 to 12 minutes or until crisp-tender, stirring ocassionally. Stir in tomato, wine, basil, salt and black pepper; cook 4 to 5 minutes, stirring once or twice.

2. Serve vegetables over spaghetti squash. Top with cheese.   *Makes 2 servings*

spaghetti squash primavera

jamaican steak

2 pounds beef flank steak
¼ cup packed brown sugar
3 tablespoons orange juice
3 tablespoons lime juice
3 cloves garlic, minced
1 piece (1½×1 inches) fresh ginger, minced
2 teaspoons grated orange peel
2 teaspoons grated lime peel
1 teaspoon salt
1 teaspoon black pepper
¼ teaspoon ground cinnamon
⅛ teaspoon ground cloves
    Shredded orange peel
    Shredded lime peel

Score both sides of beef.* Combine sugar, juices, garlic, ginger, grated peels, salt, pepper, cinnamon and cloves in 2-quart glass dish. Add beef; turn to coat. Cover and refrigerate steak at least 2 hours. Remove beef from marinade; discard marinade. Grill beef over medium-hot KINGSFORD® Briquets about 6 minutes per side until medium-rare or to desired doneness. Garnish with shredded orange and lime peels.

Makes 6 servings

To score flank steak, cut ¼-inch-deep diagonal lines about 1 inch apart in surface of steak to form diamond-shaped design.

jamaican steak

pepperoni pizza soup

nutrients per serving:

Calories: 296
Carbohydrate: 14 g
Calories From Fat: 64%
Total Fat: 21 g
Saturated Fat: 7 g
Cholesterol: 32 mg
Sodium: 1 mg
Dietary Fiber: 3 g
Protein: 15 g

1 tablespoon oil
1 cup sliced mushrooms
1 cup chopped green bell pepper
½ cup chopped onion
1 can (15 ounces) pizza sauce
1 can (14½ ounces) chicken broth
1 cup water
3 ounces sliced pepperoni
1 teaspoon dried oregano leaves
1 cup (4 ounces) shredded mozzarella cheese

1. Heat oil in large saucepan over medium heat. Add mushrooms, bell pepper and onion. Cook, stirring frequently, 7 minutes or until vegetables are tender.

2. Stir in pizza sauce, broth, water, pepperoni and oregano. Bring to a boil. Reduce heat and simmer 5 minutes. Serve with cheese.   *Makes 4 servings*

Tip: This recipe satisfies your craving for pizza with all the flavors of this popular treat and a minimum carbohydrate count.

chicken broccoli frittata

nutrients per serving:

Calories: 187
Carbohydrate: 7 g
Calories From Fat: 34%
Total Fat: 7 g
Saturated Fat: 1 g
Cholesterol: 27 mg
Sodium: 308 mg
Dietary Fiber: 2 g
Protein: 24 g

1 cup chopped fresh broccoli florets
½ cup chopped cooked chicken
¼ cup chopped tomato
¼ cup chopped onion
¼ teaspoon dried tarragon leaves
1 tablespoon FLEISCHMANN'S® Original Margarine
1 cup EGG BEATERS® Healthy Real Egg Product

In 10-inch nonstick skillet, over medium heat, sauté broccoli, chicken, tomato, onion and tarragon in margarine until broccoli is tender-crisp. Reduce heat to low. Pour Egg Beaters evenly into skillet over chicken mixture. Cover; cook for 5 to 7 minutes or until cooked on bottom and almost set on top. Slide onto serving platter; cut into wedges to serve.   *Makes 2 servings*

Prep Time: 15 minutes
Cook Time: 11 minutes

pepperoni pizza soup

poached seafood italiano

nutrients per serving:

Calories: 251
Carbohydrate: 5 g
Calories From Fat: 33%
Total Fat: 9 g
Saturated Fat: 1 g
Cholesterol: 86 mg
Sodium: 620 mg
Dietary Fiber: 1 g
Protein: 34 g

1 tablespoon olive or vegetable oil
1 large clove garlic, minced
¼ cup dry white wine or chicken broth
4 (6-ounce) salmon steaks or fillets
1 can (14.5 ounces) CONTADINA® Recipe Ready Diced Tomatoes with Italian Herbs, undrained
⅓ cup sliced olives (black, green or a combination)
2 tablespoons chopped fresh basil (optional)

1. Heat oil in large skillet. Add garlic; sauté 30 seconds. Add wine. Bring to boil.

2. Add salmon; cover. Reduce heat to medium; simmer 6 minutes.

3. Add undrained tomatoes and olives; simmer 2 minutes or until salmon flakes easily when tested with fork. Sprinkle with basil just before serving, if desired.

Makes 4 servings

chicken caesar salad

nutrients per serving:

Calories: 361
Carbohydrate: 13 g
Calories From Fat: 59%
Total Fat: 22 g
Saturated Fat: 5 g
Cholesterol: 57 mg
Sodium: 244 mg
Dietary Fiber: 1 g
Protein: 24 g

6 ounces chicken tenders
¼ cup plus 1 tablespoon Caesar salad dressing, divided
Black pepper
4 cups (about 5 ounces) prepared Italian salad mix (romaine and radicchio)
½ cup prepared croutons, divided
2 tablespoons grated Parmesan cheese

1. Cut chicken tenders in half lengthwise and crosswise. Heat 1 tablespoon salad dressing in large nonstick skillet. Add chicken; cook and stir over medium heat 3 to 4 minutes or until chicken is no longer pink. Remove chicken from skillet; sprinkle with pepper and let cool.

2. Combine salad mix, half of croutons, remaining ¼ cup salad dressing and Parmesan in serving bowl; toss to coat. Top with remaining croutons and chicken.

Makes 2 servings

Prep and Cook Time: 17 minutes

poached seafood italiano

nutrients per serving:

Calories: 158
Carbohydrate: 7 g
Calories From Fat: 15%
Total Fat: 3 g
Saturated Fat: <1 g
Cholesterol: 68 mg
Sodium: 304 mg
Dietary Fiber: 2 g
Protein: 26 g

main dish chicken soup

**1 can (49½ ounces) fat-free, reduced-sodium chicken broth OR
    3 cans (14½ ounces each) fat-free, reduced-sodium chicken broth
    plus 6 ounces of water
1 cup grated carrots
½ cup sliced green onions
½ cup diced red bell pepper
½ cup frozen green peas
1 seedless cucumber
½ teaspoon ground white pepper
12 chicken tenders (about 1 pound)**

1. Place chicken broth (and water, if using) in large 4-quart Dutch oven. Bring to a boil over high heat. Add carrots, green onions, red pepper and green peas. Bring to a boil. Reduce heat and simmer 3 minutes.

2. Meanwhile, cut ends off cucumber and discard. Using vegetable peeler, start at top and make long, noodle-like strips of cucumber. Slice any remaining cucumber pieces thinly with knife. Add cucumber strips to Dutch oven; simmer until cucumber is tender.

3. Add chicken tenders; simmer about 5 minutes or until chicken is no longer pink.

Makes 6 servings

main dish chicken soup

pork chops paprikash

2 teaspoons butter
1 medium onion, very thinly sliced
1 1/4 teaspoons paprika, divided
1 teaspoon garlic salt
1/2 teaspoon black pepper
4 (5- to 6-ounce) bone-in center cut pork chops (about 1/2 inch thick)
1/3 cup well-drained sauerkraut
1/3 cup light or regular sour cream

1. Preheat broiler.

2. Melt butter in large skillet over medum-high heat. Separate onion slices into rings; add to skillet. Cook, stirring occasionally, until golden brown and tender, about 10 minutes.

3. Meanwhile, sprinkle 1 teaspoon paprika, garlic salt and pepper over both sides of pork chops. Place chops on rack of broiler pan.

4. Broil 4 to 5 inches from heat 5 minutes. Turn; broil 4 to 5 minutes or until chops are barely pink in center.

5. Combine cooked onion with sauerkraut, sour cream and remaining 1/4 teaspoon paprika; mix well. Garnish chops with onion mixture, or spread onion mixture over chops and return to broiler. Broil just until hot, about 1 minute.   *Makes 4 servings*

pork chop paprikash

nutrients per serving:

Calories: 378
Carbohydrate: 4 g
Calories From Fat: 76%
Total Fat: 32 g
Saturated Fat: 15 g
Cholesterol: 487 mg
Sodium: 797 mg
Dietary Fiber: 1 g
Protein: 19 g

fabulous feta frittata

2 tablespoons butter or olive oil
8 eggs
¼ cup whipping cream or half-and-half
¼ cup chopped fresh basil
½ teaspoon salt
¼ teaspoon freshly ground black pepper
1 package (4 ounces) crumbled feta cheese with basil, olives and sun-dried tomatoes *or* 1 cup crumbled feta cheese
¼ cup pine nuts

1. Preheat broiler. Melt butter in 10-inch ovenproof skillet over medium heat. Tilt skillet so bottom and side are well coated with butter. Beat eggs. Add cream, basil, salt and pepper; mix well. Pour mixture into skillet. Cover; cook 8 to 10 minutes or until eggs are set around edge (center will be wet).

2. Sprinkle cheese and pine nuts evenly over frittata. Transfer to broiler; broil 4 to 5 inches from heat source for 2 minutes or until center of frittata is set and pine nuts are golden brown. Cut into wedges.   *Makes 4 servings*

Tip: If skillet is not ovenproof, wrap the handle in heavy-duty foil.

fabulous feta frittata

easy chicken salad

nutrients per serving:

Calories: 410
Carbohydrate: 16 g
Calories From Fat: 44%
Total Fat: 20 g
Saturated Fat: 8 g
Cholesterol: 130 mg
Sodium: 790 mg
Dietary Fiber: 1 g
Protein: 41 g

- ¼ **cup finely chopped celery**
- ¼ **cup mayonnaise**
- 2 **tablespoons sweet relish**
- 1 **tablespoon finely minced onion**
- ½ **teaspoon Dijon mustard**
- ⅛ **teaspoon salt**
  Black pepper to taste
- 2 **cups cubed cooked chicken**
  Salad greens (optional)

1. Combine all ingredients except chicken and salad greens in large bowl; mix well. Stir in chicken. Cover; refrigerate at least 1 hour.

2. Serve on salad greens.

Makes 2 servings

barbecued salmon

nutrients per serving:

Calories: 215
Carbohydrate: 4 g
Calories From Fat: 42%
Total Fat: 10 g
Saturated Fat: 6 g
Cholesterol: 70 mg
Sodium: 433 mg
Dietary Fiber: 0 g
Protein: 25 g

- 4 **salmon steaks, ¾ to 1 inch thick**
- 3 **tablespoons lemon juice**
- 2 **tablespoons soy sauce**
  Salt and black pepper
- ½ **cup KC MASTERPIECE™ Original Barbecue Sauce**
  Fresh oregano sprigs
  Grilled mushrooms (optional)

Rinse salmon; pat dry with paper towels. Combine lemon juice and soy sauce in shallow glass dish. Add salmon; let stand at cool room temperature no more than 15 to 20 minutes, turning salmon several times. Remove salmon from marinade; discard marinade. Season lightly with salt and pepper.

Lightly oil hot grid to prevent sticking. Grill salmon on covered grill over medium KINGSFORD® Briquets 10 to 14 minutes. Halfway through cooking time brush salmon with barbecue sauce, then turn and continue grilling until fish flakes easily when tested with fork. Remove fish from grill; brush with remaining barbecue sauce. Garnish with oregano sprigs and mushrooms.

Makes 4 servings

easy chicken salad

maple-mustard pork chops

nutrients per serving:

1 chop

Calories: 286
Carbohydrate: 14 g
Calories From Fat: 44%
Total Fat: 14 g
Saturated Fat: 3 g
Cholesterol: 70 mg
Sodium: 102 mg
Dietary Fiber: <1 g
Protein: 26 g

2 tablespoons maple syrup, divided
1 tablespoon olive oil
2 teaspoons whole-grain mustard
2 center-cut pork loin chops (6 ounces each)
Nonstick cooking spray
⅓ cup water

Preheat oven to 375°F. Combine maple syrup, olive oil and mustard in small bowl. Brush syrup mixture over both sides of pork chops. Spray medium ovenproof skillet with cooking spray; heat over medium-high heat. Add chops; brown on both sides. Add water, cover and bake 20 to 30 minutes or until barely pink in center.

Makes 2 servings

ham and beer cheese soup

nutrients per serving:

Calories: 471
Carbohydrate: 11 g
Calories From Fat: 67%
Total Fat: 35 g
Saturated Fat: 21 g
Cholesterol: 128 mg
Sodium: 1621 mg
Dietary Fiber: <1 g
Protein: 29 g

1 cup chopped onion
½ cup sliced celery
2 tablespoons butter or margarine
1 cup hot water
1 HERB-OX® chicken flavor bouillon cube *or* 1 teaspoon instant chicken boullion
3 cups half-and-half
3 cups (18 ounces) diced CURE 81® ham
1 (16-ounce) loaf pasteurized process cheese spread, cubed
1 (12-ounce) can beer
3 tablespoons all-purpose flour
Popcorn (optional)

In Dutch oven over medium-high heat, sauté onion and celery in butter until tender. In small liquid measuring cup, combine water and bouillon; set aside. Add half-and-half, ham, cheese, beer and ¾ cup broth to onion and celery mixture. Cook, stirring constantly, until cheese melts. Combine remaining ¼ cup broth and flour; stir until smooth. Add flour mixture to soup, stirring constantly. Cook, stirring constantly, until slightly thickened. Sprinkle individual servings with popcorn, if desired.

Makes 8 servings

bolognese-style pork ragú over spaghetti squash

nutrients per serving:

Calories: 333
Carbohydrate: 15 g
Calories From Fat: 59%
Total Fat: 22 g
Saturated Fat: 20 g
Cholesterol: 75 mg
Sodium: 275 mg
Dietary Fiber: 2 g
Protein: 20 g

1½ **pounds ground pork**
1 **cup finely chopped celery**
½ **cup chopped onion**
1 **teaspoon prepared crushed garlic** *or* **2 cloves garlic, minced**
2 **tablespoons tomato paste**
1 **teaspoon Italian seasoning**
1 **can (14½ ounces) low-sodium chicken broth**
½ **cup half-and-half**
1 **spaghetti squash (3 to 4 pounds)**
½ **cup grated Parmesan (optional)**

1. Brown pork in 3-quart saucepan over medium-high heat, stirring to break up meat. Add celery and onion; cook and stir 5 minutes over medium heat or until vegetables are tender. Add garlic, cook and stir 1 minute. Stir in tomato paste and Italian seasoning.

2. Stir in broth. Reduce heat. Simmer 10 to 15 minutes, stirring occasionally.

3. Add half-and-half; cook and stir until hot. Skim off excess fat.

4. Meanwhile, pierce spaghetti squash several times with knife. Microwave at HIGH (100%) 15 minutes until squash is tender (squash will yield when pressed with finger). Let cool 10 to 15 minutes. Cut in half, scoop out and discard seeds. Separate flesh into strands with fork; keep squash warm.

5. Serve ½ cup meat sauce over 1 cup spaghetti squash. Sprinkle with 1 tablespoon grated Parmesan, if desired.   *Makes 8 servings*

Tip: Sauce can be cooked the day before and refrigerated so that chilled fat can be easily removed and discarded before reheating.

nutrients per serving:

Calories: 746
Carbohydrate: 8 g
Calories From Fat: 62%
Total Fat: 50 g
Saturated Fat: 14 g
Cholesterol: 238 mg
Sodium: 1145 mg
Dietary Fiber: 1 g
Protein: 61 g

chicken tikka (tandoori-style grilled chicken)

2 chickens (3 pounds each), cut up
1 pint nonfat yogurt
½ cup *Frank's® RedHot®* Original Cayenne Pepper Sauce
1 tablespoon grated peeled fresh ginger
3 cloves garlic, minced
1 tablespoon paprika
1 tablespoon cumin seeds, crushed *or* 1½ teaspoons ground cumin
2 teaspoons salt
1 teaspoon ground coriander

Remove skin and visible fat from chicken pieces. Rinse with cold water and pat dry. Randomly poke chicken all over with tip of sharp knife. Place chicken in resealable plastic food storage bags or large glass bowl. Combine yogurt, **Frank's RedHot** Sauce, ginger, garlic, paprika, cumin, salt and coriander in small bowl; mix well. Pour over chicken pieces, turning pieces to coat evenly. Seal bags or cover bowl and marinate in refrigerator 1 hour or overnight.

Place chicken on oiled grid, reserving marinade. Grill over medium coals 45 minutes or until chicken is no longer pink near bone and juices run clear, turning and basting often with marinade. (Do not baste during last 10 minutes of cooking.) Discard any remaining marinade. Serve warm. *Makes 6 to 8 servings*

Prep Time: 15 minutes
Marinate Time: 1 hour
Cook Time: 45 minutes

chicken tikka (tandoori-style grilled chicken)

shrimp creole stew

nutrients per serving:

Calories: 131
Carbohydrate: 9 g
Calories From Fat: 10%
Total Fat: 1 g
Saturated Fat: 0 g
Cholesterol: 170 mg
Sodium: 1709 mg
Dietary Fiber: 4 g
Protein: 20 g

1½ cups raw small shrimp, shelled
  1 bag (16 ounces) **BIRDS EYE**® frozen Farm Fresh Mixtures Broccoli, Cauliflower & Red Peppers
  1 can (14½ ounces) diced tomatoes
1½ teaspoons salt
  1 teaspoon hot pepper sauce
  1 teaspoon vegetable oil

• In large saucepan, combine all ingredients.

• Cover; bring to a boil. Reduce heat to medium-low; simmer 20 minutes or until shrimp turn opaque. *Makes 4 servings*

Prep Time: 5 minutes
Cook Time: 20 minutes

pan seared halibut steaks with avocado salsa

nutrients per serving:

Calories: 169
Carbohydrate: 2 g
Calories From Fat: 36%
Total Fat: 7 g
Saturated Fat: <1 g
Cholesterol: 36 mg
Sodium: 476 mg
Dietary Fiber: 4 g
Protein: 25 g

  4 tablespoons chipotle salsa, divided
  ½ teaspoon salt, divided
  4 small (4 to 5 ounces) *or* 2 large (8 to 10 ounces) halibut steaks, cut ¾ inch thick
  ½ cup diced tomato
  ½ ripe avocado, diced
  2 tablespoons chopped cilantro (optional)
    Lime wedges (optional)

1. Combine 2 tablespoons salsa and ¼ teaspoon salt; spread over both sides of halibut.

2. Heat large nonstick skillet over medium heat until hot. Add halibut; cook 4 to 5 minutes per side or until fish is opaque in center.

3. Meanwhile, combine remaining 2 tablespoons salsa, ¼ teaspoon salt, tomato, avocado and cilantro, if desired, in small bowl. Mix well and spoon over cooked fish. Garnish with lime wedges, if desired. *Makes 4 servings*

shrimp creole stew

pasta meatball soup

10 ounces 95% ground beef sirloin
5 tablespoons acini di pepe pasta, divided
¼ cup fresh fine bread crumbs
1 egg
2 tablespoons finely chopped parsley, divided
1 teaspoon dried basil leaves, divided
¼ teaspoon salt
⅛ teaspoon black pepper
1 clove garlic, minced
2 cans (about 14 ounces each) fat-free reduced-sodium beef broth
1 (8-ounce) can tomato sauce
⅓ cup chopped onion

1. Combine beef, 2 tablespoons pasta, bread crumbs, egg, 1 tablespoon parsley, ½ teaspoon basil, salt, pepper and garlic in medium bowl. Form into approximately 28 to 30 (1-inch) meatballs.

2. Bring beef broth, tomato sauce, onion and remaining ½ teaspoon basil to a boil in large saucepan over medium-high heat. Carefully add meatballs to broth. Reduce heat to medium-low; simmer, covered, 20 minutes. Add remaining 3 tablespoons pasta; cook 10 minutes or until tender. Garnish with remaining 1 tablespoon parsley.

Makes 4 (1½-cup) servings

Tip: Acini di pepe is tiny rice-shaped pasta. You may substitute orzo pasta or pastina.

pasta meatball soup

roasted rosemary chicken legs

¼ **cup finely chopped onion**
2 **tablespoons margarine or butter, melted**
1 **tablespoon chopped fresh rosemary** *or* 1 **teaspoon dried rosemary**
½ **teaspoon salt**
¼ **teaspoon black pepper**
2 **cloves garlic, minced**
4 **chicken legs (about 1½ pounds)**
¼ **cup white wine or chicken broth**

1. Preheat oven to 375°F.

2. Combine onion, margarine, rosemary, salt, pepper and garlic in small bowl; set aside. Run finger under chicken skin to loosen. Rub onion mixture under and over skin. Place chicken, skin side up, in small shallow roasting pan. Pour wine over chicken.

3. Roast chicken 50 to 60 minutes or until chicken is browned and juices run clear, basting often with pan juices. Garnish as desired.   *Makes 4 servings*

curried chicken & zucchini salad

½ **cup nonfat plain yogurt**
⅓ **cup mayonnaise**
2 **tablespoons chili sauce**
1 **teaspoon white wine vinegar**
1 **teaspoon grated onion**
¾ **teaspoon curry powder**
¼ **teaspoon salt**
2 **cups shredded cooked chicken**
1 **cup seedless red grapes**
1 **medium zucchini, cut into matchstick-size strips**
   Leaf lettuce
¼ **cup slivered almonds, toasted**

1. Combine yogurt, mayonnaise, chili sauce, vinegar, onion, curry powder and salt in large bowl; stir until smooth. Add chicken, grapes and zucchini; toss to coat.

2. Arrange lettuce on plate. Top with chicken mixture; sprinkle with almonds.
                                                        Makes 4 servings

roasted rosemary chicken leg

salmon broccoli waldorf salad

1 bag (16 ounces) BIRDS EYE® frozen Broccoli Cuts
1 large Red Delicious apple, chopped
¼ cup thinly sliced green onions
½ cup bottled creamy roasted garlic, ranch or blue cheese dressing
1 can (14¾ ounces) salmon, drained and flaked

● In large saucepan, cook broccoli according to package directions; drain and rinse under cold water in colander.

● In large bowl, toss together broccoli, apple, onions and dressing. Gently stir in salmon; add pepper to taste.   *Makes 4 servings*

Serving Suggestion: Serve over lettuce leaves and sprinkle with toasted nuts.

BIRDS EYE IDEA: To prevent cut fruits and vegetables, such as apples and artichokes, from discoloring, try rubbing them with a lemon wedge.

Prep Time: 5 minutes
Cook Time: 7 minutes

lemon-garlic chicken

2 tablespoons olive oil
2 cloves garlic, pressed
1 teaspoon grated lemon peel
1 teaspoon lemon juice
¼ teaspoon salt
¼ teaspoon black pepper
4 skinless boneless chicken breast halves (about 1 pound)

Combine oil, garlic, lemon peel, lemon juice, salt and pepper in small bowl. Brush oil mixture over both sides of chicken to coat. Lightly oil grid to prevent sticking. Grill chicken over medium KINGSFORD® Briquets 8 to 10 minutes or until chicken is no longer pink in center, turning once.   *Makes 4 servings*

salmon broccoli waldorf salad

blackened chicken salad

nutrients per serving:

includes 1 tablespoon Ranch Salad Dressing

Calories: 222
Carbohydrate: 17 g
Calories From Fat: 16%
Total Fat: 4 g
Saturated Fat: 1 g
Cholesterol: 69 mg
Sodium: 191 mg
Dietary Fiber: 5 g
Protein: 30 g

2 cups cubed sourdough or French bread
   Nonstick cooking spray
1 tablespoon paprika
1 teaspoon onion powder
1 teaspoon garlic powder
½ teaspoon dried oregano leaves
½ teaspoon dried thyme leaves
½ teaspoon ground white pepper
½ teaspoon ground red pepper
½ teaspoon black pepper
1 pound boneless skinless chicken breasts
4 cups bite-size pieces fresh spinach leaves
2 cups bite-size pieces romaine lettuce
2 cups cubed zucchini
2 cups cubed seeded cucumber
½ cup sliced green onions with tops
1 medium tomato, cut into 8 wedges
   Ranch Salad Dressing (page 190)

1. Preheat oven to 375°F. To make croutons, spray bread cubes lightly with cooking spray; place in 15×10-inch jelly-roll pan. Bake 10 to 15 minutes or until browned, stirring occasionally. Set aside.

2. Combine paprika, onion powder, garlic powder, oregano, thyme, white pepper, red pepper and black pepper in small bowl; rub on all surfaces of chicken. Broil chicken, 6 inches from heat source, 7 to 8 minutes on each side or until chicken is no longer pink in center. Or, grill chicken, on covered grill over medium-hot coals, 10 minutes on each side or until chicken is no longer pink in center. Cool slightly. Cut chicken into thin strips.

3. Combine warm chicken, greens, zucchini, cucumber, green onions, tomato and reserved croutons in large bowl. Drizzle with Ranch Salad Dressing; toss to coat. Serve immediately. *Makes 4 servings*

Tip: If you eliminate the croutons from this salad, the grams of carbohydrate will drop to 6 grams per serving.

blackened chicken salad

sirloin with sweet caramelized onions

nutrients per serving:

Calories: 159
Carbohydrate: 7 g
Calories From Fat: 28%
Total Fat: 5 g
Saturated Fat: 2 g
Cholesterol: 60 mg
Sodium: 118 mg
Dietary Fiber: 1 g
Protein: 21 g

Nonstick cooking spray
1 medium onion, very thinly sliced
1 boneless beef top sirloin steak (about 1 pound)
¼ cup water
2 tablespoons Worcestershire sauce
1 tablespoon sugar

1. Lightly coat 12-inch skillet with cooking spray; heat over high heat until hot. Add onion; cook and stir 4 minutes or until browned. Remove from skillet and set aside. Wipe out skillet with paper towel.

2. Coat same skillet with cooking spray; heat until hot. Add beef; cook 10 to 13 minutes for medium-rare to medium, turning once. Remove from heat and transfer to cutting board; let stand 3 minutes before slicing.

3. Meanwhile, return skillet to high heat until hot; add onion, water, Worcestershire sauce and sugar. Cook 30 to 45 seconds or until most liquid has evaporated.

4. Thinly slice beef on the diagonal and serve with onions. *Makes 4 servings*

ranch salad dressing

nutrients per serving:

1 tablespoon

Calories: 18
Carbohydrate: 1 g
Calories From Fat: 84%
Total Fat: 2 g
Saturated Fat: <1 g
Cholesterol: 0 mg
Sodium: 99 mg
Dietary Fiber: <1 g
Protein: <1 g

¼ cup water
3 tablespoons reduced-fat cucumber-ranch salad dressing
1 tablespoon reduced-fat mayonnaise or salad dressing
1 tablespoon lemon juice
2 teaspoons finely chopped parsley
⅛ teaspoon salt
⅛ teaspoon black pepper

In small jar with tight-fitting lid, combine all ingredients; shake well. Refrigerate until ready to use; shake before using. *Makes about ½ cup*

sirloin with sweet caramelized onions

provençal grilled tuna salad

nutrients per serving:

Calories: 332
Carbohydrate: 6 g
Calories From Fat: 48%
Total Fat: 17 g
Saturated Fat: 3 g
Cholesterol: 54 mg
Sodium: 143 mg
Dietary Fiber: 2 g
Protein: 35 g

4 (5- to 6-ounce) tuna steaks, ¾ to 1 inch thick
3 tablespoons white wine or fish broth
3 tablespoons olive oil
2 tablespoons red wine vinegar
½ teaspoon chopped fresh rosemary *or* ¼ teaspoon dried rosemary
½ teaspoon black pepper
⅛ teaspoon salt
1 clove garlic, minced
   Vegetable cooking spray
6 cups packed, torn salad greens
1 cup halved cherry tomatoes

Measure thickness of fish to determine cooking time; place in glass dish. To make vinaigrette, combine wine, oil, vinegar, rosemary, pepper and salt in jar with tight-fitting lid. Shake well. Pour 2 tablespoons vinaigrette over fish; add garlic and turn to coat. Marinate 15 to 30 minutes, turning once. Reserve remaining vinaigrette for salad dressing.

Coat grill rack with cooking spray and place on grill to heat 1 minute. Place tuna on grill 4 to 6 inches over hot coals. Cover with lid or tent with foil. Cook, turning once, just until tuna begins to flake easily when tested with fork, about 7 minutes. Discard marinade.

Meanwhile, arrange salad greens on 4 plates. Place hot tuna on greens and add cherry tomatoes. Shake remaining vinaigrette and drizzle over salads.

Makes 4 servings

Note: Halibut, swordfish or shark can be substituted for tuna.

Favorite recipe from *National Fisheries Institute*

provençal grilled tuna salad

blue cheese-stuffed sirloin patties

nutrients per serving:

Calories: 463
Carbohydrate: 3 g
Calories From Fat: 62%
Total Fat: 32 g
Saturated Fat: 16 g
Cholesterol: 131 mg
Sodium: 548 mg
Dietary Fiber: 1 g
Protein: 38 g

1½ pounds ground beef sirloin
½ cup (2 ounces) shredded sharp Cheddar cheese
¼ cup crumbled blue cheese
¼ cup finely chopped parsley
2 teaspoons Dijon mustard
1 teaspoon Worcestershire sauce
1 clove garlic, minced
¼ teaspoon salt
2 teaspoons olive oil
1 medium red bell pepper, cut into thin strips

1. Shape beef into 8 patties, about 4 inches in diameter and ¼ inch thick.

2. Combine cheeses, parsley, mustard, Worcestershire sauce, garlic and salt in small bowl; toss gently to blend.

3. Mound ¼ cheese mixture on each of 4 patties (about 3 tablespoons per patty). Top with remaining 4 patties; pinch edges of patties to seal completely. Set aside.

4. Heat oil in 12-inch nonstick skillet over medium-high heat until hot. Add pepper strips; cook and stir until edges of peppers begin to brown. Sprinkle with salt. Remove from skillet and keep warm.

5. Add beef patties to same skillet; cook on medium-high 5 minutes. Turn patties; top with peppers. Cook 4 minutes or until patties are no longer pink in centers (160°F).

Makes 4 servings

blue cheese-stuffed sirloin patty

nutrients per serving:

1 fillet

Calories: 162
Carbohydrate: <1 g
Calories From Fat: 49%
Total Fat: 9 g
Saturated Fat: 2 g
Cholesterol: 56 mg
Sodium: 41 mg
Dietary Fiber: <1 g
Protein: 17 g

vermouth salmon

2 (10×10-inch) sheets of heavy-duty foil
2 salmon fillets or steaks (3 ounces each)
   Pinch of salt and black pepper
4 sprigs fresh dill
2 slices lemon
1 tablespoon vermouth

1. Preheat oven to 375°F. Turn up the edges of 1 sheet of foil so juices will not run out. Place salmon in the center of the foil. Sprinkle with salt and pepper. Place dill on top of salmon and lemon slices on top of the dill. Pour vermouth evenly over fish pieces.

2. Cover fish with second sheet of foil. Crimp edges of foil together to seal packet. Place packet on baking sheet. Bake 20 to 25 minutes or until salmon flakes easily when tested with fork.

Makes 2 servings

nutrients per serving:

Calories: 577
Carbohydrate: 3 g
Calories From Fat: 73%
Total Fat: 46 g
Saturated Fat: 8 g
Cholesterol: 108 mg
Sodium: 382 mg
Dietary Fiber: <1 g
Protein: 36 g

grilled chicken with chimichurri salsa

4 boneless skinless chicken breasts (6 ounces each)
½ cup plus 4 teaspoons olive oil
   Salt and black pepper
½ cup finely chopped parsley
¼ cup white wine vinegar
2 tablespoons finely chopped onion
3 cloves garlic, minced
1 fresh or canned jalapeño pepper, finely chopped
2 teaspoons dried oregano leaves

1. Prepare grill for direct grilling.

2. Brush chicken with 4 teaspoons olive oil; season with salt and black pepper. Place on oiled grid. Grill, covered, over medium heat 5 to 8 minutes on each side or until chicken is no longer pink in center.

3. To prepare sauce, combine parsley, vinegar, onion, garlic, jalapeño pepper, oregano, ½ cup olive oil, and salt and pepper to taste. Serve over chicken.

Makes 4 servings

Tip: Chimichurri salsa has a fresh, green color. Serve it with grilled steak or fish as well as chicken.

vermouth salmon

nutrients per serving:

Calories: 371
Carbohydrate: 7 g
Calories From Fat: 57%
Total Fat: 23 g
Saturated Fat: 9 g
Cholesterol: 105 mg
Sodium: 854 mg
Dietary Fiber: <1 g
Protein: 33 g

spinach, cheese and prosciutto-stuffed chicken breasts

4 boneless skinless chicken breasts (about 4 ounces each)
 Salt and black pepper
4 slices (½ ounce each) prosciutto*
4 slices (½ ounce each) smoked provolone
1 cup spinach leaves, chopped
4 tablespoons all-purpose flour, divided
1 tablespoon olive oil
1 tablespoon butter
1 cup chicken broth
1 tablespoon heavy cream

Prosciutto, an Italian ham, is seasoned, cured and air-dried, not smoked. Look for imported or less expensive domestic prosciutto in delis and Italian food markets.

1. Preheat oven to 350°F.

2. To form pocket, cut each chicken breast horizontally almost to opposite edge. Fold back top half of chicken breast; sprinkle chicken lightly with salt and pepper. Place 1 slice prosciutto, 1 slice provolone and ¼ cup spinach on each chicken breast. Fold top half of breasts over filling.

3. Spread 3 tablespoons flour on plate. Holding chicken breast closed, coat with flour; shake off excess. Lightly sprinkle chicken with salt and pepper.

4. Heat oil and butter in large skillet over medium heat. Place chicken in skillet; cook about 4 minutes on each side or until browned.

5. Transfer chicken to shallow baking dish. Bake in oven 10 minutes or until chicken is no longer pink in center and juices run clear.

6. Whisk chicken broth and cream into remaining 1 tablespoon flour in small bowl. Pour chicken broth mixture into same skillet; heat over medium heat, stirring constantly, until sauce thickens, about 3 minutes. Spoon sauce onto serving plates; top with chicken breasts. *Makes 4 servings*

Tip: Swiss, Gruyére or mozzarella cheese may be substituted for the smoked provolone. Thinly sliced deli ham may be substituted for the prosciutto.

spinach, cheese and prosciutto-stuffed chicken breast

stir-fry beef & vegetable soup

1 boneless beef top sirloin or top round steak (about 1 pound)
2 teaspoons dark sesame oil, divided
3 cans (about 14 ounces each) reduced-sodium beef broth
1 package (16 ounces) frozen stir-fry vegetables
3 green onions, thinly sliced
¼ cup stir-fry sauce

1. Slice beef lengthwise in half, then crosswise into ⅛-inch-thick strips.

2. Heat Dutch oven over high heat. Add 1 teaspoon sesame oil and tilt pan to coat bottom. Add half the beef in single layer; cook 1 minute, without stirring, until slightly browned on bottom. Turn and brown other side about 1 minute. Remove beef from pan; set aside. Repeat with remaining 1 teaspoon sesame oil and beef; set aside.

3. Add broth to Dutch oven; cover and bring to a boil over high heat. Add vegetables; reduce heat and simmer 3 to 5 minutes or until vegetables are heated through. Add beef, green onions and stir-fry sauce; simmer 1 minute.

Makes 6 servings

Prep and Cook Time: 22 minutes

stir-fry beef & vegetable soup

snapper veracruz

Nonstick cooking spray
1 teaspoon olive oil
¼ large onion, thinly sliced
⅓ cup low sodium fish or vegetable broth, defatted* and divided
2 cloves garlic, minced
1 cup GUILTLESS GOURMET® Roasted Red Pepper Salsa
20 ounces fresh red snapper, tilapia, sea bass or halibut fillets

*To defat broth, simply chill the canned broth thoroughly. Open the can and use a spoon to lift out any solid fat floating on the surface of the broth.

Preheat oven to 400°F. Coat baking dish with cooking spray. (Dish needs to be large enough for fish to fit snugly together.) Heat oil in large nonstick skillet over medium heat until hot. Add onion; cook and stir until onion is translucent. Stir in 3 tablespoons broth. Add garlic; cook and stir 1 minute more. Stir in remaining broth and salsa. Bring mixture to a boil. Reduce heat to low; simmer about 2 minutes or until heated through.

Wash fish thoroughly; pat dry with paper towels. Place in prepared baking dish, overlapping thin edges to obtain an overall equal thickness. Pour and spread salsa mixture over fish.

Bake 15 minutes or until fish turns opaque and flakes easily when tested with fork. Serve hot.

Makes 4 servings

nutrients per serving:

Calories: 184
Carbohydrate: 6 g
Calories From Fat: 16%
Total Fat: 3 g
Saturated Fat: <1 g
Cholesterol: 52 mg
Sodium: 353 mg
Dietary Fiber: 0 g
Protein: 30 g

snapper veracruz

mediterranean shrimp soup

2 cans (14½ ounces each) reduced-sodium chicken broth
1 can (14½ ounces) whole tomatoes, undrained and coarsely chopped
1 can (8 ounces) tomato sauce
1 medium onion, chopped
½ medium green bell pepper, chopped
½ cup orange juice
½ cup dry white wine (optional)
1 jar (2½ ounces) sliced mushrooms
¼ cup ripe olives, sliced
2 cloves garlic, minced
1 teaspoon dried basil leaves
2 bay leaves
¼ teaspoon fennel seeds, crushed
⅛ teaspoon black pepper
1 pound medium shrimp, peeled

Slow Cooker Directions

Place all ingredients except shrimp in slow cooker. Cover and cook on LOW 4 to 4½ hours or until vegetables are crisp-tender. Stir in shrimp. Cover; cook 15 to 30 minutes or until shrimp are opaque. Remove and discard bay leaves.

Makes 6 servings

Note: For a heartier soup, add some fish. Cut 1 pound of whitefish or cod into 1-inch pieces. Add the fish to the slow cooker 45 minutes before serving. Cover and cook on LOW.

mediterranean shrimp soup

nutrients per serving:
Calories: 267
Carbohydrate: 7 g
Calories From Fat: 51%
Total Fat: 15 g
Saturated Fat: 10 g
Cholesterol: 69 mg
Sodium: 308 mg
Dietary Fiber: 5 g
Protein: 28 g

pork curry over cauliflower couscous

3 tablespoons olive oil, divided
2 tablespoons mild curry powder
2 teaspoons prepared crushed garlic
1½ pounds pork (boneless shoulder, loin or chops), cubed
1 red or green bell pepper, seeded and diced
1 tablespoon cider vinegar
½ teaspoon salt
2 cups water
1 large head cauliflower

1. Heat 2 tablespoons oil over medium heat in large saucepan. Add curry powder and garlic; cook and stir 1 to 2 minutes until garlic is golden.

2. Add pork; stir to coat completely with curry and garlic. Cook and stir 5 to 7 minutes or until pork cubes are barely pink in center. Add bell pepper and vinegar; cook and stir 3 minutes or until bell pepper is soft. Sprinkle with salt.

3. Add water; bring to a boil. Reduce heat and simmer 30 to 45 minutes, stirring occasionally, until liquid is reduced and pork is tender, adding additional water as needed.

4. Meanwhile, trim and core cauliflower; cut into equal pieces. Place in food processor fitted with metal blade. Process using on/off pulsing action until cauliflower is in small uniform pieces about the size of cooked couscous. *Do not purée.*

5. Heat remaining 1 tablespoon oil over medium heat in 12-inch nonstick skillet. Add cauliflower; cook and stir 5 minutes or until cooked crisp-tender. *Do not overcook.* Serve pork curry over cauliflower.   *Makes 6 servings*

pork curry over cauliflower couscous

chicken marsala

4 BUTTERBALL® Boneless Skinless Chicken Breast Fillets
3 cups sliced fresh mushrooms
2 tablespoons sliced green onion
2 tablespoons water
¼ teaspoon salt
¼ cup dry Marsala wine
1 teaspoon cornstarch

Flatten chicken fillets between two pieces of plastic wrap. Spray nonstick skillet with nonstick cooking spray; heat over medium heat until hot. Add chicken; cook 2 to 3 minutes on each side or until no longer pink in center. Transfer to platter; keep warm. Add mushrooms, onion, water and salt to skillet. Cook 3 minutes or until most of the liquid has evaporated. Combine wine and cornstarch in small bowl; add to skillet. Heat, stirring constantly, until thickened. Spoon over chicken. *Makes 4 servings*

Prep Time: 15 to 20 minutes

southwest skillet

1 cup cubed cooked chicken breast
1 bag (16 ounces) BIRDS EYE® frozen Pasta Secrets Zesty Garlic
1 cup chunky salsa
½ teaspoon chili powder
½ cup chopped green or red bell pepper

- In large skillet, combine all ingredients.
- Cook over medium heat 10 to 15 minutes or until heated through.

Makes 4 servings

Cheesy Southwest Skillet: Stir in ½ cup shredded Cheddar cheese during last 5 minutes. Cook until cheese is melted.

Creamy Southwest Skillet: Remove skillet from heat. Stir in ¼ cup sour cream before serving.

Prep Time: 5 minutes
Cook Time: 15 minutes

chicken marsala

nutrients per serving:

Calories: 583
Carbohydrate: 9 g
Calories From Fat: 69%
Total Fat: 45 g
Saturated Fat: 18 g
Cholesterol: 516 mg
Sodium: 922 mg
Dietary Fiber: 2 g
Protein: 36 g

crustless southwestern quiche

8 ounces chorizo sausage*
8 eggs
1 package (10 ounces) frozen chopped spinach, thawed and squeezed dry
1 cup crumbled queso fresco or 1 cup (4 ounces) shredded Cheddar or pepper Jack cheese
½ cup whipping cream or half-and-half
¼ cup salsa

Chorizo, a spicy Mexican pork sausage, is flavored with garlic and chilies. It is available in most supermarkets. If it is not available, substitute 8 ounces bulk pork sausage plus ¼ teaspoon cayenne pepper.

1. Preheat oven to 400°F. Butter 10-inch quiche dish or deep-dish pie plate.

2. Remove sausage from casings. Crumble sausage into medium skillet. Cook over medium heat until sausage is browned, stirring to break up meat. Remove from heat; pour off drippings. Cool 5 minutes.

3. Beat eggs in medium bowl. Add spinach, cheese, cream and sausage; mix well. Pour into prepared quiche dish. Bake 20 minutes or until center is set. Let stand 5 minutes before cutting into wedges. Serve with salsa. *Makes 4 servings*

crustless southwestern quiche

oriental steak salad

nutrients per serving:

Calories: 449
Carbohydrate: 14 g
Calories From Fat: 56%
Total Fat: 28 g
Saturated Fat: 6 g
Cholesterol: 90 mg
Sodium: 389 mg
Dietary Fiber: 3 g
Protein: 36 g

1 package (3 ounces) Oriental flavor instant ramen noodles, uncooked
4 cups water
1 bag (16 ounces) BIRDS EYE® frozen Farm Fresh Mixtures Cauliflower, Carrots & Snow Pea Pods
2 tablespoons vegetable oil
1 pound boneless beef top loin steak, cut into thin strips
⅓ cup Oriental sesame salad dressing
¼ cup chow mein noodles
Lettuce leaves

• Reserve seasoning packet from noodles.

• In large saucepan, bring water to boil. Add ramen noodles and vegetables; return to boil and cook 5 minutes, stirring occasionally. Drain.

• Heat remaining oil in large nonstick skillet over medium-high heat. Add beef; cook and stir about 8 minutes or until browned.

• Stir in reserved seasoning packet until beef is well coated.

• In large bowl, toss together beef, vegetables, ramen noodles and salad dressing. Sprinkle with chow mein noodles. Serve over lettuce.   *Makes 4 servings*

Serving Suggestion: Salad also can be served chilled. Moisten with additional salad dressing, if necessary. Sprinkle with chow mein noodles and spoon over lettuce just before serving.

Prep Time: 10 minutes
Cook Time: 12 to 15 minutes

oriental steak salad

nutrients per serving:

Calories: 389
Carbohydrate: 9 g
Calories From Fat: 38%
Total Fat: 16 g
Saturated Fat: 4 g
Cholesterol: 164 mg
Sodium: 797 mg
Dietary Fiber: 2 g
Protein: 49 g

tandoori-style seafood kabobs

½ pound each salmon fillet, tuna steak and swordfish steak*
 1 teaspoon salt
 1 teaspoon ground cumin
¼ teaspoon black pepper
   Dash ground cinnamon
   Dash ground cloves
   Dash ground nutmeg
   Dash ground cardamom (optional)
½ cup plain low-fat yogurt
¼ cup lemon juice
 1 piece (1-inch cube) peeled fresh ginger, minced
 1 tablespoon olive oil
 2 cloves garlic, minced
½ jalapeño pepper, seeded and minced
½ pound large shrimp, shelled with tails intact, deveined
 1 each red and green bell pepper, cut into bite-size pieces
   Fresh parsley sprigs
   Fresh chives

Any firm fish can be substituted for any fish listed above.

Cut fish into 1½-inch cubes; cover and refrigerate. Heat salt and spices in small skillet over medium heat until fragrant (or spices may be added to marinade without heating); place spices in 2-quart glass dish. Add yogurt, lemon juice, ginger, oil, garlic and jalapeño pepper; mix well. Add fish and shrimp; turn to coat. Cover and refrigerate at least 1 hour but no longer than 2 hours. Thread a variety of seafood onto each metal or wooden skewer, alternating with bell peppers. (Soak wooden skewers in hot water 30 minutes to prevent burning.) Grill kabobs over medium-hot KINGSFORD® Briquets about 2 minutes per side until fish flakes easily when tested with fork and shrimp are pink and opaque. Remove seafood and peppers from skewers. Garnish with parsley and chives. *Makes 4 servings*

braciola

1 can (28 ounces) tomato sauce
2½ teaspoons dried oregano leaves, divided
1¼ teaspoons dried basil leaves, divided
1 teaspoon salt
½ pound bulk hot Italian sausage
½ cup chopped onion
¼ cup grated Parmesan cheese
2 cloves garlic, minced
1 tablespoon dried parsley flakes
1 to 2 beef flank steaks (about 2½ pounds)

nutrients per serving:

Calories: 349
Carbohydrate: 9 g
Calories From Fat: 44%
Total Fat: 17 g
Saturated Fat: 10 g
Cholesterol: 78 mg
Sodium: 1182 mg
Dietary Fiber: 2 g
Protein: 38 g

Slow Cooker Directions

1. Combine tomato sauce, 2 teaspoons oregano, 1 teaspoon basil and salt in medium bowl; set aside.

2. Cook sausage in large nonstick skillet over medium-high heat until no longer pink stirring to separate; drain well. Combine sausage, onion, cheese, garlic, parsley, remaining ½ teaspoon oregano and ¼ teaspoon basil in medium bowl; set aside.

3. Place steak on countertop between two pieces waxed paper. Pound with meat mallet until steak is ⅛ to ¼ inch thick. Cut steak into about 3-inch wide strips.

4. Spoon sausage mixture evenly onto each steak strip. Roll up, jelly-roll style, securing meat with toothpicks. Place each roll in slow cooker. Pour tomato sauce mixture over meat. Cover; cook on LOW 6 to 8 hours.

5. Cut each roll into slices. Arrange slices on dinner plates. Top with hot tomato sauce. *Makes 8 servings*

Prep Time: 35 minutes
Cook Time: 6 to 8 hours

chicken teriyaki

8 large chicken drumsticks (about 2 pounds)
⅓ cup teriyaki sauce
2 tablespoons brandy or apple juice
1 green onion, minced
1 tablespoon vegetable oil
1 teaspoon ground ginger
½ teaspoon sugar
¼ teaspoon garlic powder
   Prepared sweet and sour sauce (optional)

1. Remove skin from drumsticks, if desired, by pulling skin toward end of leg using paper towel; discard skin.

2. Place chicken in large resealable plastic food storage bag. Combine teriyaki sauce, brandy, onion, oil, ginger, sugar and garlic powder in small bowl; pour over chicken. Close bag securely, turning to coat. Marinate in refrigerator at least 1 hour or overnight, turning occasionally.

3. Prepare grill for indirect cooking.

4. Drain chicken; reserve marinade. Place chicken on grid directly over drip pan. Grill, covered, over medium-high heat 60 minutes or until chicken is no longer pink in center and juices run clear, turning and brushing with reserved marinade every 20 minutes. *Do not brush with marinade during last 5 minutes of grilling.* Discard remaining marinade. Serve with sweet and sour sauce, if desired.

Makes 4 servings

chicken teriyaki

southwest ham 'n cheese quiche

   4 (8-inch) flour tortillas
   2 tablespoons butter or margarine, melted
   2 cups pizza 4-cheese blend
1½ cups (8 ounces) diced CURE 81® ham
   ½ cup sour cream
   ¼ cup salsa
   3 eggs, beaten
      Salsa
      Sour cream

Heat oven to 350°F. Cut 3 tortillas in half. Place remaining whole tortilla in bottom of greased 10-inch quiche dish or tart pan; brush with melted butter. Arrange tortilla halves around edge of dish, rounded sides up, overlapping to form pastry shell. Brush with remaining butter. Place 9-inch round cake pan inside quiche dish. Bake 5 minutes. Cool; remove cake pan. In large bowl, combine cheese and ham. Stir in sour cream, salsa and eggs. Pour into tortilla shell. Bake 55 to 60 minutes or until knife inserted in center comes out clean. Let stand 5 minutes. Serve with additional salsa and sour cream.   *Makes 6 servings*

orange vinaigrette grilled chicken salad

1¼ cups prepared fat-free red wine vinaigrette salad dressing
   ¼ cup MRS. DASH® Lemon Pepper Seasoning
   1 pound boneless, skinless chicken breast halves
   1 bunch romaine lettuce, torn
   1 (11-ounce) can mandarin oranges, drained
      Chopped fresh vegetables of your choice

Whisk together salad dressing and Mrs. Dash. Reserve ¾ cup mixture. Brush chicken with remaining ½ cup dressing mixture. Grill, turning and brushing occasionally, until chicken is no longer pink in center, about 15 to 20 minutes. Cut chicken into strips. Serve over lettuce with oranges and desired vegetables. Drizzle reserved dressing over salad.   *Makes 4 servings*

Prep Time: 5 minutes
Cook Time: 20 minutes

southwest ham 'n cheese quiche

nutrients per serving:

Calories: 135
Carbohydrate: 6 g
Calories From Fat: 21%
Total Fat: 3 g
Saturated Fat: 1 g
Cholesterol: 46 mg
Sodium: 307 mg
Dietary Fiber: 2 g
Protein: 19 g

asian chicken kabobs

1 pound boneless skinless chicken breasts
2 small zucchini or yellow squash, cut into 1-inch slices
8 large fresh mushrooms
1 cup red, yellow or green bell pepper pieces
2 tablespoons reduced-sodium soy sauce
2 tablespoons dry sherry
1 teaspoon dark sesame oil
2 cloves garlic, minced
2 large green onions, cut into 1-inch pieces

1. Cut chicken into 1½-inch pieces; place in large plastic bag. Add zucchini, mushrooms and bell pepper to bag. Combine soy sauce, sherry, oil and garlic in cup; pour over chicken and vegetables. Close bag securely; turn to coat. Marinate in refrigerator at least 30 minutes or up to 4 hours.

2. Soak 4 (12-inch) skewers in water to cover 20 minutes.

3. Drain chicken and vegetables; reserve marinade. Alternately thread chicken and vegetables with onions onto skewers.

4. Place on rack of broiler pan. Brush with half of reserved marinade. Broil 5 to 6 inches from heat 5 minutes. Turn kabobs over; brush with remaining marinade. Broil 5 minutes or until chicken is no longer pink. Garnish with green onion brushes, if desired.

Makes 4 servings

asian chicken kabobs

nutrients per serving:

Calories: 304
Carbohydrate: 18 g
Calories From Fat: 30%
Total Fat: 10 g
Saturated Fat: 3 g
Cholesterol: 67 mg
Sodium: 836 mg
Dietary Fiber: 3 g
Protein: 37 g

lime-poached fish with corn and chili salsa

4 swordfish steaks, 1 inch thick (about 1½ pounds)*
1 cup baby carrots, cut lengthwise into halves
2 green onions, cut into 1-inch pieces
3 tablespoons lime juice
½ teaspoon salt, divided
½ teaspoon chili powder
1½ cups chopped tomatoes
1 cup frozen corn, thawed
1 can (4 ounces) chopped green chilies, drained
2 tablespoons chopped fresh cilantro
1 tablespoon margarine or butter

Tuna or halibut steaks can be substituted.

1. Place fish and carrots in saucepan just large enough to hold them in single layer. Add onions, lime juice, ¼ teaspoon salt and chili powder. Add enough water to just cover fish.

2. Bring to a simmer over medium heat. Cook 8 minutes or until center of fish begins to flake easily when tested with fork. Transfer to serving plates with spatula.

3. Meanwhile, to prepare salsa, combine tomatoes, corn, chilies, cilantro and remaining ¼ teaspoon salt in medium bowl; toss well.

4. Drain carrots; add margarine. Transfer to serving plates; serve with salsa.

Makes 4 servings

Tip: If time allows, prepare the salsa in advance so the flavors have more time to develop. Do not add salt until ready to serve. Cover and refrigerate salsa up to 1 day before serving.

Prep and Cook Time: 15 minutes

lime-poached fish with corn and chili salsa

salmon, asparagus and shiitake salad

¼ **cup cider vinegar**
¼ **cup extra-virgin olive oil**
  Grated peel and juice of 1 lemon
4 **teaspoons Dijon mustard, divided**
1 **clove garlic, minced**
¼ **teaspoon salt**
¼ **teaspoon black pepper**
2 **teaspoons minced fresh tarragon** *or* ¾ **teaspoon dried tarragon leaves**
1 **pound small salmon fillets, skinned**
1 **medium red onion, thinly sliced**
1 **pound asparagus, ends trimmed**
¼ **pound shiitake mushrooms or button mushrooms**
  Additional salt and black pepper
8 **cups lightly packed torn romaine and red leaf lettuce**

Combine vinegar, oil, peel, juice, 2 teaspoons mustard, garlic, ¼ teaspoon salt and ¼ teaspoon pepper in medium bowl; spoon 3 tablespoons dressing into 2-quart glass dish to use as marinade. Reserve remaining dressing. Add tarragon and 2 teaspoons remaining mustard to marinade in glass dish; blend well. Add salmon; turn to coat. Cover and refrigerate 1 hour. Transfer 3 tablespoons reserved dressing to medium bowl; add onion, tossing to coat. Thread asparagus and mushrooms onto wooden skewers. (Soak skewers in hot water 30 minutes to prevent burning.)

Remove salmon from marinade; discard marinade. Season salmon to taste with additional salt and pepper. Lightly oil hot grid to prevent sticking. Grill salmon over medium-hot KINGSFORD® Briquets 2 to 4 minutes per side or until fish flakes when tested with fork. Grill asparagus and mushrooms over medium-hot briquets 5 to 8 minutes or until crisp-tender. Cut asparagus into 2-inch pieces and slice mushrooms; add to onion mixture. Let stand 10 minutes. Toss lettuce with onion mixture in large bowl; arrange lettuce on platter. Break salmon into 2-inch pieces; arrange salmon and vegetables over lettuce. Drizzle with remaining reserved dressing. Serve immediately.

Makes 4 main-dish servings

salmon, asparagus and shiitake salad

nutrients per serving:

Calories: 188
Carbohydrate: 15 g
Calories From Fat: 24%
Total Fat: 5 g
Saturated Fat: 1 g
Cholesterol: 54 mg
Sodium: 704 mg
Dietary Fiber: 2 g
Protein: 22 g

chicken and vegetable chowder

    1 pound boneless skinless chicken breasts, cut into 1-inch pieces
10 ounces frozen broccoli cuts
    1 cup sliced carrots
    1 jar (4½ ounces) sliced mushrooms, drained
  ½ cup chopped onion
  ½ cup whole kernel corn
    2 cloves garlic, minced
  ½ teaspoon dried thyme leaves
    1 can (14½ ounces) reduced-sodium chicken broth
    1 can (10¾ ounces) condensed cream of potato soup
  ⅓ cup half-and-half

Slow Cooker Directions

1. Combine all ingredients except half-and-half in slow cooker. Cover and cook on LOW 5 hours or until vegetables are tender and chicken is no longer pink in center.

2. Stir in half-and-half. Turn to HIGH. Cover and cook 15 minutes or until heated through. *Makes 6 servings*

Variation: If desired, add ½ cup (2 ounces) shredded Swiss or Cheddar cheese to thickened chowder, stirring over LOW heat until melted.

chicken and vegetable chowder

mexican tortilla soup

Nonstick cooking spray
2 pounds boneless skinless chicken breasts, cut into ½-inch strips
4 cups diced carrots
2 cups sliced celery
1 cup chopped green bell pepper
1 cup chopped onion
4 cloves garlic, minced
1 jalapeño pepper,* seeded and sliced
1 teaspoon dried oregano leaves
½ teaspoon ground cumin
8 cups fat-free reduced-sodium chicken broth
1 large tomato, seeded and chopped
4 to 5 tablespoons lime juice
2 (6-inch) corn tortillas, cut into ¼-inch strips
Salt (optional)
3 tablespoons finely chopped fresh cilantro

*Jalapeño peppers can sting and irritate the skin; wear rubber gloves when handling peppers and do not touch eyes. Wash hands after handling.

1. Preheat oven to 350°F. Spray large nonstick Dutch oven with cooking spray; heat over medium heat. Add chicken; cook and stir about 10 minutes or until browned and no longer pink in center. Add carrots, celery, bell pepper, onion, garlic, jalapeño pepper, oregano and cumin; cook and stir over medium heat 5 minutes.

2. Stir in chicken broth, tomato and lime juice; heat to a boil. Reduce heat to low; cover and simmer 15 to 20 minutes.

3. Meanwhile, spray tortilla strips lightly with cooking spray; sprinkle very lightly with salt, if desired. Place on baking sheet. Bake about 10 minutes or until browned and crisp, stirring occasionally.

4. Stir cilantro into soup. Ladle soup into bowls; top evenly with tortilla strips.
Makes 8 servings

mexican tortilla soup

sensational side dishes

cucumber tomato salad

½ cup rice vinegar*
3 tablespoons EQUAL® SPOONFUL**
3 cups unpeeled ¼-inch-thick sliced cucumbers, quartered (about 2 medium)
2 cups chopped tomato (about 1 large)
½ cup chopped red onion
Salt and pepper to taste

*Distilled white vinegar may be substituted for rice vinegar.

**May substitute 4½ packets Equal® sweetener.

● Combine vinegar and Equal®. Add cucumbers, tomato and onion. Season to taste with salt and pepper; mix well. Refrigerate, covered, at least 30 minutes before serving.   *Makes 6 servings*

sesame broccoli

1 bag (16 ounces) BIRDS EYE® frozen Broccoli Cuts
1 tablespoon sesame seeds
1 tablespoon oil
Dash soy sauce (optional)

● Cook broccoli according to package directions.

● Cook sesame seeds in oil 1 to 2 minutes or until golden brown, stirring frequently.

● Toss broccoli with sesame seed mixture. Add soy sauce, salt and pepper to taste.
                                                              Makes 4 to 6 servings

Prep Time: 1 minute
Cook Time: 8 to 9 minutes

cucumber tomato salad

jalapeño wild rice cakes

⅓ **cup wild rice**
¾ **cup water**
½ **teaspoon salt, divided**
1 **tablespoon all-purpose flour**
½ **teaspoon baking powder**
1 **egg**
1 **jalapeño pepper,* finely chopped**
2 **tablespoons minced onion**
1 **tablespoon freshly grated ginger** *or* **2 teaspoons ground ginger**
2 **tablespoons vegetable or olive oil**

*Jalapeño peppers can sting and irritate the skin; wear rubber gloves when handling peppers and do not touch eyes. Wash hands after handling.

1. Combine rice, water and ¼ teaspoon salt in medium saucepan. Bring to a boil. Reduce heat; cover and simmer 40 to 45 minutes or until rice is tender. Drain rice, if necessary; place in medium bowl. Add flour, baking powder and remaining ¼ teaspoon salt; mix until blended.

2. Whisk egg, jalapeño pepper, onion and ginger together in small bowl. Pour egg mixture over rice; mix until well blended.

3. Heat oil in large nonstick skillet over medium heat. Spoon 2 tablespoons rice mixture into pan and shape into cake. Cook, 4 cakes at a time, 3 minutes on each side or until golden brown. Transfer to paper towels. Serve immediately or refrigerate rice cakes for up to 24 hours. *Makes 8 (3-inch diameter) rice cakes*

Tip: To reheat cold rice cakes, preheat oven to 400°F. Place rice cakes in single layer on baking sheet; heat 5 minutes.

jalapeño wild rice cakes

strawberry blueberry salsa

nutrients per serving:

Calories: 19
Carbohydrate: 5 g
Calories From Fat: 7%
Total Fat: <1 g
Saturated Fat: <1 g
Cholesterol: 0 mg
Sodium: 2 mg
Dietary Fiber: 1 g
Protein: <1 g

¾ cup chopped strawberries
⅓ cup chopped blueberries
2 tablespoons chopped green bell pepper
2 tablespoons chopped carrot
1 tablespoon chopped onion
2 teaspoons cider vinegar
1 teaspoon minced jalapeño pepper*
⅛ teaspoon ground ginger

*Jalapeño peppers can sting and irritate the skin; wear rubber gloves when handling peppers and do not touch eyes. Wash hands after handling.

Combine all ingredients in small bowl. Let stand 20 minutes to allow flavors to blend. Serve with grilled chicken, pork or fish. *Makes 4 servings*

lemony cabbage slaw with curry

nutrients per serving:

Calories: 28
Carbohydrate: 7 g
Calories From Fat: 6%
Total Fat: <1 g
Saturated Fat: 0 g
Cholesterol: 0 mg
Sodium: 189 mg
Dietary Fiber: 2 g
Protein: 1 g

4 cups shredded green or white cabbage
2 tablespoons chopped green bell pepper
2 tablespoons chopped red bell pepper
1 green onion, thinly sliced
2 tablespoons cider vinegar
1 tablespoon lemon juice
1 tablespoon sugar
1 teaspoon curry powder
½ teaspoon salt
½ teaspoon celery seeds
Green and red bell pepper rings for garnish

1. Mix cabbage, bell peppers and green onion in large bowl. Combine vinegar, lemon juice, sugar, curry powder, salt and celery seeds in small bowl. Pour over cabbage mixture; mix well.

2. Refrigerate, covered, at least 4 hours or overnight, stirring occasionally. Garnish with bell pepper rings. *Makes 6 servings*

strawberry blueberry salsa

sun-dried tomato scones

nutrients per serving:

1 scone

Calories: 75
Carbohydrate: 10 g
Calories From Fat: 36%
Total Fat: 3 g
Saturated Fat: 1 g
Cholesterol: 2 mg
Sodium: 209 mg
Dietary Fiber: <1 g
Protein: 2 g

2 cups buttermilk baking mix
¼ cup (1 ounce) grated Parmesan cheese
1½ teaspoons dried basil
⅔ cup reduced-fat (2%) milk
½ cup chopped drained oil-packed sun-dried tomatoes
¼ cup chopped green onions

1. Preheat oven to 450°F. Combine baking mix, cheese and basil in medium bowl.

2. Stir in milk, tomatoes and onions. Mix just until dry ingredients are moistened. Drop by heaping teaspoonfuls onto greased baking sheet.

3. Bake 8 to 10 minutes or until light golden brown. Remove baking sheet to cooling rack; let stand 5 minutes. Remove scones and serve warm or at room temperature.

Makes 1½ dozen scones

Prep and Cook Time: 20 minutes

red and greens salad

nutrients per serving:

⅛ of total recipe

Calories: 46
Carbohydrate: 4 g
Calories From Fat: 65%
Total Fat: 4 g
Saturated Fat: <1 g
Cholesterol: 0 mg
Sodium: 75 mg
Dietary Fiber: 2 g
Protein: <1 g

2 tablespoons raspberry vinegar
1 teaspoon white pepper
1 teaspoon sugar
¼ teaspoon salt
2 tablespoons olive or canola oil
1 bag (4 to 6 ounces) mixed baby salad greens
1 carton (6 ounces) fresh raspberries

1. To prepare dressing, whisk together vinegar, pepper, sugar and salt in small bowl until salt and sugar dissolve. Add oil and whisk to blend. Reserve.

2. Place greens in large salad bowl. Add reserved dressing and toss gently to coat greens. Add raspberries and toss gently to mix and coat with dressing. Divide salad evenly among 8 plates.

Makes 8 servings

Tip: As raspberries are gently tossed, they will release a little of their juice and enhance the flavor of the dressing.

sun-dried tomato scones

tabbouleh

½ **cup uncooked bulgur wheat**
¾ **cup boiling water**
¼ **teaspoon salt**
5 **teaspoons lemon juice**
2 **teaspoons olive oil**
½ **teaspoon dried basil leaves**
¼ **teaspoon black pepper**
1 **green onion, thinly sliced**
½ **cup chopped cucumber**
½ **cup chopped green bell pepper**
½ **cup chopped tomato**
¼ **cup chopped fresh parsley**
2 **teaspoons chopped mint (optional)**

1. Rinse bulgur thoroughly in colander under cold water, picking out any debris. Drain well; transfer to medium heatproof bowl. Stir in boiling water and salt. Cover; let stand 30 minutes. Drain well.

2. Combine lemon juice, oil, basil and black pepper in small bowl. Pour over bulgur; mix well.

3. Layer bulgur, onion, cucumber, bell pepper and tomato in clear glass bowl; sprinkle with parsley and mint, if desired.

4. Refrigerate, covered, at least 2 hours to allow flavors to blend. Serve layered or toss before serving.

Makes 8 servings

broccoli italian style

1¼ pounds broccoli
2 tablespoons lemon juice
1 teaspoon olive oil
1 clove garlic, minced
1 teaspoon chopped fresh parsley
Dash pepper

1. Trim broccoli, disgarding tough part of stems. Cut broccoli into florets with 2-inch stems. Peel remaining broccoli stems; cut into ½-inch-thick slices.

2. Bring 1 quart water to a boil in large saucepan over high heat. Add broccoli; return to a boil. Reduce heat to medium-high. Cook, uncovered, 3 to 5 minutes or until broccoli is fork-tender. Drain; arrange evenly in serving dish.

3. Combine lemon juice, oil, garlic, parsley and pepper in small bowl. Pour over broccoli, turning to coat. Let stand, covered, 1 to 2 hours before serving to allow flavors to blend. *Makes 4 servings*

nutrients per serving:

Calories: 44
Carbohydrate: 7 g
Calories From Fat: 26%
Total Fat: 2 g
Saturated Fat: <1 g
Cholesterol: 0 mg
Sodium: 29 mg
Dietary Fiber: 3 g
Protein: 3 g

dilly beans

¾ cup white wine vinegar
3 tablespoons olive oil
1 teaspoon SPLENDA® Granular
1 tablespoon minced fresh dill
1½ pounds green beans, trimmed and rinsed

1. In large bowl, whisk together vinegar, oil, SPLENDA® and dill. Set aside.

2. Bring large saucepan of water to a boil; add green beans and cook until crisp-tender, about 3 minutes. Drain well.

3. Add beans to dressing, tossing and stirring to coat beans. Add salt and pepper to taste. Cool beans to room temperature, stirring occasionally.

4. Serve immediately or refrigerate until needed. *Makes 6 servings*

Prep Time: 15 minutes

nutrients per serving:

1 cup

Calories: 101
Carbohydrate: 7 g
Calories From Fat: 63%
Total Fat: 7 g
Saturated Fat: 1 g
Cholesterol: 0 mg
Sodium: 8 mg
Dietary Fiber: 3 g
Protein: 2 g

cranberry salad

2 cups cranberries
1 cup water
1 cup EQUAL® SPOONFUL*
1 small package cranberry or cherry sugar-free gelatin
1 cup boiling water
1 cup diced celery
1 can (7¼ ounces) crushed pineapple, in juice
½ cup chopped walnuts

May substitute 24 packets Equal® sweetener.

● Bring cranberries and 1 cup water to a boil. Remove from heat when cranberries have popped open. Add Equal® and stir. Set aside to cool.

● Dissolve gelatin with 1 cup boiling water. Add cranberry sauce; mix thoroughly. Add celery, pineapple and walnuts. Pour into mold or bowl. Place in refrigerator until set.   *Makes 8 servings*

saucy herb dressing

1 cup nonfat cottage cheese
¼ cup skim milk
2 tablespoons red wine vinegar
2 teaspoons CRISCO® Oil*
¼ cup chopped green onions with tops
¼ cup chopped fresh parsley
1 clove garlic, minced
¼ teaspoon dried oregano leaves
¼ teaspoon dried basil leaves
¼ teaspoon black pepper
⅛ teaspoon cayenne pepper

Use your favorite Crisco Oil product.

1. Combine cottage cheese, milk, vinegar and oil in blender or food processor container. Process until smooth.

2. Add green onions, parsley, garlic, oregano, basil, black pepper and cayenne. Process until blended. Serve over crisp salad greens.   *Makes 1⅔ cups*

cranberry salad

grilled vegetables

nutrients per serving:

Calories: 34
Carbohydrate: 8 g
Calories From Fat: 6%
Total Fat: <1 g
Saturated Fat: <1 g
Cholesterol: 0 mg
Sodium: 190 mg
Dietary Fiber: 2 g
Protein: 1 g

¼ cup minced fresh herbs, such as parsley, thyme, rosemary, oregano or basil
1 small eggplant (about ¾ pound), cut into ¼-inch-thick slices
½ teaspoon salt
Nonstick cooking spray
1 each red, green and yellow bell pepper, quartered and seeded
2 zucchini, cut lengthwise into ¼-inch-thick slices
1 fennel bulb, cut lengthwise into ¼-inch-thick slices

1. Combine herbs in small bowl; let stand 3 hours or overnight.

2. Place eggplant in large colander over bowl; sprinkle with salt. Drain 1 hour.

3. Heat grill until coals are glowing red. Spray vegetables with cooking spray and sprinkle with herb mixture. Grill 10 to 15 minutes or until fork-tender and lightly browned on both sides. (Cooking times vary depending on vegetable; remove vegetables as they are done to avoid overcooking.)   *Makes 6 servings*

stilton salad dressing

nutrients per serving:

Calories: 51
Carbohydrate: 2 g
Calories From Fat: 55%
Total Fat: 3 g
Saturated Fat: 2 g
Cholesterol: 8 mg
Sodium: 265 mg
Dietary Fiber: <1 g
Protein: 4 g

½ cup buttermilk
¼ cup silken firm tofu
2 ounces Stilton cheese
1 teaspoon lemon juice
1 clove garlic, peeled
¼ teaspoon salt
⅛ teaspoon black pepper
2 tablespoons low-fat (1%) cottage cheese
Romaine lettuce hearts, torn into bite-size pieces (optional)
Toasted chopped walnuts (optional)

1. Place buttermilk, tofu, Stilton cheese, lemon juice, garlic, salt and pepper in blender or food processor; process until smooth. Pour mixture into small bowl; fold in cottage cheese.

2. Store in airtight container and refrigerate 3 hours or overnight before serving. Serve with romaine lettuce and toasted walnuts, if desired.   *Makes 6 servings*

grilled vegetables

nutrients per serving:

1 tablespoon

Calories: 5
Carbohydrate: 1 g
Calories From Fat: 17%
Total Fat: <1 g
Saturated Fat: <1 g
Cholesterol: <1 mg
Sodium: 12 mg
Dietary Fiber: <1 g
Protein: <1 g

buttermilk-herb dressing

½ cup plus 1 tablespoon nonfat buttermilk
3 tablespoons raspberry-flavored vinegar
1 tablespoon chopped fresh basil leaves
1½ teaspoons snipped fresh chives
¼ teaspoon minced garlic

Place all ingredients in small bowl; stir to combine. Store, covered, in refrigerator up to 2 days. *Makes about ¾ cup*

nutrients per serving:

½ cup

Calories: 37
Carbohydrate: 4 g
Calories From Fat: 29%
Total Fat: 1 g
Saturated Fat: <1 g
Cholesterol: 3 mg
Sodium: 184 mg
Dietary Fiber: 1 g
Protein: 3 g

autumn casserole

¼ cup fat-free reduced-sodium chicken broth or water
2 cups sliced mushrooms
2 cups chopped stemmed and washed fresh spinach
1 cup diced red bell pepper
1 clove garlic, minced
1 cup cooked spaghetti squash
¼ teaspoon salt
¼ teaspoon black pepper
⅛ teaspoon dried Italian seasoning
⅛ teaspoon red pepper flakes (optional)
¼ cup grated Parmesan cheese

1. Preheat oven to 350°F. Spray 1-quart casserole with nonstick cooking spray.

2. Heat chicken broth in medium saucepan. Add mushrooms, spinach, bell pepper and garlic. Cook 10 minutes or until vegetables are tender, stirring frequently. Stir in squash. Add salt, black pepper, Italian seasoning and red pepper flakes, if desired.

3. Spoon into prepared casserole. Sprinkle with cheese. Bake 5 to 10 minutes or until cheese melts. *Makes 6 servings*

Note: For 1 cup cooked spaghetti squash, place half small spaghetti squash in microwavable dish and add ¼ cup water. Microwave at HIGH 8 to 10 minutes or until squash is tender when pierced with a fork. Discard seeds and scrape out strands of squash. Or, bake in preheated 350°F oven 45 minutes or until tender.

buttermilk-herb dressing

nutrients per serving:

Calories: 72
Carbohydrate: 9 g
Calories From Fat: 45%
Total Fat: 4 g
Saturated Fat: <1 g
Cholesterol: 0 mg
Sodium: 163 mg
Dietary Fiber: 2 g
Protein: 2 g

marinated tomato salad

Marinade
 1½ cups tarragon or white wine vinegar
  ½ teaspoon salt
  ¼ cup finely chopped shallots
  2 tablespoons finely chopped chives
  2 tablespoons fresh lemon juice
  ¼ teaspoon white pepper
  2 tablespoons extra-virgin olive oil

Salad
  6 plum tomatoes, quartered vertically
  2 large yellow tomatoes,* sliced horizontally into ½-inch slices
 16 red cherry tomatoes, halved vertically
 16 small yellow pear tomatoes,* halved vertically

Substitute 10 plum tomatoes, quartered vertically, for yellow tomatoes and yellow pear tomatoes, if desired.

1. To prepare marinade, combine vinegar and salt in large bowl; stir until salt is completely dissolved. Add shallots, chives, lemon juice and white pepper; mix well. Slowly whisk in oil until well blended.

2. Add tomatoes to marinade; toss well. Cover and let stand at room temperature 2 to 3 hours.

3. To serve, place 3 plum tomato quarters on each of 8 salad plates. Add 2 slices yellow tomato, 4 cherry tomato halves and 4 pear tomato halves. Garnish each plate with sunflower sprouts, if desired. (Or, place all marinated tomatoes on large serving plate.)
Makes 8 servings

marinated tomato salad

nutrients per serving:

Calories: 75
Carbohydrate: 4 g
Calories From Fat: 60%
Total Fat: 5 g
Saturated Fat: 2 g
Cholesterol: 6 mg
Sodium: 286 mg
Dietary Fiber: 2 g
Protein: 4 g

oven-roasted asparagus

1 bunch (12 to 14 ounces) asparagus spears
1 tablespoon olive oil
½ teaspoon salt
¼ teaspoon ground black pepper
¼ cup shredded Asiago or Parmesan cheese

1. Preheat oven to 425°F.

2. Trim off and discard tough ends of asparagus spears. Peel stem ends of asparagus with vegetable peeler, if desired. Arrange asparagus in shallow baking dish. Drizzle oil onto asparagus; turn stalks to coat. Sprinkle with salt and pepper.

3. Bake until asparagus is tender, about 12 to 18 minutes depending on thickness of asparagus. Chop or leave spears whole. Sprinkle with cheese.   *Makes 4 servings*

nutrients per serving:

1 tablespoon

Calories: 20
Carbohydrate: 5 g
Calories From Fat: 1%
Total Fat: <1 g
Saturated Fat: 0 g
Cholesterol: 0 mg
Sodium: 2 mg
Dietary Fiber: 1 g
Protein: <1 g

peach freezer jam

2 pounds peaches, peeled, pitted and coarsely chopped
1 package (1¾ ounces) no-sugar-needed pectin
1 to 1½ cups unsweetened apple juice
1 to 1½ cups EQUAL® SPOONFUL*

*May substitute 24 to 36 packets Equal® sweetener.

● Coarsely mash peaches in large bowl with potato masher or pastry blender (about 2½ cups).

● Gradually stir pectin into apple juice in medium saucepan. Heat mixture to a rolling boil (one that does not stop when being stirred) over high heat, stirring constantly; boil, stirring constantly, 1 minute.

● Stir hot mixture into peaches; stir in Equal®. Fill jars, allowing ½ inch headspace. Cool jam; seal and freeze up to 3 months.   *Makes 3 (½-pint) jars*

equal® cinnamon cream cheese

8 ounces whipped cream cheese
⅔ cup EQUAL® SPOONFUL*
1¼ teaspoons ground cinnamon

May substitute16 packets Equal® sweetener.

● Combine cream cheese with Equal® and cinnamon.

● Spread mixture on celery sticks, apple slices, bread and crackers.

● For variety, stir in 1 or 2 tablespoons of the following: raisins, chopped nuts, mini chocolate chips, chopped fresh apple, dried cherries, dried cranberries or mixed dried fruits. *Makes 11 servings*

nutrients per serving:
2 tablespoons

Calories: 97
Carbohydrate: 5 g
Calories From Fat: 74%
Total Fat: 8 g
Saturated Fat: 5 g
Cholesterol: 46 mg
Sodium: 101 mg
Dietary Fiber: 0 g
Protein: 2 g

savory green bean casserole

2 teaspoons CRISCO® Oil*
1 medium onion, chopped
½ medium green bell pepper, chopped
1 package (10 ounces) frozen green beans, thawed
1 can (8 ounces) tomatoes, drained
2 tablespoons nonfat mayonnaise dressing
¼ teaspoon salt
⅛ teaspoon crushed red pepper
⅛ teaspoon garlic powder
¼ cup plain dry bread crumbs

Use your favorite Crisco Oil product.

1. Heat oven to 375°F. Oil 1-quart casserole lightly. Place cooling rack on countertop.

2. Heat 2 teaspoons oil in large skillet on medium heat. Add onion and green pepper. Cook and stir until tender.

3. Add beans, tomatoes, mayonnaise dressing, salt, red pepper and garlic powder. Heat thoroughly, stirring occasionally.

4. Spoon into casserole. Sprinkle with bread crumbs. Bake at 375°F for 30 minutes. *Do not overbake.* Remove casserole to cooling rack. Serve warm.

Makes 8 servings

nutrients per serving:
½ cup casserole

Calories: 51
Carbohydrate: 8 g
Calories From Fat: 26%
Total Fat: 1 g
Saturated Fat: <1 g
Cholesterol: 0 mg
Sodium: 179 mg
Dietary Fiber: 2 g
Protein: 1 g

stir-fried asparagus

½ pound asparagus
1 tablespoon olive or canola oil
1 cup celery slices
½ cup bottled roasted red peppers, drained and diced
¼ teaspoon black pepper
¼ cup sliced almonds, toasted*

To toast almonds, place in small dry skillet. Cook over medium heat, stirring constantly, until almonds are lightly browned.

1. Trim ends from asparagus; cut stalks diagonally into 1-inch pieces.

2. Heat oil in 12-inch nonstick skillet over medium-high heat. Add celery; stir-fry 2 minutes. Add asparagus and red peppers. Stir-fry 3 to 4 minutes or until asparagus is crisp tender.

3. Add black pepper and almonds; mix until blended.   *Makes 6 servings*

triple-berry jam

4 cups fresh strawberries or thawed frozen unsweetened strawberries
2 cups fresh raspberries or thawed frozen unsweetened raspberries
1 cup fresh blueberries or thawed frozen unsweetened blueberries
1 package (1¾ ounces) no-sugar-needed pectin
¾ cup EQUAL® SPOONFUL*

May substitute 18 packets Equal® sweetener.

● Mash strawberries, raspberries and blueberries by hand or with food processor to make 4 cups pulp. Stir in pectin; let mixture stand 10 minutes, stirring frequently.

● Transfer to large saucepan. Cook and stir over medium heat until mixture comes to a boil. Cook and stir 1 minute more. Remove from heat; stir in Equal®. Skim off foam, if necessary.

● Immediately fill containers, leaving ½-inch headspace. Seal and let stand at room temperature until firm (several hours). Store up to 2 weeks in refrigerator or 3 months in freezer.   *Makes 8 (½-pint) jars*

stir-fried asparagus

broccoli with creamy lemon sauce

nutrients per serving:

Calories: 44
Carbohydrate: 7 g
Calories From Fat: 18%
Total Fat: 1 g
Saturated Fat: <1 g
Cholesterol: 4 mg
Sodium: 216 mg
Dietary Fiber: 2 g
Protein: 2 g

  2 tablespoons fat-free mayonnaise
4½ teaspoons reduced-fat sour cream
  1 tablespoon fat-free (skim) milk
  1 to 1½ teaspoons lemon juice
  ⅛ teaspoon ground turmeric
1¼ cups hot cooked broccoli florets

Combine all ingredients except broccoli in top of double boiler. Cook over simmering water 5 minutes or until heated through, stirring constantly. Serve over hot cooked broccoli.

Makes 2 servings

vegetable napoleon

nutrients per serving:

Calories: 78
Carbohydrate: 9 g
Calories From Fat: 25%
Total Fat: 2 g
Saturated Fat: 1 g
Cholesterol: 6 mg
Sodium: 105 mg
Dietary Fiber: 3 g
Protein: 6 g

  1 teaspoon salt-free garlic and herb seasoning mix
  ¼ teaspoon black pepper
  ¼ teaspoon garlic powder
  1 large yellow squash, thinly sliced lengthwise
  1 large zucchini, thinly sliced lengthwise
  ¼ cup (1 ounce) shredded reduced-fat mozzarella cheese
  1 large tomato, thinly sliced*

For easier slicing, use a serrated bread knife to slice tomatoes.

1. Preheat oven to 350°F. Lightly spray small loaf pan with cooking spray. Combine seasoning mix, pepper and garlic powder, in small bowl.

2. Place one layer of squash and zucchini in bottom of loaf pan. Sprinkle with ⅓ of seasoning mixture and 1 tablespoon cheese. Layer tomato slices over squash. Top with ⅓ of seasoning mixture and 1 tablespoon of cheese. Top with remaining squash, seasoning mixture and cheese.

3. Bake 35 minutes or until vegetables are tender and cheese is melted. Remove from oven and cool slightly before slicing.

Makes 2 servings

broccoli with creamy lemon sauce

nutrients per serving:

⅙ of total recipe (without garnish)

Calories: 40
Carbohydrate: 7 g
Calories From Fat: 22%
Total Fat: 1 g
Saturated Fat: <1 g
Cholesterol: 0 mg
Sodium: 198 mg
Dietary Fiber: 1 g
Protein: 2 g

indian-style vegetable stir-fry

1 teaspoon canola oil
1 teaspoon curry powder
1 teaspoon ground cumin
⅛ teaspoon red pepper flakes
1 ½ teaspoons minced seeded jalapeño pepper*
2 cloves garlic, minced
¾ cup chopped red bell pepper
¾ cup thinly sliced carrots
3 cups cauliflower florets
½ cup water, divided
½ teaspoon salt
2 teaspoons finely chopped fresh cilantro (optional)

Jalapeño peppers can sting and irritate the skin; wear rubber gloves when handling peppers and do not touch eyes. Wash hands after handling.

1. Heat oil in large nonstick skillet over medium-high heat. Add curry powder, cumin and red pepper flakes; cook and stir about 30 seconds.

2. Stir in jalapeño pepper and garlic. Add bell pepper and carrots; mix well. Add cauliflower; reduce heat to medium.

3. Stir in ¼ cup water; cook and stir until water evaporates. Add remaining ¼ cup water; cover and cook about 8 to 10 minutes or until vegetables are crisp-tender, stirring occasionally.

4. Add salt; mix well. Sprinkle with cilantro and garnish with mizuna and additional red bell pepper, if desired. *Makes 6 servings*

indian-style vegetable stir-fry

spicy deviled eggs

6 eggs
3 tablespoons heavy cream
1 green onion, finely chopped
1 tablespoon white wine vinegar
2 teaspoons Dijon mustard
½ teaspoon curry powder
½ teaspoon hot pepper sauce
3 tablespoons crisply cooked chopped bacon
1 tablespoon chopped fresh chives or parsley, for garnish

1. Place eggs into small saucepan; cover with cold water. Bring to a boil over high heat. Cover and remove from heat. Let stand 15 minutes. Drain; rinse under cold water. Peel eggs; cool completely.

2. Slice eggs in half lengthwise. Remove yolks to small bowl; set whites aside. Mash yolks with fork. Stir in cream, onion, vinegar, mustard, curry powder and pepper sauce until blended.

3. Spoon or pipe egg yolk mixture into centers of egg whites. Arrange eggs on serving plate. Garnish eggs with bacon and chives.   *Makes 12 deviled eggs*

tartar sauce

1 cup nonfat sour cream alternative
½ cup sweet pickle relish, drained
¼ cup finely chopped green onions with tops
1 teaspoon CRISCO® Oil*

*Use your favorite Crisco Oil product.

Combine "sour cream," pickle relish, onions and oil in small bowl. Stir to blend. Garnish, if desired. Cover and refrigerate leftover sauce.   *Makes 1¼ cups*

Hint: Prepare and refrigerate at least 2 hours before serving for best flavor.

zucchini salad

1 pound zucchini, unpeeled
1 medium sweet onion, sliced thinly
1 medium orange bell pepper, sliced
½ cup cider vinegar
⅓ cup water
1 tablespoon vegetable oil
½ cup EQUAL® SPOONFUL*
¼ teaspoon salt
¼ teaspoon ground black pepper
¼ teaspoon dried marjoram or tarragon, crushed (optional)
6 cups salad greens
12 arugula leaves
3 tablespoons pine nuts, optional

May substitute 12 packets Equal® sweetener.

- Cut zucchini into ⅛-inch slices. Combine with onion and bell pepper; set aside.

- Combine vinegar, water, oil, Equal®, salt, pepper and marjoram in quart-size container with lid. Pour over vegetables. Chill overnight.

- Spoon vegetables over salad greens using slotted spoon. Top with bits of arugula and sprinkle with pine nuts. *Makes 6 servings*

nutrients per serving:
Calories: 62
Carbohydrate: 9 g
Calories From Fat: 31%
Total Fat: 3 g
Saturated Fat: <1 g
Cholesterol: 0 mg
Sodium: 106 mg
Dietary Fiber: 3 g
Protein: 2 g

balsamic vinaigrette

¼ cup balsamic vinegar
¼ cup water
3 tablespoons olive oil
2 tablespoons finely chopped red or green onion
3 cloves garlic, minced
¾ teaspoon dried chervil leaves
½ teaspoon celery seeds

Combine all ingredients in jar with tight-fitting lid; refrigerate until serving time. Shake well before using. *Makes about ⅔ cup*

nutrients per serving:
1 tablespoon
Calories: 38
Carbohydrate: 1 g
Calories From Fat: 87%
Total Fat: 4 g
Saturated Fat: 1 g
Cholesterol: 0 mg
Sodium: 1 mg
Dietary Fiber: <1 g
Protein: <1 g

super snacks

nutrients per serving:

Calories: 363
Carbohydrate: 4 g
Calories From Fat: 50%
Total Fat: 30 g
Saturated Fat: 12 g
Cholesterol: 69 mg
Sodium: 699 mg
Dietary Fiber: <1 g
Protein: 20 g

jerk wings with ranch dipping sauce

½ **cup mayonnaise**
½ **cup plain yogurt or sour cream**
1½ **teaspoons salt, divided**
1¼ **teaspoons garlic powder, divided**
½ **teaspoon black pepper, divided**
¼ **teaspoon onion powder**
2 **tablespoons orange juice**
1 **teaspoon sugar**
1 **teaspoon dried thyme leaves**
1 **teaspoon paprika**
¼ **teaspoon ground nutmeg**
¼ **teaspoon ground red pepper**
2½ **pounds chicken wings (about 10 wings)**

1. Preheat oven to 450°F. For Ranch Dipping Sauce, combine mayonnaise, yogurt, ½ teaspoon salt, ¼ teaspoon garlic powder, ¼ teaspoon black pepper and onion powder in small bowl.

2. Combine orange juice, sugar, thyme, paprika, nutmeg, red pepper, remaining 1 teaspoon salt, 1 teaspoon garlic powder and ¼ teaspoon black pepper in small bowl.

3. Cut tips from wings; discard. Place wings in large bowl. Drizzle with orange juice mixture; toss to coat.

4. Transfer chicken to greased broiler pan. Bake 25 to 30 minutes or until juices run clear and skin is crisp. Serve with Ranch Dipping Sauce.   *Makes 6 to 7 servings*

Serving Suggestion: Serve with celery sticks.

jerk wings with ranch dipping sauce

wild wedges

2 (8-inch) fat-free flour tortillas
    Nonstick cooking spray
⅓ cup shredded reduced-fat Cheddar cheese
⅓ cup chopped cooked chicken or turkey
1 green onion, thinly sliced
2 tablespoons mild, thick and chunky salsa

1. Heat large nonstick skillet over medium heat until hot.

2. Spray one side of one flour tortilla with cooking spray; place, sprayed side down, in skillet. Top with cheese, chicken, green onion and salsa. Place remaining tortilla over mixture; spray with cooking spray.

3. Cook 2 to 3 minutes per side or until golden brown and cheese is melted. Cut into 8 triangles.   *Makes 4 servings*

bacon & cheese dip

2 packages (8 ounces each) reduced-fat cream cheese, softened, cut into cubes
4 cups (16 ounces) shredded reduced-fat sharp Cheddar cheese
1 cup evaporated skimmed milk
2 tablespoons prepared mustard
1 tablespoon chopped onion
2 teaspoons Worcestershire sauce
½ teaspoon salt
¼ teaspoon hot pepper sauce
1 pound turkey bacon, crisp-cooked and crumbled

Slow Cooker Directions

Place cream cheese, Cheddar cheese, evaporated milk, mustard, onion, Worcestershire sauce, salt and pepper sauce into slow cooker. Cover; cook, stirring occasionally, on LOW 1 hour or until cheese melts. Stir in bacon; adjust seasonings. Serve with fruit and vegetable dippers.   *Makes about 4 cups*

wild wedges

roasted garlic spread with three cheeses

2 medium heads garlic
2 packages (8 ounces each) fat-free cream cheese, softened
1 package (3½ ounces) goat cheese
2 tablespoons (1 ounce) crumbled blue cheese
1 teaspoon dried thyme leaves

1. Preheat oven to 400°F. Cut tops off garlic heads to expose tops of cloves. Place garlic in small baking pan; bake 45 minutes or until garlic is very tender. Remove from pan; cool completely. Squeeze garlic into small bowl; mash with fork.

2. Beat cream cheese and goat cheese in small bowl until smooth; stir in blue cheese, garlic and thyme. Cover; refrigerate 3 hours or overnight. Spoon dip into serving bowl; serve with cucumbers, radishes, carrots or yellow bell peppers, if desired. Garnish with fresh thyme and red bell pepper strip, if desired.

Makes 21 servings

peaches and creamy dip with waffle wedges

4 ounces reduced-fat cream cheese
⅓ cup sugar-free peach preserves
1 tablespoon fat-free (skim) milk
2 packages sugar substitute
½ teaspoon vanilla
4 low-fat toaster waffles
  Ground cinnamon to taste

1. Place all ingredients, except waffles and cinnamon, in blender and process until smooth. Set aside.

2. Toast waffles and cut each waffle into 6 wedges.

3. Place cream cheese mixture in small serving bowl and sprinkle with cinnamon. Serve with waffle wedges for dipping.

Makes 24 wedges and about ¾ cup cream cheese mixture

roasted garlic spread with three cheeses

angelic deviled eggs

6 eggs
¼ cup low-fat (1%) cottage cheese
3 tablespoons prepared fat-free ranch dressing
2 teaspoons Dijon mustard
2 tablespoons minced fresh chives or dill
1 tablespoon diced well-drained pimiento or roasted red pepper

1. Place eggs in medium saucepan; add enough water to cover. Bring to a boil over medium heat. Remove from heat; cover. Let stand 15 minutes. Drain. Add cold water to eggs in saucepan; let stand until eggs are cool. Drain. Remove shells from eggs.

2. Cut eggs lengthwise in half. Remove yolks, reserving 3 yolk halves. Discard remaining yolks or reserve for another use. Place egg whites, cut sides up, on serving plate; cover with plastic wrap. Refrigerate while preparing filling.

3. Combine cottage cheese, dressing, mustard and reserved yolk halves in mini food processor; process until smooth. (Or, place in small bowl and mash with fork until well blended.) Transfer cheese mixture to small bowl; stir in chives and pimiento. Spoon into egg whites. Cover and chill at least 1 hour. Garnish, if desired.

Makes 12 servings

picante vegetable dip

⅔ cup reduced-fat sour cream
½ cup picante sauce
⅓ cup mayonnaise or reduced-fat mayonnaise
¼ cup finely chopped green or red bell pepper
2 tablespoons finely chopped green onion
¾ teaspoon garlic salt
Assorted fresh vegetable dippers

Combine sour cream, picante sauce, mayonnaise, bell pepper, green onion and garlic salt in medium bowl until well blended. Cover; refrigerate several hours or overnight to allow flavors to blend. Serve with dippers.

Makes about 1⅔ cups

angelic deviled eggs

confetti tuna in celery sticks

1 (3-ounce) pouch of STARKIST® Premium Albacore or Chunk Light Tuna
½ cup shredded red or green cabbage
½ cup shredded carrot
¼ cup shredded yellow squash or zucchini
3 tablespoons reduced-calorie cream cheese, softened
1 tablespoon plain low-fat yogurt
½ teaspoon dried basil, crushed
Salt and pepper to taste
10 to 12 (4-inch) celery sticks, with leaves if desired

1. In a small bowl toss together tuna, cabbage, carrot and squash.

2. Stir in cream cheese, yogurt and basil. Add salt and pepper to taste.

3. With small spatula spread mixture evenly into celery sticks.

Makes 10 to 12 servings

Prep Time: 20 minutes

monterey wedges

2 (6-inch) corn tortillas
¼ cup (1 ounce) shredded reduced-fat Monterey Jack or sharp Cheddar cheese
½ teaspoon chili powder
½ cup chopped green bell pepper
1 plum tomato, chopped (about ¼ cup)
2 tablespoons chopped canned green chilies
¼ cup sliced ripe olives, drained

1. Preheat oven 425°F. Coat nonstick baking sheet with nonstick cooking spray.

2. Place tortillas on baking sheet; top each with 2 tablespoons cheese, half the chili powder, bell pepper, tomato, chilies and olives. Top with remaining 2 tablespoons cheese.

3. Bake 5 minutes or until cheese melts. Remove from oven and let stand on baking sheet 3 minutes for easier handling. Cut into 4 wedges. *Makes 4 servings*

confetti tuna in celery sticks

taco popcorn olé

nutrients per serving:

1½ cups

Calories: 48
Carbohydrate: 10 g
Calories From Fat: 10%
Total Fat: 1 g
Saturated Fat: <1 g
Cholesterol: 0 mg
Sodium: 199 mg
Dietary Fiber: 2 g
Protein: 2 g

9 cups air-popped popcorn
  Butter-flavored cooking spray
1 teaspoon chili powder
½ teaspoon salt
½ teaspoon garlic powder
⅛ teaspoon ground red pepper (optional)

1. Preheat oven to 350°F. Line 15×10-inch jelly-roll pan with foil.

2. Place popcorn in single layer in prepared pan. Coat lightly with cooking spray.

3. Combine chili powder, salt, garlic powder and red pepper, if desired, in small bowl; sprinkle over popcorn. Mix lightly to coat evenly.

4. Bake 5 minutes or until hot, stirring gently after 3 minutes. Spread mixture in single layer on large sheet of foil to cool. *Makes 6 (1½-cup) servings*

Tip: Store popcorn mixture in tightly covered container at room temperature up to 4 days.

cheesy chips

nutrients per serving:

5 chips

Calories: 75
Carbohydrate: 9 g
Calories From Fat: 38%
Total Fat: 3 g
Saturated Fat: 1 g
Cholesterol: 4 mg
Sodium: 92 mg
Dietary Fiber: <1 g
Protein: 2 g

10 wonton wrappers
2 tablespoons powdered American cheese or grated Parmesan cheese
2 teaspoons olive oil
⅛ teaspoon garlic powder

1. Preheat oven to 375°F. Spray baking sheet with nonstick cooking spray.

2. Diagonally cut each wonton wrapper in half, forming two triangles. Place in single layer on prepared baking sheet.

3. Combine cheese, oil and garlic powder in small bowl. Sprinkle over wonton triangles.

4. Bake 6 to 8 minutes or until golden brown and crisp. Remove from oven. Cool completely. *Makes 4 servings*

taco popcorn olé

chilled shrimp in chinese mustard sauce

1 cup water
½ cup dry white wine
2 tablespoons reduced-sodium soy sauce
½ teaspoon Szechuan or black peppercorns
1 pound raw large shrimp, peeled and deveined
¼ cup prepared sweet and sour sauce
2 teaspoons hot Chinese mustard

1. Combine water, wine, soy sauce and peppercorns in medium saucepan. Bring to a boil over high heat. Add shrimp; reduce heat to medium. Cover and simmer 2 to 3 minutes or until shrimp are opaque. Drain well. Cover and refrigerate until chilled.

2. Combine sweet and sour sauce and mustard in small bowl; mix well. Serve as a dipping sauce for shrimp. *Makes 6 servings*

Health Note: Shellfish, such as shrimp, is an excellent source of low-calorie, low-fat protein. It's also rich in the minerals iron, copper and zinc, yet low in sodium.

grilled turkey ham quesadillas

Nonstick cooking spray
¼ cup salsa
4 (7-inch) flour tortillas
½ cup (1 ounce) shredded reduced-sodium reduced-fat Monterey Jack cheese
¼ cup finely chopped turkey ham
1 can (4 ounces) diced green chilies, drained
Additional salsa (optional)
Fat-free sour cream (optional)

1. To prevent sticking, spray grid with cooking spray. Prepare coals for grilling.

2. Spread 1 tablespoon salsa onto each tortilla. Sprinkle cheese, turkey ham and chilies equally over half of each tortilla; fold over uncovered half to make "sandwich"; spray tops and bottoms of tortilla "sandwiches" with cooking spray.

3. Grill quesadillas on uncovered grill over medium coals 1½ minutes per side or until cheese is melted and tortillas are golden brown, turning once. Quarter each quesadilla and serve with additional salsa and nonfat sour cream, if desired.

Makes 8 servings

chilled shrimp in chinese mustard sauce

buffalo chicken tenders

3 tablespoons Louisiana-style hot sauce
½ teaspoon paprika
¼ teaspoon ground red pepper
1 pound chicken tenders
½ cup fat-free blue cheese dressing
¼ cup reduced-fat sour cream
2 tablespoons crumbled blue cheese
1 medium red bell pepper, cut into ½-inch slices

1. Preheat oven to 375°F. Combine hot sauce, paprika and ground red pepper in small bowl; brush on all surfaces of chicken. Place chicken in greased 11×7-inch baking dish. Cover; marinate in refrigerator 30 minutes.

2. Bake, uncovered, about 15 minutes or until chicken is no longer pink in center.

3. Combine blue cheese dressing, sour cream and blue cheese in small serving bowl. Garnish as desired. Serve with chicken and bell pepper for dipping.

Makes 10 servings

nutrients per serving:

about 2 chicken tenders plus 1½ tablespoons dipping sauce

Calories: 83
Carbohydrate: 5 g
Calories From Fat: 27%
Total Fat: 2 g
Saturated Fat: 1 g
Cholesterol: 27 mg
Sodium: 180 mg
Dietary Fiber: 0 g
Protein: 9 g

chicken nachos

22 (about 1 ounce) GUILTLESS GOURMET® Baked Tortilla Chips (yellow, red or blue corn)
½ cup (4 ounces) cooked and shredded boneless chicken breast
¼ cup chopped green onions
¼ cup (1 ounce) shredded Cheddar cheese
Sliced green and red chilies (optional)

Microwave Directions

Spread tortilla chips on flat microwave-safe plate. Sprinkle chicken, onions and cheese over chips. Microwave on HIGH 30 seconds until cheese starts to bubble. Serve hot. Garnish with chilies, if desired.

Conventional Directions

Preheat oven to 325°F. Spread tortilla chips on baking sheet. Sprinkle chicken, onions and cheese over chips. Bake about 5 minutes or until cheese starts to bubble. Serve hot.

Makes 22 nachos

nutrients per serving:

1 nacho

Calories: 20
Carbohydrate: 1 g
Calories From Fat: 32%
Total Fat: 1 g
Saturated Fat: <1 g
Cholesterol: 6 mg
Sodium: 21 mg
Dietary Fiber: <1 g
Protein: 2 g

buffalo chicken tenders

easiest three-cheese fondue

nutrients per serving:

Calories: 207
Carbohydrate: 3 g
Calories From Fat: 74%
Total Fat: 17 g
Saturated Fat: 10 g
Cholesterol: 48 mg
Sodium: 334 mg
Dietary Fiber: <1 g
Protein: 10 g

   1 tablespoon margarine
¼ cup finely chopped onion
   2 cloves garlic, minced
   1 tablespoon all-purpose flour
¾ cup reduced-fat (2%) milk
   2 cups (8 ounces) shredded mild or sharp Cheddar cheese
   1 package (3 ounces) cream cheese, cut into cubes
½ cup (2 ounces) crumbled blue cheese
⅛ teaspoon ground red pepper
   4 to 6 drops hot pepper sauce
     Assorted fresh vegetables for dipping

1. Heat margarine in small saucepan over medium heat until melted. Add onion and garlic; cook and stir 2 to 3 minutes or until tender. Stir in flour; cook 2 minutes, stirring constantly.

2. Stir milk into saucepan; bring to a boil. Boil, stirring constantly, about 1 minute or until thickened. Reduce heat to low; add cheeses, stirring until melted. Stir in red pepper and pepper sauce. Pour fondue into serving dish. Serve with dippers.

Makes 8 (3-tablespoon) servings

Hint: For a special touch, sprinkle fondue with parsley and ground red pepper.

Lighten Up: To reduce the total fat, replace the Cheddar cheese and cream cheese with reduced-fat Cheddar and cream cheeses.

Prep and Cook Time: 20 minutes

easiest three-cheese fondue

turkey-broccoli roll-ups

2 pounds fresh broccoli spears
⅓ cup fat-free sour cream
¼ cup reduced-fat mayonnaise
2 tablespoons thawed frozen orange juice concentrate
1 tablespoon Dijon mustard
1 teaspoon dried basil leaves
1 pound smoked turkey, very thinly sliced

1. Arrange broccoli spears in single layer in large, shallow microwavable dish. Add 1 tablespoon water. Cover dish tightly with plastic wrap; vent. Microwave at HIGH 6 to 7 minutes or just until broccoli is crisp-tender, rearranging spears after 4 minutes. Carefully remove plastic wrap; drain broccoli. Immediately place broccoli in cold water to stop cooking; drain well. Pat dry with paper towels.

2. Combine sour cream, mayonnaise, juice concentrate, mustard and basil in small bowl; mix well.

3. Cut turkey slices into 2-inch-wide strips. Spread sour cream mixture evenly on strips. Place 1 broccoli piece at short end of each strip. Starting at short end, roll up tightly (allow broccoli spear to protrude from one end). Place on serving platter; cover with plastic wrap. Refrigerate until ready to serve. Garnish just before serving, if desired. *Makes 20 servings*

Note: To blanch broccoli on stove top, bring small amount of water to a boil in saucepan. Add broccoli spears; cover. Simmer 2 to 3 minutes or until broccoli is crisp-tender; drain. Cool; continue as directed.

turkey-broccoli roll-ups

hummus-stuffed vegetables

1 can (15 ounces) chick-peas, rinsed and drained
1 medium clove garlic
1 tablespoon lemon juice
1 tablespoon olive oil
½ teaspoon ground cumin
¼ teaspoon salt
¼ teaspoon black pepper
1 cup Chinese pea pods (about 24)
¾ pound medium fresh mushrooms (about 24)

1. Combine chick-peas, garlic, lemon juice, oil, cumin, salt and pepper in food processor. Process until smooth. Transfer to piping bag fitted with fluted tip.

2. Remove strings from pea pods. Carefully split pea pods with tip of paring knife. Remove stems from mushrooms; discard.

3. Pipe bean mixture into pea pods and into cavities of inverted mushrooms. Store loosely covered in refrigerator until ready to serve. Garnish just before serving, if desired. *Makes 12 servings*

Variation: Substitute cucumber slices or red or green bell peppers, cut into 1½-inch triangles, for pea pods and mushrooms.

hummus-stuffed vegetables

swimming tuna dip

1 cup low-fat (1%) cottage cheese
1 tablespoon reduced-fat mayonnaise
1 tablespoon lemon juice
2 teaspoons dry ranch-style salad dressing mix
1 can (3 ounces) chunk white tuna packed in water, drained and flaked
2 tablespoons sliced green onion or chopped celery
1 teaspoon dried parsley flakes
1 package (12 ounces) peeled baby carrots

Combine cottage cheese, mayonnaise, lemon juice and salad dressing mix in food processor or blender. Cover and blend until smooth. Stir in tuna, green onion and parsley. Serve with carrots. *Makes 4 servings*

curly lettuce wrappers

4 green leaf lettuce leaves
¼ cup reduced-fat sour cream
4 turkey bacon slices, crisp-cooked and crumbled
½ cup (2 ounces) crumbled feta or blue cheese
8 ounces thinly sliced deli turkey breast
4 whole green onions
½ medium red or green bell pepper, thinly sliced
1 cup broccoli sprouts

1. Rinse lettuce leaves and pat dry.

2. Combine sour cream and bacon in small bowl. Spread ¼ of sour cream mixture evenly over center third of one lettuce leaf. Sprinkle 2 tablespoons cheese over sour cream. Top with 2 ounces turkey.

3. Cut off green portion of each green onion, reserving white onion bottoms for later use. Place green portion of 1 onion, ¼ of bell pepper slices and ¼ cup sprouts on top of turkey.

4. Fold right edge of lettuce over filling; fold bottom edge up over filling. Loosely roll up from folded right edge, leaving left edge of wrap open. Repeat with remaining ingredients. *Makes 4 servings*

Travel Tip: Wrap individually in plastic wrap. Store in cooler with ice.

swimming tuna dip

mini marinated beef skewers

nutrients per serving:

3 skewers (without cherry tomatoes and lettuce)

Calories: 120
Carbohydrate: 2 g
Calories From Fat: 30%
Total Fat: 4 g
Saturated Fat: 1 g
Cholesterol: 60 mg
Sodium: 99 mg
Dietary Fiber: <1 g
Protein: 20 g

1 beef top round steak (about 1 pound)
2 tablespoons reduced-sodium soy sauce
1 tablespoon dry sherry
1 teaspoon dark sesame oil
2 cloves garlic, minced
18 cherry tomatoes (optional)

1. Cut beef crosswise into ⅛-inch slices. Place in large resealable plastic food storage bag. Combine soy sauce, sherry, oil and garlic in cup; pour over steak. Seal bag; turn to coat. Marinate in refrigerator at least 30 minutes or up to 2 hours.

2. Soak 18 (6-inch) skewers in water 20 minutes.

3. Drain steak; discard marinade. Weave beef accordion-style onto skewers. Place on rack of broiler pan.

4. Broil 4 to 5 inches from heat 2 minutes. Turn skewers over; broil 2 minutes or until beef is barely pink.

5. If desired, garnish each skewer with 1 cherry tomato. Place skewers on lettuce-lined platter. Serve warm. *Makes 6 servings (3 skewers each)*

chunky hawaiian spread

nutrients per serving:

1 tablespoon

Calories: 28
Carbohydrate: 5 g
Calories From Fat: 22%
Total Fat: 1 g
Saturated Fat: <1 g
Cholesterol: 2 mg
Sodium: 33 mg
Dietary Fiber: <1 g
Protein: 1 g

1 package (3 ounces) light cream cheese, softened
½ cup fat free or light sour cream
1 can (8 ounces) DOLE® Crushed Pineapple, well-drained
¼ cup mango chutney*
Low fat crackers

*If there are large pieces of fruit in chutney, cut into small pieces.

● Beat cream cheese, sour cream, crushed pineapple and chutney in bowl until blended. Cover and chill 1 hour or overnight. Serve with crackers. Refrigerate any leftover spread in airtight container for up to one week. *Makes 2½ cups*

mini marinated beef skewers

nutrients per serving:
8 pieces
Calories: 145
Carbohydrate: 3 g
Calories From Fat: 81%
Total Fat: 13 g
Saturated Fat: 12 g
Cholesterol: 40 mg
Sodium: 263 mg
Dietary Fiber: <1 g
Protein: 5 g

ham and cheese "sushi" rolls

4 thin slices deli ham (about 4×4 inches)
1 package (8 ounces) cream cheese, softened
1 seedless cucumber, quartered lengthwise and cut into 4-inch lengths
4 thin slices (about 4×4 inches) American or Cheddar cheese, room temperature
1 red bell pepper, cut into thin 4-inch-long strips

1. For ham sushi: Pat each ham slice with paper towel to remove excess moisture. Spread each ham slice to edges with 2 tablespoons cream cheese.

2. Pat 1 cucumber quarter with paper towel to remove excess moisture; place at edge of ham slice. Roll tightly. Seal by pressing gently. Roll in plastic wrap; refrigerate. Repeat with remaining three ham slices.

3. For cheese sushi: Spread each cheese slice to edges with 2 tablespoons cream cheese.

4. Place 2 strips red pepper even with one edge of one cheese slice. Roll tightly. Seal by pressing gently. Roll in plastic wrap; refrigerate. Repeat with remaining 3 cheese slices.

5. To serve: Remove plastic wrap from ham and cheese rolls. Cut each roll into 8 (½-inch-wide) pieces. Arrange on platter. *Makes 8 servings*

ham and cheese "sushi" rolls

nutrients per serving:

Calories: 168
Carbohydrate: 2 g
Calories From Fat: 86%
Total Fat: 16 g
Saturated Fat: 5 g
Cholesterol: 64 mg
Sodium: 128 mg
Dietary Fiber: <1 g
Protein: 5 g

best of the wurst spread

1 tablespoon butter or margarine
½ cup finely chopped onion
1 package (16 ounces) liverwurst
¼ cup mayonnaise or salad dressing
¼ cup finely chopped dill pickle
2 teaspoons horseradish mustard or spicy brown mustard
1 tablespoon drained capers
2 teaspoons dried dill weed
¼ small dill pickle, cut into strips
  Cocktail rye bread for serving

1. Heat butter in small saucepan over medium heat until melted. Add onion; cook and stir 5 minutes or until tender. Mash liverwurst with fork in medium bowl; beat in onion, mayonnaise, chopped dill pickle, mustard, capers and dill weed.

2. Form liverwurst mixture into football shape on serving plate; decorate with dill pickle strips to look like football laces. Serve with bread.

Makes 12 (3-tablespoon) servings

Serve It With Style!: For added flavor, serve the spread with mustard toast instead of rye bread. To prepare mustard toast, lightly spread horseradish mustard or spicy brown mustard on cocktail rye bread slices. Broil, 4 inches from heat, until lightly browned.

Prep and Cook Time: 15 minutes

mini burgers

1 pound ground chicken
¼ cup Italian-style dry bread crumbs
¼ cup chili sauce
1 egg white
1 tablespoon white Worcestershire sauce
2 teaspoons Dijon-style mustard
½ teaspoon dried thyme leaves
¼ teaspoon garlic powder
32 thin slices plum tomatoes (about 3 medium)
½ cup sweet onion slices (about 1 small)
16 slices cocktail rye or pumpernickel bread
Mustard (optional)
Pickle slices (optional)
Snipped chives or green onion tops (optional)

1. Preheat oven to 350°F. Combine chicken, bread crumbs, chili sauce, egg white, Worcestershire sauce, mustard, thyme and garlic powder in medium bowl. Form mixture into 16 patties.

2. Place patties in 15×10-inch jelly-roll pan. Bake, uncovered, 10 to 15 minutes or until patties are no longer pink in centers.

3. Place 2 tomato slices and 1 onion slice on each bread slice. Top each with 1 patty; add dollops of mustard, pickle slices and chives, if desired.

Makes 16 servings

nutrients per serving:
1 burger

Calories: 74
Carbohydrate: 7 g
Calories From Fat: 27%
Total Fat: 2 g
Saturated Fat: 1 g
Cholesterol: 14 mg
Sodium: 149 mg
Dietary Fiber: 1 g
Protein: 6 g

dazzling desserts

café au lait ice cream sundae

3 cups whipping cream, divided
4 egg yolks, lightly beaten
1 tablespoon instant coffee granules
½ cup plus 2 tablespoons no-calorie sugar substitute for baking, divided
½ teaspoon vanilla
½ cup chopped walnuts or pecans

1. Pour 2 cups cream into medium saucepan. Whisk egg yolks and coffee granules into cream. Heat 10 minutes over low heat, stirring constantly, until mixture reaches 160°F. Mixture will thicken as it cooks.

2. Pour mixture into bowl, stir in ½ cup sugar substitute until well blended. Refrigerate 2 to 3 hours or until cold. Pour chilled mixture into ice cream maker; process according to manufacturer's directions.

3. Whip remaining 1 cup cream, 2 tablespoons sugar substitute and vanilla until stiff. Scoop ice cream into serving bowls; top with whipped cream. Sprinkle with nuts just before serving. *Makes 4 servings*

tapioca pudding

2¾ cups low-fat milk
½ cup SPLENDA® Granular
¼ cup egg substitute
3 tablespoons quick-cooking tapioca
⅛ teaspoon salt
1½ teaspoons vanilla

1. In large saucepan, combine milk, SPLENDA®, egg substitute, tapioca and salt. Stir until blended, about 30 seconds. Let stand for 5 minutes.

2. Heat over medium heat, stirring constantly, until pudding comes to a full boil.

3. Remove from heat and stir in vanilla. Cool at room temperature for 20 minutes. Stir once and serve. *Makes 6 servings*

Prep Time: 25 minutes
Cook Time: 15 minutes

café au lait ice cream sundae

chocolate peanut butter ice cream sandwiches

nutrients per serving:

1 cookie

Calories: 129
Carbohydrate: 15 g
Calories From Fat: 49%
Total Fat: 7 g
Saturated Fat: 3 g
Cholesterol: 4 mg
Sodium: 124 mg
Dietary Fiber: 1 g
Protein: 4 g

2 tablespoons creamy peanut butter
8 chocolate wafer cookies
⅔ cup no-sugar-added vanilla ice cream, softened

1. Spread peanut butter over flat sides of all cookies.

2. Spoon ice cream over peanut butter on 4 cookies. Top with remaining 4 cookies, peanut butter sides down. Press down lightly to force ice cream to edges of sandwich.

3. Wrap each sandwich in foil; seal tightly. Freeze at least 2 hours or up to 5 days.

Makes 4 servings

chocolate flan

nutrients per serving:

⅛ of total recipe

Calories: 82
Carbohydrate: 13 g
Calories From Fat: 17%
Total Fat: 2 g
Saturated Fat: <1 g
Cholesterol: 56 mg
Sodium: 93 mg
Dietary Fiber: <1 g
Protein: 7 g

2 eggs, lightly beaten
24 packets NatraTaste® Brand Sugar Substitute
2 heaping tablespoons unsweetened cocoa powder
1 tablespoon cornstarch
1 teaspoon almond extract
1 (15-ounce) can evaporated skim milk
1 cup fat-free milk

1. Preheat oven to 350°F. Coat a 3-cup mold with nonstick cooking spray.

2. In a medium bowl, whisk together eggs, NatraTaste®, cocoa, cornstarch and almond extract until smooth. Stir in evaporated milk and fat-free milk. Pour mixture into mold. Place mold in a baking pan. Pour enough water into the baking pan to reach halfway up sides of mold.*

3. Bake 2 hours. Mixture will not look completely set, but will become firm upon cooling. Let cool at room temperature 1 hour, then refrigerate for several hours. To serve, invert mold onto a plate, or spoon flan from the mold.   *Makes 8 servings*

Baking mold in water helps cook the flan evenly without cracking.

chocolate peanut butter ice cream sandwiches

strawberry-topped cheesecake cups

nutrients per serving:

Calories: 205
Carbohydrate: 15 g
Calories From Fat: 66%
Total Fat: 15 g
Saturated Fat: 9 g
Cholesterol: 36 mg
Sodium: 127 mg
Dietary Fiber: <1 g
Protein: 3 g

1 cup sliced strawberries
10 packages sugar substitute, divided
1 teaspoon vanilla, divided
½ teaspoon grated orange peel
¼ teaspoon grated fresh ginger
1 package (8 ounces) cream cheese, softened
½ cup sour cream
2 tablespoons granulated sugar
16 vanilla wafers, crushed

1. Combine strawberries, 1 package sugar substitute, ¼ teaspoon vanilla, orange peel and grated ginger in medium bowl; toss gently. Let stand 20 minutes to allow flavors to blend.

2. Meanwhile, combine cream cheese, sour cream, remaining 9 packets sugar substitute and granulated sugar in medium mixing bowl. Add remaining ¾ teaspoon vanilla; beat 30 seconds on low speed of electric mixer. Increase to medium speed; beat 30 seconds or until smooth.

3. Spoon cream cheese mixture into 8 individual ¼-cup ramekins. Top each with about 2 tablespoons vanilla wafer crumbs and about 2 tablespoons strawberry mixture.   *Makes 8 servings*

easy raspberry ice cream

nutrients per serving:

½ cup

Calories: 193
Carbohydrate: 15 g
Calories From Fat: 68%
Total Fat: 15 g
Saturated Fat: 9 g
Cholesterol: 54 mg
Sodium: 15 mg
Dietary Fiber: 3 g
Protein: 2 g

8 ounces (1¾ cups) frozen unsweetened raspberries (not frozen in syrup or juice)
2 to 3 tablespoons powdered sugar
½ cup whipping cream

In food processor fitted with steel blade, process raspberries 15 minutes using on/off pulsing action or until they resemble coarse crumbs. Add sugar and process about 5 seconds or until thoroughly blended. With machine running, slowly add cream and process about 10 seconds or until well combined and raspberries have lightened in color. Serve immediately.   *Makes 3 servings*

strawberry-topped cheesecake cups

speedy pineapple-lime sorbet

nutrients per serving:

½ cup sorbet

Calories: 56
Carbohydrate: 15 g
Calories From Fat: 5%
Total Fat: <1 g
Saturated Fat: <1 g
Cholesterol: 0 mg
Sodium: 1 mg
Dietary Fiber: 1 g
Protein: <1 g

1 ripe pineapple, cut into cubes (about 4 cups)
⅓ cup frozen limeade concentrate, thawed
1 to 2 tablespoons fresh lime juice
1 teaspoon grated lime peel

1. Arrange pineapple in single layer on large baking sheet; freeze at least 1 hour or until very firm. Use metal spatula to transfer pineapple to resealable plastic freezer food storage bags; freeze up to 1 month.

2. Combine frozen pineapple, limeade, lime juice and lime peel in food processor; process until smooth and fluffy. If pineapple doesn't become smooth and fluffy, let stand 30 minutes to soften slightly; then repeat processing. Serve immediately.

Makes 8 servings

Note: This dessert is best if served immediately; but it may be made ahead, stored in the freezer, then softened several minutes before being served.

cherry-peach pops

nutrients per serving:

1 pop

Calories: 52
Carbohydrate: 11 g
Calories From Fat: 1%
Total Fat: <1 g
Saturated Fat: <1 g
Cholesterol: 1 mg
Sodium: 34 mg
Dietary Fiber: <1 g
Protein: 2 g

⅓ cup peach nectar or apricot nectar
1 teaspoon unflavored gelatin
1 (15-ounce) can sliced peaches in light syrup, drained
1 (6- or 8-ounce) carton fat-free sugar-free peach or cherry yogurt
1 (6- or 8-ounce) carton fat-free sugar-free cherry yogurt

1. Combine nectar and unflavored gelatin in small saucepan; let stand 5 minutes. Heat and stir over low heat just until gelatin dissolves.

2. Combine nectar mixture, drained peaches and yogurts in food processor. Cover and process until smooth.

3. Pour into 7 (3-ounce) paper cups, filling each about ⅔ full. Place in freezer; freeze 1 hour. Insert wooden stick into center of each cup. Freeze at least 3 more hours.

4. Let stand at room temperature 10 minutes before serving. Tear away paper cups to serve.

Makes 7 servings

speedy pineapple-lime sorbet

rich chocolate cheesecake

1 cup chocolate wafer crumbs
3 tablespoons EQUAL® SPOONFUL*
3 tablespoons stick butter or margarine, melted
3 packages (8 ounces each) reduced-fat cream cheese, softened
1 ¼ cups EQUAL® SPOONFUL**
2 eggs
2 egg whites
2 tablespoons cornstarch
¼ teaspoon salt
1 cup reduced-fat sour cream
2 teaspoons vanilla
4 ounces (4 squares) semi-sweet chocolate, melted and slightly cooled

*May substitute 4½ packets Equal® sweetener.

**May substitute 30 packets Equal® sweetener.

● Mix chocolate crumbs, 3 tablespoons Equal® Spoonful and melted butter in bottom of 9-inch springform pan. Pat mixture evenly onto bottom of pan. Bake in preheated 325°F oven 8 minutes. Cool on wire rack.

● Beat cream cheese and 1¼ cups Equal® Spoonful in large bowl until fluffy; beat in eggs, egg whites, cornstarch and salt. Beat in sour cream and vanilla until well blended. Gently fold in melted chocolate. Pour batter into crust.

● Bake in 325°F oven 40 to 45 minutes or until center is almost set. Remove cheesecake to wire rack. Gently run metal spatula around rim of pan to loosen cake. Let cheesecake cool completely; cover and refrigerate several hours or overnight before serving. To serve, remove side of springform pan.   *Makes 16 servings*

rich chocolate cheesecake

nutrients per serving:

Calories: 110
Carbohydrate: 12 g
Calories From Fat: 33%
Total Fat: 4 g
Saturated Fat: 2 g
Cholesterol: 15 mg
Sodium: 100 mg
Dietary Fiber: <1 g
Protein: 4 g

chocolate swirled cheesecake

Yogurt Cheese (recipe follows)
2 tablespoons graham cracker crumbs
1 package (8 ounces) Neufchâtel cheese (⅓ less fat cream cheese), softened
1½ teaspoons vanilla extract
¾ cup sugar
1 tablespoon cornstarch
1 container (8 ounces) liquid egg substitute
¼ cup HERSHEY'S Cocoa
¼ teaspoon almond extract

1. Prepare Yogurt Cheese.

2. Heat oven to 325°F. Spray bottom of 8- or 9-inch springform pan with vegetable cooking spray. Sprinkle graham cracker crumbs on bottom of pan.

3. Beat Yogurt Cheese, Neufchâtel cheese and vanilla in large bowl on medium speed of mixer until smooth. Add sugar and cornstarch; beat just until well blended. Gradually add egg substitute, beating on low speed until blended.

4. Transfer 1½ cups batter to medium bowl; add cocoa. Beat until well blended. Stir almond extract into vanilla batter. Alternately spoon vanilla and chocolate batters into prepared pan. With knife or metal spatula, cut through batters for marble effect.

5. Bake 35 minutes for 8-inch pan, 40 minutes for 9-inch pan or until edge is set. With knife, loosen cheesecake from side of pan. Cool completely in pan on wire rack.

6. Cover; refrigerate at least 6 hours before serving. Just before serving, remove side of pan. Garnish as desired. Cover; refrigerate leftover cheesecake.

Makes 16 servings

Yogurt Cheese: Use one 16-ounce container plain lowfat yogurt, no gelatin added. Line non-rusting colander or sieve with large piece of double thickness cheesecloth or large coffee filter; place colander over deep bowl. Spoon yogurt into prepared colander; cover with plastic wrap. Refrigerate until liquid no longer drains from yogurt, about 24 hours. Remove yogurt from cheesecloth and place in separate bowl; discard liquid.

chocolate swirled cheesecake

currant cheesecake bars

½ cup (1 stick) butter, softened
1 cup all-purpose flour
½ cup packed light brown sugar
½ cup finely chopped pecans
1 package (8 ounces) cream cheese, softened
¼ cup granulated sugar
1 egg
1 tablespoon milk
2 teaspoons grated lemon peel
⅓ cup currant jelly or seedless raspberry jam

Preheat oven to 350°F. Grease 9-inch square baking pan. Beat butter in medium bowl with electric mixer at medium speed until smooth. Add flour, brown sugar and pecans; beat at low speed until well blended. Press mixture into bottom and partially up sides of prepared pan.

Bake about 15 minutes or until light brown. If sides of crust have slumped down, press back up and reshape with spoon. Let cool 5 minutes on wire rack.

Meanwhile, beat cream cheese in large bowl with electric mixer at medium speed until smooth. Add granulated sugar, egg, milk and lemon peel; beat until well blended.

Heat jelly in small saucepan over low heat 2 to 3 minutes or until smooth, stirring occasionally.

Pour cream cheese mixture over crust. Drizzle jelly in 7 to 8 horizontal strips across filling with spoon. Swirl jelly through filling with knife to create marbled effect.

Bake 20 to 25 minutes or until filling is set. Cool completely on wire rack before cutting into bars. Store in airtight container in refrigerator up to 1 week.

Makes about 32 bars

currant cheesecake bars

chocolate-caramel s'mores

nutrients per serving:

1 s'more

Calories: 72
Carbohydrate: 14 g
Calories From Fat: 23%
Total Fat: 2 g
Saturated Fat: 1 g
Cholesterol: 0 mg
Sodium: 77 mg
Dietary Fiber: 0 g
Protein: 1 g

12 chocolate wafer cookies or chocolate graham cracker squares
2 tablespoons fat-free caramel topping
6 large marshmallows

1. Prepare coals for grilling. Place 6 wafer cookies top down on plate. Spread 1 teaspoon caramel topping in center of each wafer to within about ¼ inch of edge.

2. Spear 1 to 2 marshmallows onto long wood-handled skewer.* Hold several inches above coals 3 to 5 minutes or until marshmallows are golden and very soft, turning slowly. Push 1 marshmallow off into center of caramel. Top with plain wafer. Repeat with remaining marshmallows and wafers. *Makes 6 servings*

*If wood-handled skewers are unavailable, use oven mitt to protect hand from heat.

Note: S'mores, a favorite campfire treat, got their name because everyone who tasted them wanted "some more." In the unlikely event of leftover S'Mores, they can be reheated in the microwave at HIGH 15 to 30 seconds.

frozen berry ice cream

nutrients per serving:

½ cup

Calories: 69
Carbohydrate: 15 g
Calories From Fat: 2%
Total Fat: <1 g
Saturated Fat: <1 g
Cholesterol: 0 mg
Sodium: 23 mg
Dietary Fiber: 1 g
Protein: 3 g

8 ounces frozen unsweetened strawberries, partially thawed
8 ounces frozen unsweetened peaches, partially thawed
4 ounces frozen unsweetened blueberries, partially thawed
6 packets sugar substitute
2 teaspoons vanilla
2 cups no-sugar-added light vanilla ice cream
16 blueberries
4 small strawberries, halved
8 peach slices

1. Combine frozen strawberries, peaches, blueberries, sugar substitute and vanilla in food processor. Process until coarsely chopped.

2. Add ice cream; process until well blended.

3. Serve immediately for semi-soft texture or freeze until needed and allow to stand 10 minutes to soften slightly. Garnish each serving with 2 blueberries, 1 strawberry half and 1 peach slice. *Makes 8 servings*

chocolate-caramel s'mores

luscious chocolate cheesecake

2 cups (1 pound) nonfat cottage cheese
¾ cup liquid egg substitute
⅔ cup sugar
4 ounces (½ of 8-ounce package) Neufchâtel cheese (⅓ less fat
  cream cheese), softened
⅓ cup HERSHEY'S Cocoa or HERSHEY'S Dutch Processed Cocoa
½ teaspoon vanilla extract
  Yogurt Topping (recipe follows)
  Sliced strawberries or mandarin orange segments (optional)

1. Heat oven to 300°F. Spray 9-inch springform pan with vegetable cooking spray.

2. Place cottage cheese, egg substitute, sugar, Neufchâtel cheese, cocoa and vanilla in food processor; process until smooth. Pour into prepared pan.

3. Bake 35 minutes or until edges are set.

4. Meanwhile, prepare Yogurt Topping. Carefully spread topping over cheesecake. Continue baking 5 minutes. Remove from oven to wire rack. With knife, loosen cheesecake from side of pan. Cool completely.

5. Cover; refrigerate until chilled. Remove side of pan. Serve with strawberries or mandarin orange segments, if desired. Refrigerate leftover cheesecake.

Makes 12 servings

nutrients per serving:

1 slice cheesecake (1/12 of total recipe) without strawberries or mandarin orange segments

Calories: 84
Carbohydrate: 6 g
Calories From Fat: 27%
Total Fat: 2 g
Saturated Fat: 1 g
Cholesterol: 7 mg
Sodium: 199 mg
Dietary Fiber: <1 g
Protein: 8 g

yogurt topping

⅔ cup plain nonfat yogurt
2 tablespoons sugar

Stir together yogurt and sugar in small bowl until well blended.

luscious chocolate cheesecake

pineapple-ginger bavarian

1 can (8 ounces) crushed pineapple in juice, drained and liquid reserved
1 package (4 serving size) sugar-free orange gelatin
1 cup sugar-free ginger ale
1 cup plain nonfat yogurt
¾ teaspoon grated fresh ginger
½ cup whipping cream
1 packet sugar substitute
¼ teaspoon vanilla

1. Combine reserved pineapple juice with enough water to equal ½ cup liquid. Pour into small saucepan. Bring to a boil over high heat.

2. Place gelatin in medium bowl. Add pineapple juice mixture; stir until gelatin is completely dissolved. Add ginger ale and half of crushed pineapple; stir until well blended. Add yogurt; whisk until well blended. Pour into 5 individual ramekins. Cover each ramekin with plastic wrap; refrigerate until firm.

3. Meanwhile, combine remaining half of pineapple with ginger in small bowl. Cover with plastic wrap; refrigerate.

4. Just before serving, beat cream in small deep bowl on high speed of electric mixer until soft peaks form. Add sugar substitute and vanilla; beat until stiff peaks form.

5. To serve, top bavarian with 1 tablespoon whipped topping and 1 tablespoon pineapple mixture. *Makes 5 servings*

Tip: Use 2 tablespoons ready-made whipped topping to garnish, if desired.

pineapple-ginger bavarian

strawberry bavarian deluxe

nutrients per serving:

Calories: 82
Carbohydrate: 15 g
Calories From Fat: 14%
Total Fat: 1 g
Saturated Fat: <1 g
Cholesterol: 0 mg
Sodium: 25 mg
Dietary Fiber: 2 g
Protein: 3 g

½ bag whole frozen unsweetened strawberries (1 mounded quart), partially thawed
¼ cup low-sugar strawberry preserves
¼ cup granular sucralose
2 tablespoons balsamic vinegar
¾ cup water, divided
2 envelopes (7g each) unflavored gelatin
1 tablespoon honey
½ cup pasteurized liquid egg whites or 4 egg whites*
½ teaspoon cream of tartar
1 teaspoon vanilla
1 pint strawberries, washed, dried and hulled
1 cup thawed frozen light whipped topping
Mint sprigs (optional)

Use only clean, uncracked eggs.

1. Place strawberries, preserves and sucralose in food processor fitted with steel blade. Process until smooth. Transfer mixture to bowl. Set aside.

2. Combine vinegar with ¼ cup water in small saucepan. Sprinkle in gelatin and let stand until softened. Stir in remaining ½ cup water and honey. Cook and stir over medium heat until gelatin dissolves.

3. Whisk gelatin mixture into berry mixture in bowl. Refrigerate, covered, until mixture is soupy, but not set.

4. Meanwhile, combine liquid egg whites and cream of tartar in bowl. When berry-gelatin mixture is soupy, whip egg whites until soft peaks form.

5. Gently fold egg whites, ⅓ at a time, into chilled berry mixture until mixture is uniform in color. Pour mousse into prechilled 2-quart mold, such as nonstick Bundt pan. Refrigerate covered for at least 8 hours or overnight.

6. To serve, run tip of knife around top of mold. Dip mold briefly into large bowl of hot water to loosen. To unmold, center flat serving plate on top of mold, hold firmly so mold doesn't shift, and invert plate and mold. Shake gently to release. Remove mold and refrigerate 10 to 15 minutes. Garnish with fresh strawberries and mint sprigs, if desired. Cut into wedges and serve with 2 tablespoons whipped topping.

Makes 10 servings

strawberry bavarian deluxe

nutrients per serving:

1 square (⅑ of total recipe)

Calories: 98
Carbohydrate: 11 g
Calories From Fat: 24%
Total Fat: 3 g
Saturated Fat: 2 g
Cholesterol: 8 mg
Sodium: 223 mg
Dietary Fiber: 1 g
Protein: 7 g

streusel-topped strawberry cheesecake squares

1 container (8 ounces) strawberry-flavored nonfat yogurt with aspartame sweetener
1 package (8 ounces) fat-free cream cheese
4 ounces reduced-fat cream cheese
6 packets sugar substitute _or_ equivalent of ¼ cup sugar
1 packet unflavored gelatin
2 tablespoons water
1 cup fresh chopped strawberries
1 tablespoon sugar
1 cup fresh sliced strawberries
⅓ cup low-fat granola

1. Line 9-inch square baking pan with plastic wrap, leaving 4-inch overhang on 2 opposite sides.

2. Combine yogurt, cream cheese and sugar substitute in medium bowl; beat until smooth. Set aside.

3. Combine gelatin and water in small microwavable bowl; let stand 2 minutes. Microwave at HIGH 40 seconds to dissolve gelatin. Beat gelatin into yogurt mixture. Combine chopped strawberries and sugar in small bowl. Add to yogurt mixture.

4. Pour yogurt mixture evenly into prepared pan. Refrigerate 1 hour or until firm.

5. Just before serving, arrange 1 cup sliced strawberries on top; sprinkle with granola.

6. Gently lift cheesecake out of pan with plastic wrap. Pull plastic wrap away from sides; cut into 9 to 12 squares.   _Makes 9 to 12 servings_

METRIC CONVERSION CHART

VOLUME MEASUREMENTS (dry)

1/8 teaspoon = 0.5 mL
1/4 teaspoon = 1 mL
1/2 teaspoon = 2 mL
3/4 teaspoon = 4 mL
1 teaspoon = 5 mL
1 tablespoon = 15 mL
2 tablespoons = 30 mL
1/4 cup = 60 mL
1/3 cup = 75 mL
1/2 cup = 125 mL
2/3 cup = 150 mL
3/4 cup = 175 mL
1 cup = 250 mL
2 cups = 1 pint = 500 mL
3 cups = 750 mL
4 cups = 1 quart = 1 L

VOLUME MEASUREMENTS (fluid)

1 fluid ounce (2 tablespoons) = 30 mL
4 fluid ounces (1/2 cup) = 125 mL
8 fluid ounces (1 cup) = 250 mL
12 fluid ounces (1 1/2 cups) = 375 mL
16 fluid ounces (2 cups) = 500 mL

WEIGHTS (mass)

1/2 ounce = 15 g
1 ounce = 30 g
3 ounces = 90 g
4 ounces = 120 g
8 ounces = 225 g
10 ounces = 285 g
12 ounces = 360 g
16 ounces = 1 pound = 450 g

DIMENSIONS

1/16 inch = 2 mm
1/8 inch = 3 mm
1/4 inch = 6 mm
1/2 inch = 1.5 cm
3/4 inch = 2 cm
1 inch = 2.5 cm

OVEN TEMPERATURES

250°F = 120°C
275°F = 140°C
300°F = 150°C
325°F = 160°C
350°F = 180°C
375°F = 190°C
400°F = 200°C
425°F = 220°C
450°F = 230°C

BAKING PAN SIZES

Utensil	Size in Inches/Quarts	Metric Volume	Size in Centimeters
Baking or Cake Pan (square or rectangular)	8×8×2	2 L	20×20×5
	9×9×2	2.5 L	23×23×5
	12×8×2	3 L	30×20×5
	13×9×2	3.5 L	33×23×5
Loaf Pan	8×4×3	1.5 L	20×10×7
	9×5×3	2 L	23×13×7
Round Layer Cake Pan	8×1½	1.2 L	20×4
	9×1½	1.5 L	23×4
Pie Plate	8×1¼	750 mL	20×3
	9×1¼	1 L	23×3
Baking Dish or Casserole	1 quart	1 L	—
	1½ quart	1.5 L	—
	2 quart	2 L	—

acknowledgments

The publisher would like to thank the companies and organizations listed below for the use of their recipes and photographs in this publication.

BelGioioso® Cheese, Inc.
Birds Eye®
Bob Evans®
Butterball® Turkey
Del Monte Corporation
Dole Food Company, Inc.
Egg Beaters®
Equal® sweetener
Guiltless Gourmet®
Heinz North America
Hershey Foods Corporation
Hillshire Farm®
Hormel Foods, LLC
The Kingsford Products Company
Mrs. Dash®
National Fisheries Institute
NatraTaste® is a registered trademark of Stadt Corporation
Reckitt Benckiser Inc.
The J.M. Smucker Company
Splenda® is a registered trademark of McNeil Nutritionals
StarKist® Seafood Company
Unilever Bestfoods North America

recipe index

general index